Hotel Scarface

WHERE COCAINE COWBOYS PARTIED AND PLOTTED TO CONTROL MIAMI

Roben Farzad

CORGI BOOKS

TRANSWORLD PUBLISHERS
61–63 Uxbridge Road, London W5 5SA
www.penguin.co.uk

Transworld is part of the Penguin Random House group of companies
whose addresses can be found at global.penguinrandomhouse.com

First published in Great Britain in 2018 by Bantam Press
an imprint of Transworld Publishers
Corgi edition published 2019

Published by arrangement with Gotham Books,
a member of Penguin Group (USA) LLC, a Penguin Random House Company

Title page art: silhouette of palm trees © Champ008/Shutterstock.com

Book design by Tiffany Estreicher

A CIP catalogue record for this book
is available from the British Library.

ISBN 9780552171540

Typeset in Mercury.
Printed and bound in Great Britain by Clays Ltd, Elcograf S.p.A.

Penguin Random House is committed to a sustainable
future for our business, our readers and our planet. This book
is made from Forest Stewardship Council® certified paper.

1 3 5 7 9 10 8 6 4 2

For Karen and my Bears
For Mom and Dad
For my hometown and our scars . . .

Memory / is another name for ghosts and their awful hunger.

—EUGENE GLORIA

Contents

CONTENTS

CONTENTS

Introduction

IN 2001, OUR documentary *Raw Deal: A Question of Consent*, which examined a case of alleged rape at a University of Florida fraternity house, premiered at the Sundance Film Festival to an avalanche of audience and critical acclaim. The *New York Post* splashed *Raw Deal* on its cover with the headline "Sundance Shocker." We were twenty-two years old, among the youngest filmmakers ever invited to the festival and the only ones ever invited from South Florida, and now our film was the talk of Sundance. Agents and managers were calling, asking us if we were heading to New York or Los Angeles. We thought that was ridiculous: we were heading home to Miami.

Miami's reputation as a city that welcomed the movie industry was cemented in the 1990s with a string of films that traded on the gorgeous backdrop the city provided: *The Birdcage*, *Bad Boys*, *Ace Ventura: Pet Detective* and *The Specialist*. But what Miami didn't have were homegrown filmmakers telling Miami stories. Carl Hiaasen and Edna Buchanan chronicled the city in the pages of the

Miami Herald and later in novels, but there was no equivalent of what Woody Allen or Spike Lee is to New York or what Barry Levinson is to Baltimore. We were going to become those guys. And the story we wanted to tell first was the story of Miami's cocaine boom in the 1980s, the story of the Cocaine Cowboys.

Even though we both were still in elementary school when the 1980s ended, growing up in Miami during that decade made an indelible impression on us. While the rest of the country was suffering through oil shocks and usurious interest rates, Miami's economy was buoyed by a white powder that could be bought for one thousand dollars a kilo in Medellín and sold for fifty thousand dollars a kilo in Coconut Grove. The city was awash in cash, and everyone seemed to know someone who drove a Mercedes yet had no visible means of support. Miami was a boomtown: not since the discovery of gold nuggets in the Sacramento Valley in 1848 led to the California Gold Rush had there been such massive wealth generated so quickly in one place. As a result, law and order broke down so completely that one federal judge declared that Miami was "on the ragged edge of anarchy."

We started with the thesis that contemporary Miami—"the Gateway to the Americas," as the civic boosters called it—was built on the back of the cocaine industry. Yet when we began doing research in 2003, it was shocking how little of the city's history from just twenty years prior had been documented and analyzed. There were only two nonfiction books written by journalists who covered Miami during the good-ol'-bad-ol' days and one autobiography by a former trafficker turned snitch. And since our research began at the dawn of the Google Age, all of the contemporaneous news reporting was stored away on microfiche in filing cabinets at the city's main library. Our questions about how the cocaine industry impacted the development of Miami seemed to puzzle one of the city's premier historians. It seemed that by the end of the 1980s, as the crack cocaine scourge was destroying entire neighborhoods and politicians were proposing the death penalty for drug kingpins, interest in the subject of Miami's cocaine boom died.

Documenting the underworld is always tricky. The gangsters of Miami's cocaine wars knew that the only way you exited the business was in a box or to a cell, and they left behind precious little evidence with which to piece together their lives. We relied on police intelligence reports, surveillance photos and court testimony to verify the stories of the subjects we interviewed for *Cocaine Cowboys*. But because the drug business is so compartmentalized and there were precious few first-person accounts, it was difficult to see the big picture and how people and events tied together. That's why Roben Farzad's *Hotel Scarface* is such an accomplishment.

Using the infamous Mutiny Club, the Rick's Café of Miami during the cocaine wars, to tie three generations of Cuban exile smugglers together, Farzad pulls back the curtain on an underworld populated by smugglers and assassins, dope lawyers and drug agents, snitches and party girls. Fueled by marching powder and Dom Pérignon and secured with MAC-10s, the Mutiny was a world that few entered and even fewer left unscathed.

Hotel Scarface is an unflinching account of the social, economic and political forces that merged into a perfect storm and threatened to destroy the morality of a major American city. It almost makes you want to empty the contents of your Deering grinder onto a mirror and roll up a hundred-dollar bill. If it were 1980.

—Billy Corben and Alfred Spellman,
  producers of the documentary series *Cocaine Cowboys*

Cast of Characters

The Mutiny at Sailboat Bay: A hot hotel and club in Coconut Grove, Florida.

Ricardo "Monkey" Morales: CIA-trained bomber, assassin, drug dealer and informant.

Rodolfo "Rudy Redbeard" Rodriguez Gallo: Cuban-born cocaine kingpin.

Carlos "Carlene" Quesada: Redbeard's childhood friend and co-kingpin.

Mollie Hampton: Evangelical turned lipstick lesbian hostess and chauffeur to Mutiny coke lords.

A. Guillermo "Willie" Falcon and Salvador "Sal" Magluta: Cuban-born Miami high school dropouts turned two-billion-dollar cocaine lords.

Mariel & Co.: 1980 boatlift refugees Coca-Cola, Weetchie, Albertico, Kiki et al.

CAST OF CHARACTERS

Raul Diaz: Miami homicide and narcotics cop; Monkey Morales's handler.

Raul Martinez: Miami cop pursuing Redbeard's gang.

Bernardo de Torres: Bay of Pigs veteran; Mutiny VIP; arms dealer.

Wayne Black: A cop listening in to the Mutiny from a van across the street.

Burton Goldberg: Developer; founder and mostly absentee owner of the Mutiny.

Baruch Vega: Goldberg's fashion photographer son-in-law; informant.

Ramon "Mon" Perez Lamas: Internationally wanted hit man working for Redbeard.

Ray Corona: Miami's cocaine banker-in-chief; laundered kingpin cash; major user.

Nelson Aguilar: Young cocaine dealer; tight with Rick James and the Miami Dolphins.

Owen "Bar Mitzvah" Band: Salutatorian of Boston University turned cocaine dealer.

Fernando Puig: Mutiny's "head of security"; Bay of Pigs veteran.

Rafael Leon "Amilcar" Rodriguez: Venezuelan cocaine kingpin and assassin.

Jorge Valdes: Star accounting student and Federal Reserve staffer turned cocaine cowboy.

Miguel Miranda: Serial killer; voodoo worshipper; Mutiny member.

Caesar: Blinged-out chimp.

Hotel Scarface

Preface

IT WAS AUTUMN 1980 in Miami, and Willy Gomez, a tall, thickly bearded twentysomething who looked like a disco conquistador, was working security at the Mutiny at Sailboat Bay, a club and hotel in Coconut Grove, just south of downtown. Outside, a long line snaked by the poolside entrance to the Mutiny Club. If everyone in Miami claimed to know Willy—his gig won him side jobs from VIPs and action from a smorgasbord of chicks—it was because they wanted inside, where the action was.

Gomez, you could say, was living the dream.

Save for tonight.

As he came down the stairs from the club to the hotel's lobby, he heard a commotion.

Coño tu madre! [Fuck your mother!]

Come mierda! [Eat shit!]

Hijo de puta! [Son of a whore!]

Come plomo, maricón! [Eat lead, faggot!]

"Fuck me," thought Gomez, stifling the urge to piss himself.

Ricardo "Monkey" Morales, a Mutiny regular, was pointing his gun at some other thug. So intense was the vitriol that spit was flying in the air.

"I knew Ricky was a CIA guy—an informant," Gomez said of Morales. "I knew he was a problem. I knew he was a rat."

He also knew his .38 Colt revolver was downright *Gunsmoke* compared with the Monkey's semiautomatic: "No way I could let him turn on me with that."

The domino tables of Little Havana echoed with cigar-smoked tales of *el Mono* (the Monkey) meting out and cheating death: about how once, in broad daylight, he emptied seventeen rounds from a machine gun into another exile; how there was still shrapnel embedded in the busy Miami street where nine years earlier he had walked away from a car bombing that should have at least severed his legs; how Morales, the lucky bastard, later survived a drive-by shooting that nearly blew out his brains by rolling out of his car and regrouping until he could kill his would-be assassin with gunshots to the face.

Morales's menacing appearance—dead gaze, gorilla-sloped back, huge ears and hands—resembled that of some early hominid you might see re-created in the pages of *National Geographic*.

Which was seemingly the only publication that hadn't profiled him. Morales had been featured in *Esquire*, and cover treatments by both *Newsday*'s magazine and *Harper's* were in the pipeline. The *Miami Herald* and the *Miami News* had filing cabinets dedicated to this mythical exile: informant, bomber, drug dealer, assassin, quoter of military histories. Literary agents were calling.

The Mutiny was where Monkey Morales held court, his bloodstream coursing with cocaine, THC, Quaaludes, Valium, alcohol and caffeine.

And two decades of Cuban-American rage.

He always snuck in the back of the hotel and in through the kitchen, where he'd hand Chef Manny—"Manolito!"—choice little briquettes of cocaine. And maybe a lobster or hog snapper that he had personally speared.

So, Willy Gomez, security conquistador, hardly ever crossed paths with this guy—and he was fine with that. But tonight, for whatever reason, Monkey Morales felt the need to go apeshit a couple of yards from the hotel's front desk.

"Police!" yelled Gomez, hand on his gun. "Call the police."

But the lobby had completely emptied out, save for the three of them. Music from the club wafted downstairs:

I got to ride, ride like the wind
To be free again

"If I blink," Gomez thought to himself, "this psychopath will kill me."

He resolved to squeeze the trigger. "Monkey was already dead, as far as I was concerned. I was worried his brains would splatter on the artwork."

The future flashed before Gomez. Burton Goldberg, the Mutiny's hard-assed owner, would throw the mother of all shit fits when crime-scene photographers captured the mess in his lobby. He had paid tens of thousands of dollars for Hollywood-caliber set lighting to showcase his art and orchids, micromanaging the scene down to the last lumen. "I hired the guy that lit up the Statue of Liberty in 'seventy-six," Goldberg would always boast to guests.

Gomez would then have to quit his job, assuming the Mutiny survived the shooting. You didn't just plug Monkey Morales and go on with your life like nothing happened. Yes, many in Miami who hated Morales would send Gomez drinks and introduce the dapper *caballero* to their daughters and sisters.

But the Monkey had too many friends in dangerous places—spooks, arms dealers, mercenaries, soldiers of fortune—who would put a retaliatory hit out on his killer, justified circumstances or not.

("Or," Willy Gomez thought, "if you keep thinking about all this, the Monkey will fucking turn around and kill you himself. Focus!")

Then the elevator door opened.

"Police!" yelled Gomez, with renewed desperation.

Out walked Rafael Villaverde, Morales's tablemate. As the scene came into focus through his tinted glasses, the paunchy exile grimaced, bit a knuckle and took hesitating steps forward. Willy Gomez now had his gun at Morales's head.

Villaverde held out his hand. "No police!" he pleaded, looking at Gomez. "Ricky. Ricky. Hey. Look. *Mira*. . . ."

Villaverde then carefully walked up to Morales and whispered something.

Gomez was still convinced the Monkey would blow him away with a flick of his wrist. He imagined his head in a puddle of blood.

But Morales rapidly tucked his semiautomatic back into his pants. His rival bolted, but Gomez didn't put away his revolver.

"Get the *fuck* out of here, Ricky!" he yelled to Morales, panting, almost hyperventilating. "Try! If you even *try* to fucking come back . . ."

"You know who you talking to?" shot back Morales, snarling. "Do. You. Know?"

He pulled back his coat to reveal a giant grenade on his belt. It was practically the size of a Florida avócado.

The Monkey flashed a deranged grin and took his time walking out the front of the Mutiny.

Outside, an oblivious and unruly crowd would likely have formed. Giggling groupies checking the shrubs and walkways for the club's gilded matchboxes, looking inside for Quaaludes and nose candy.

The air would have been pungent with cigarette smoke, preparty rum, various overpowering perfumes, colognes and hair sprays, high-tide salt water, sweaty rayon, joints.

Desperation.

Aspiration.

Ferraris, Porsches, Rollses, Benzes, Maseratis and Lambos pulled up, windows wide-open, blasting Blondie, Donna Summer and "Funkytown." The Mutiny's valets were tipped to the cuffs to take their time, hog the curb along South Bayshore Drive and keep the beats pumping.

Opposite the hotel, a marina led out to a bay containing more than one hundred boats, sails flapping, the occasional manatee scraping up against the bows. Giant yachts ferried area regulars—who at times could include names like the Bee Gees and Richard Nixon—to land.

In the shallows, you were bound to find a recently arrived Cuban refugee swatting away mosquitoes with a cigarette, desperate to snag a small shark or ray on a handline. Anything bigger he'd hawk a mile north at the big intersection on US-1, where others from the Mariel boatlift emigration of Cubans that spring and summer were selling fruit and hog trotters.

Abutting this vista were Miami City Hall and the police station.

Back across South Bayshore Drive—"Rubberneck Avenue," wags were now calling it—a scene of intense star watching was taking place outside the Mutiny. Recently spotted:

Mr. Universe, Arnold Schwarzenegger, his head appearing freakishly small atop the boulder that was his midsection. The tiny waitress from Michigan he'd hit on wondered to a girlfriend *how* she could possibly mount this beast.

Paul Newman, small as a jockey, and Sally Field were in town with star director Sydney Pollack to shoot the film *Absence of Malice*. Newman drank so much of the Mutiny's Château Lafite that he passed out and literally had to be carried up to his suite by a hostess. A brooding Burt Reynolds kept a watchful eye on Sally.

Playboy hopefuls visited for casting calls in one of the hotel's 130 fantasy-themed rooms and its Playboy Video set. *Penthouse* used the joint, too.

The Eagles had just recorded an album in the studio next door. Waitresses gossiped about which member tipped—and bedded—the best.

You'd see Frankie Valli, in boosting disco heels—not to be confused with *Dance Fever* host Deney Terrio, who reminded everyone at the Mutiny that, hey, you know, he coached Travolta for *Saturday Night Fever*.

And "Super Freak"–destined Rick James, traveling with a delegation of coke whores and a croc-skin man purse full of dainty gold utensils for cutting and sniffing lines. It's true: every other word out of his mouth was "bitch." "Slick Rick" laid into a waitress who accidentally called him "miss."

Ted Kennedy, fresh off conceding the Democratic presidential nomination, had often been deep in his cups at the Mutiny, where he hated bumping into Jimmy Carter wingman Hamilton Jordan, who was constantly in Miami to negotiate asylum in Panama for the deposed shah of Iran. Kennedy picked a fight with the club's DJ, who was helping Julio Iglesias, a Mutiny resident, hype his latest record. You catch all that?

The Doobie Brothers partied hard at the Mutiny, where the

joke was they were into way more than just doobies—no: the pow-
dery stuff was what inspired band members and their roadies to
mindlessly throw cash down from their windows.

And always wandering the grounds like a lost dog was David
Crosby of Crosby, Stills, Nash & Young—his mustache and teeth nasty
from constantly smoking freebase cocaine with a small blowtorch.

For all the intense people watching at 2951 South Bayshore Drive,
however, the true players at the Mutiny had nothing to do with Hollywood or Motown or the Beltway.

They were Miami's ruling drug lords. With bullets flying everywhere there at all hours of the day, the town was increasingly being
called Dodge City. And so these guys were its "cocaine cowboys," the
Latin masterminds of the era's go-go wonder drug: *yeyo*, *perico*, toot,
snow, white pony. Cocaine. And the Mutiny was their favorite saloon.

It was in this parallel universe that the Mutiny's free-spending co-
caine lords swapped their old-world names (say, Wilfredo Perez del
Cayo) for Cubano goodfella handles like Carlene, Redbeard, Coca-Cola,
el Loco, the Boys, *Recotado* ("Stocky"), *Veneno* ("Venom"). Weetchie,
Chunky, *Peloo*, *Perro* ("Dog"), Mungy. *Venao* ("Deer"), *Raspao* ("Snow
Cone"), the Big Blonde, *Super Papi*. *Chino*, Albertico, Kiki.

Even their pets lived extra large.

Kingpin Mario Tabraue had a chimp named Caesar, whom he
adorned with a gold-rope necklace holding a fifty-peso gold coin,
an eighteen-karat ID bracelet with his name in diamonds and a
ladies' Rolex Presidential. The primate was partial to turtlenecks
and a New York baseball cap, and proudly rode shotgun in his
owner's Benz while waving a Cuban cigar.

They'd shuttle to and from Tabraue's mansion around the corner, where panthers, pythons, raptors and even a toucan roamed
the grounds. Tabraue fed live rats to a two-headed snake and an

owl he kept in a Plexiglas cage. He would sometimes answer the door with a tarantula peeking out from under his cap.

"Every known narcotic trafficker in Miami would be at the Mutiny," recalled Diosdado "D. C." Diaz, a Miami police detective. "You'd see their wives and mistresses there. Their hit men. They'd throw a big celebration every time they brought in a load; they'd send Cristal and Dom to dealers at other tables. I'd follow the bottles and jot down their license plate numbers."

So vital was the Mutiny for watching the interplay of dealers, informants, celebs and public figures, he says, that authorities were understandably loath to disturb the ecosystem. "Why stir up the pot and scare them all away?" Diaz said.

Indeed, just as Monkey Morales was about to get his brains blown out by the bouncer in the lobby, his tablemate, one of Miami's biggest cocaine dealers, attempted to bribe D. C. Diaz with a Rolex and an antique World War II–issue gun. However, the kingpin refused to part ways with a silencer-equipped MAC-10 submachine gun that Monkey had lent him and wanted back.

In the very week Morales stared down Gomez, owner Burton Goldberg threw a raucous Halloween bash at the club.

Yes, you could argue Miami was now devolving into a third-world republic that was bound to break off and sink into the Atlantic. But the Mutiny at Sailboat Bay, adorned with lush, carefully lit foliage and stunning women, was raking it in.

And so the woolly-chested Goldberg donned two-inch eyelashes, a flowing blond wig and a long white gown, and skipped around tapping guests with his wand—a fairy godmother pretending to sprinkle magic pixie dust.

Subtle.

Chapter One

HEAVEN IN HELL

BURTON GOLDBERG'S MUTINY at Sailboat Bay was one of the country's most lucrative hotels, perennially overbooked and sending off armored trucks with sacks of its cash profits, albeit in the new murder-and-drug capital of America, a city that had been ravaged by race riots, gun killings and the sudden arrival of 125 thousand Cuban refugees, many of them sprung right from Fidel Castro's jails.

By the turn of the decade, the 130-room hotel and club was a criminal free-trade zone of sorts where gangsters could both revel in Miami's danger and escape from it.

"All roads led back to the Mutiny," said Wayne Black, an undercover cop who listened in to dope deals from a tinted van across the street, often wearing nothing but BVDs to cope with the stifling heat and humidity. "The druggies," he said, "the celebs, the crooked pols, spies, the informants, cops—good and bad—were all there."

America in the late 1970s and early 'eighties was in a pronounced funk: inflation and unemployment were high; consumer sentiment was in the dumps. But so exceptional was Miami's cocaine economy that dopers were paying banks to accept suitcases full of cash (while certificates of deposit were yielding 20 percent, on top of your choice of toaster or alarm clock). According to one study from Florida International University in Miami, at least one-third of the city's economic output was derived from narcotics at the time.

So much hot money was sloshing around Miami that the Mutiny was selling more bottles of Dom Pérignon than any other establishment on the planet, according to the bubbly's distributor, whose executives visited in disbelief at the turn of the decade. They heard right: a suite at the hotel was converted into a giant walk-in cooler; beautiful women would *ooh* and *ahh* at tabletop cascades of bubbly in stacks of flutes; dopers bought bottles for the house when their loads came in and management often flew out the Mutiny's private plane at the last minute to procure even more from other cities.

Internationally wanted hit men and mercenaries chilled at the Mutiny. Frequent visitors kept their guns tucked in the cushions, and cases of cash and cocaine in their suites. Bullets flew. Thugs were nabbed. Refugees snuck in. Cops were bribed. Dopers were recorded. Pilots were hired. Contracts were placed. Plots were hatched.

You might recognize this backdrop as the Babylon Club in the movie *Scarface*, whose creators, Oliver Stone and Brian De Palma, stayed at the Mutiny and sought permission to film there. In Stone's screenplay, he accidentally referenced the Mutiny Club; stars Al Pacino, Steven Bauer and other supporting cast checked in at the hotel.

Miami Vice stars were also gravitationally pulled to the Mutiny.

Don Johnson partied there, and Philip Michael Thomas moved in with his family and insisted on parking his purple imitation Ferrari out front on the curb. The hit show's creators studied agents and kingpins at the Mutiny; one cooperating drug lord even finagled his way onto two episodes.

The Miami of the Mutiny's heyday abounded with the surreal.

So much marijuana was getting confiscated in the waters around South Florida that the Florida Power & Light Company was opportunistically burning tons of it to run its generators: 732 pounds of pot could replace a barrel of crude. Take that, energy crisis!

Area McDonald's restaurants were running out of their tiny spoon-tipped coffee stirrers—they were perfect, it turned out, for portioning and sniffing cocaine. Mutiny dopers wore bronzed ones around their necks to advertise how far they'd come.

Burger King, meanwhile, loaned the overwhelmed county morgue a refrigerated truck. Bodies were turning up in gator-infested canals; in duffel bags alongside the turnpike; bobbing out of drums, bins and shopping carts in marinas along Biscayne Bay.

Machine-gun fire rained over the parking lot of the city's busiest mall.

All of which would soon land Miami on the cover of *Time* magazine as "Paradise Lost."

The Mutiny stood out as a lush oasis within this apocalypse. The Magic City was now the planet's cocaine entrepôt—its Federal Reserve branch was showing a five-billion-dollar cash surplus—and so this hotel and club became *the* place south of Studio 54 to blow illegal tender.

The club's seventy-five-dollar metal membership card, embossed with the Mutiny's winking pirate logo, got you in the door and certainly came in handy for cutting and snorting lines.

But it was cash—lots and lots of it—that got you everything else:

Cases of 150-dollar-a-bottle Dom Pérignon emptied into your hot tub? Right away!

A private jet for jaunts to the islands, stocked with Mutiny girls, a five-man crew and stone crab claws on dry ice? No sweat.

Your machine guns, bullets and silencers discreetly locked in a chest? *Sin problema*. Plus, a hostess would hide your piece in her skirt if the cops showed up, while another Mutiny girl was adept at clicking her stilettos against guys on the dance floor to check for ankle holsters.

"We couldn't just walk into the Mutiny with a cheap rubber watch," said Wayne Black, the undercover cop who would borrow a Rolex from the police evidence locker before going there. "You'd be buying Dom with the bad guys. You owned a Pinto but drove home a Jag. 'Daddy,' your kid would say, 'the neighbors say you sell drugs.'"

None of which would ever make the press release that the otherwise media-shy Mutiny felt the need to put out to start 1981, the year when Miami became America's murder capital.

THE MOST UNUSUAL HOTEL IN THE COUNTRY
Coconut Grove, Fla.

A hotel room is a hotel room is a hotel room.

This variation of the noted Gertrude Stein quotation is a frequent complaint of jaded travelers who are convinced that all hotel rooms look alike.

One hotel, located just 15 minutes south of Miami—the Hotel Mutiny at Sailboat Bay in Coconut Grove—is proof, in the words of Ira Gershwin, that "it ain't necessarily so."

At the Mutiny, no two rooms look alike. Every room and suite is decorated with its own unduplicated, luxurious and, frequently, exotic motif.

Decorative themes are based on various ideas. Some are inspired by faraway locales, some sound like titles to novels, some to states of mind and others to flights of fancy.

"Marakesh," "Coconut Grove," "Singapore," "Zapata's Retreat," "House of the Setting Sun," "Midnight Express," "Cloud 9," "Lunar Dreams" and "Fourth Dimension" are among them.

Themes are not developed with a single picture or ornament. Rather, the furniture, draperies, art, artifacts, and the basic layout of the rooms all conform to the individual motifs.

A full-time staff of six works at decorating the Mutiny. Two members of the decorating staff work full-time on flower arrangements. As guests walk down the halls, often covered in Oriental rugs, it is not uncommon for them to see elaborate arrangements of rare flowers—Peruvian lilies, birds-of-paradise and the like.

Roman baths and mirrored ceilings are found in some rooms, and many have panoramic views of Sailboat Bay.

Recently opened rooms include "Shoko," done on the theme of a Japanese inn or ryokan, "Balinese Isle," a two-bedroom suite with a setting of a rain forest in Bali, and the Moroccan wing with "Zirka," "Tlata Ketama," "Marakesh" and "Bourabech," all named for Moroccan cities.

"Shoko" is designed like a room in a Japanese ryokan. Behind the bed is a wall of shoji screens, a framed kimono is mounted on a wall, a blue-and-white country fabric is used to upholster the furniture and walls and there are carved stone statues from Japan. A low custom-made table is surrounded by cushions on the floor.

"Balinese Isle" is a two-bedroom suite designed around a large screen painted by hand with a scene from a rain forest, highlighted by bamboo lights. The suite includes original Balinese oil paintings, and a tiki bar and furniture custom-made in the hotel from natural rattan.

Throughout the Moroccan wing, a guest will see a combination of terra-cotta floors and carpeting and plasterwork deliberately designed to give the impression of old Moorish architecture, with walls that have lost part of their plaster. A specially designed emblem was pressed repeatedly in cement to create the effect; then four layers of plaster were laid over that, with occasional areas left uncovered. On each layer, several coats of oil were applied, seasoned, waxed and buffed.

"Zirka," named for a city famous for its fountains, has in the room a large round tub designed to look like a fountain with light streaming down on it. Moroccan arches surround the tub as well as the bed, and backlighted stained glass is embedded in the plaster of the arches. Wrought iron doors and accessories complete the effect.

"Tlata Ketama" is a large city in Morocco. The room concentrates on the use of copper, including custom-made copper light fixtures, copper-treated furniture and copper-glazed Moroccan tiles around the tub. The room also has large plaster columns with capitals created by a Spanish artist living in Florida.

Dining at the Mutiny is as unusual as its rooms. There are no "walk-in" dinner guests. Each diner must be a member of the Mutiny Club or a hotel guest. The club's large international membership is sustained by the quality of the food and the service.

Hostesses and waitresses at the club, who do not wear uniforms, wear fashionable gowns, and at lunch, often wear broad-brimmed tropical hats.

Following dinner, the music starts for disco dancing. During the course of the late evening, the club has sophisticated shows.

Service at the Mutiny is on a par with the setting and the cuisine. In the morning, guests are brought a festive complimentary continental breakfast that includes five or six fresh fruits, freshly squeezed orange juice and butter croissants, along with the morning newspaper.

Coconut Grove is one of the most interesting communities in southern Florida with a widely diverse population that includes many working artists. Magnificent flowers and trees in the area surround the Mutiny in subtropical abundance. Guests can relax in a large wooden hot tub in the middle of a hanging garden, beneath a waterfall or around the swimming pool, where an alfresco lunch is served.

Chapter Two

MONKEY IN THE MIDDLE

OWNING A FANTASYLAND for outlaws in the hellscape that was Cocaine Miami had hardly been in the cards for New Jersey–born Burton Goldberg when the forty-year-old developer set his sights on Coconut Grove in the mid-1960s. True, his father, Sol, part-owned midtown Manhattan's Navarro Hotel, where mafiosi like Meyer Lansky and Lucky Luciano had held court in the 1950s. But Goldberg is adamant that he had "absolutely nothing" to do with the Navarro, and bristles at any suggestions of mob ties.

Coconut Grove, founded in the mid-nineteenth century as *Cocoanut* Grove and annexed by the city of Miami in 1925, was an offbeat bohemian village whose residents left their doors open and allowed strangers to pluck mangoes off their trees. In 1882, its Bay View House (later renamed the Peacock Inn) became the first hotel on the South Florida mainland below Palm Beach. Up until its turn-of-the-century conversion into a school, the inn was a hub for Miami's first community organizers.

The great hurricane of 1926 obliterated Coconut Grove and hit the reset button on the rest of Miami.

A parcel of land overlooking the water at the corner of South Bayshore Drive and McFarlane Road used to house the Peacock Inn's general store. In 1966, Burton Goldberg bought the plot from its eventual inheritor, a New England Christian Scientist.

By then, Coconut Grove was Miami's hippie central. Women with hairy armpits sunned topless in the park by the marina. Its Dinner Key Auditorium is where Doors front man Jim Morrison infamously exposed himself to a sellout crowd. The joke in the Grove's head shops and incense bodegas was that the most violent things in those parts were the wild roosters that chased the mailmen.

The neighborhood was a sleepy escape from the mayhem a few miles away: downtown Miami and Little Havana were getting shot up and bombed by characters like Ricardo Morales.

Nineteen sixties South Florida played host to the mob's internecine "bookie wars," while thousands of Cuban exiles in and around Miami channeled their testosterone into what they assumed would be a chance to take out Fidel Castro and reclaim Cuba. Miami hosted dozens of CIA-run paramilitary camps and dummy companies that could procure and ship any matériel at a moment's notice. Swift boats. Demolition. Underwater sabotage. Machine guns, plastic explosives and recoilless rifles. Cuban men and adolescents alike were steeped in the agency's dark arts of regime change.

Cuban exiles and the American Mafia had a shared history. During the prerevolutionary dictatorship of Fulgencio Batista, Cuba was the playground of the mob, a sort of Vegas in the Caribbean. Overlords like Luciano, Lansky and Florida-based Santo Trafficante owned many of Havana's casino resorts. They flew and cruised into the island to dine on manatee and flamingo steaks;

whore with every shape, size and color of *chica*; buy cops and judges and watch live sex shows that would have gotten them arrested in the States. It was hedonism with no consequences, as long as you paid off the right people.

In 1959, when Fidel Castro wrested control of Cuba, he nationalized the resorts and had their slot machines smashed in the streets. During the ensuing purge, Ricardo Morales, a twenty-year-old law school student, signed up for Castro's secret police.

Al pared! Al pared! ("To the wall!") The Cuban street bayed for more bodies to be brought before the firing squads. The old regime's cronies, enforcers and accused traitors were dragged out and stood up against pockmarked walls. Some of the condemned were drained of their blood—syringe after syringe—until they were about to pass out, the better to use fewer precious bullets in finishing them off.

Morales quickly grew disenchanted with the secret police and wanted out of Castro's Cuba. He might also have been flipped by the CIA, which had assets on the ground in Havana, just as Fidel Castro had moles up in Miami.

Either way, South Florida echo-chambered with rumors that the White House would soon take out Castro, much as it had snuffed out other third-world regimes that it didn't like. Fathers, sons and brothers in Miami's exile community disappeared for days on end into training camps in the Everglades and to run drills miles off the coast. Something was coming down the pike. "I had to choose between Moscow and Washington," Morales later quipped. In 1960, he finally defected through the Brazilian embassy and escaped to South Florida.

In Miami, Morales signed up for Operation 40, an assassination group that targeted Castro loyalists and assets in Cuba and abroad.

In the early 1960s, Miami's CIA branch—stocked with exiles, case agents, front companies, munitions and real estate—grew into the world's biggest.

Morales's aunt and seven-year-old niece lived in a small apartment in Little Havana, just west of downtown Miami. An overgrown mango tree touched the bedroom window. Inside, under the bed, Morales left a bomb and a couple of guns with instructions that if he ever came running through the apartment, whoever was at home had to race to the bedroom, throw him the guns and escape down the mango tree. The last one out had to pull the pin on the bomb. His aunt constantly rehearsed the drill with his niece, Lynette. "I still see that thing under the bed," she said. "Let me tell you: it was not a small bomb. It is hilarious to think back on it, and then you just shake your head."

But Miami exiles' belief that taking back Cuba was a fait accompli was smashed in April of 1961, when Castro's forces thwarted Brigade 2506—the 1,400 CIA-trained paramilitaries (most of them South Florida exiles) who attempted to invade Cuba at the Bay of Pigs.

It wasn't even close. The Kennedy administration, which inherited the top secret invasion from Dwight Eisenhower's CIA, opted not to provide air reinforcements. The anti-Castro "Brigadesmen"—Cuba's would-be *libertadores*—who weren't killed or repelled out to sea were taken prisoner.

News of which put Miami in a state of shock and mourning. The mayor went on television to plead in Spanish: "We urge the Cuban colony exiles that are here to remain calm and composed, and we pray to God that Cuba's freedom will flourish from the blood that is being shed."

It was an all-around catastrophe for Washington: Fidel Castro thumped his chest and inspired leftists the world over, Cuban-Americans seethed at President Kennedy for abandoning their men, and Havana was now blowing kisses to Soviet Russia.

To pile on the insult, Castro leveraged more than 1,100 Bay of Pigs captives to shake down the US for 53 million dollars in cash, food and medical supplies—all of which were critical to the young regime's survival. The Bay of Pigs was a coup . . . for Fidel Castro.

Even so, most everyone in Miami operated under the assumption that there would be a rematch. Kennedy himself came to Miami's Orange Bowl in late 1962 to assure returning prisoners that Brigade 2506's flag would be returned to Havana. The CIA maintained a campaign of secret exile-led raids.

In 1963, Morales regaled the *Miami Herald* with the story of how he and nine fellow exiles in two fast boats nearly destroyed a refinery on the coast of Cuba. He was desperate to see more action—and crushed when the CIA under President Lyndon B. Johnson wound down its clandestine campaign against Castro.

A year later, a restless Morales reluctantly agreed to be shipped to the Belgian Congo, where he and a top secret brigade of Cuban exiles battled leftist rebels allied with Soviet-trained Cuban troops. Many of the Congolese soldiers were armed with nothing more than spears, having been brainwashed by witch doctors. The Cuban-American mercenaries had such an easy time mowing them down that Morales's comrades compared their weapons to fire hoses.

Morales took a bullet to the spine, but kept shooting. For much of this commando tour, a terrified little Congolese girl latched onto his shoulders and slept in his arms at night. The memory would forever haunt the father of four.

In 1965, Morales returned to Miami, disillusioned and traumatized. So much for the rematch against Fidel Castro—Kennedy was dead and the Vietnam War was now front and center in the Cold War.

South Florida, meanwhile, still teemed with spies, double agents, arms smugglers, Mafia men and retired dictators, providing no shortage of gigs for orphaned mercenaries.

Morales took a job parking cars at a mob-owned steak house in Miami Beach and let it be known that this was where he kept office hours and solicited contract work.

Fifteen miles down the coastline in Coconut Grove: in 1967, Burton Goldberg hired a crane to park a houseboat on the bend of South Bayshore Drive. The vessel would serve as a quirky preconstruction sales office for his forthcoming building, Sailboat Bay.

This was while Ricardo Morales, acting as a freelance bomber, scuba dived up to the back of a mobster's house in Miami Beach. A rival wanted the homeowner offed so he could move in on his wife, a Playboy Bunny. It turned out that the gangster, his wife and four children were sleeping inside when a pair of bombs ripped apart the carport. All survived. Maybe Morales wanted it this way. Who knows?

The *Miami Herald* ran a "Bombing Box Score" of recent explosions, perpetrators still at large. (Morales, it turned out, was responsible for at least half of the incidents, including the dynamiting of a Miami cop's front lawn and the double bombing of a numbers racket in South Beach.)

In another contract hit, Morales shot a convicted jewel hustler in the face. The victim survived, and Monkey was never charged.

Later in 1967, for reasons unknown, Morales pulled up to a Cuban exile in broad Little Havana daylight and sprayed him with seventeen rounds from a silencer-equipped .45-caliber M3 submachine gun. Again, the victim somehow managed to live. He never pressed charges. Morales bragged about the episode as "just another day at the office."

In 1968, Morales bombed a firm that forwarded food and medicine to Cuba. This time, however, police found his fingerprints on C-4 explosive. In his house, they seized a bomb and detonator. Finally arrested, the Monkey was facing serious time.

But the wily Morales promised the FBI an even bigger catch: the terrorists who had just attempted to attack a Polish freighter at the Port of Miami with a shoulder-held bazooka. The shell dented the ship's hull, and the State Department had to issue an official apology to (Communist) Poland.

Morales infiltrated the gang, supplying the men and women with phony dynamite as the FBI recorded his conversations with the ringleaders. Morales testified against the culprits and won his freedom. "Chubby-cheeked Morales," as a front-page story in the *Miami Herald* described him, "testified that he didn't ask to get paid for his services to the FBI, nor did he get any promises for his undercover work."

He did, however, now have an FBI bodyguard shadowing him. Morales, twenty-nine, was a marked man in Miami, having betrayed nearly a dozen fellow exiles who were widely regarded as freedom fighters for targeting that freighter. Whispers echoed that he was still in the employ of Fidel Castro.

Down in Coconut Grove, Burton Goldberg cut the ribbon on his twelve-story Sailboat Bay, billed as the Grove's first high-rise apartment. He touted how residents would be privy to a panorama of security cameras that transmitted various live angles to an in-house TV channel.

Sailboat Bay's aesthetic was decidedly white and white-collar.

The attorney who represented Linda Lovelace, star of the porn film *Deep Throat*—much of which was shot in a house around the corner—kept an office upstairs.

Earl Smalley Jr., the majority owner of the league-dominating Miami Dolphins, scored a suite overlooking the pool. By his bed was a pink pneumatic fuck bench that beach babes could saddle up on after long days on his speedboat, which was docked in adjacent Dinner Key Marina.

In late 1971, Goldberg opened a small club and restaurant atop the lobby. He called it the Mutiny. He also wanted to convert Sailboat Bay's mixed-apartment-and-office concept into a boutique hotel called the Mutiny at Sailboat Bay. "I'd call it the Sex Hotel if I could," he said. "This was all about the sexual revolution. The pill. Boy meets girl. I wanted swingers." But it had to be upscale and classy.

Goldberg's timing could not have been better: the Republican nominating convention was coming back to Miami Beach. Richard Nixon's best friend, banker Bebe Rebozo, often wined and dined guests at the Mutiny while his yacht was out front. E. Howard Hunt, the GOP operative who was chief political officer for the CIA when Castro rose to power, lived in Coconut Grove and drank at the Mutiny's bar. Baron Joseph "Sepy" De Bicske Dobronyi—the internationally renowned aristocrat, nude sculptor and ladies' man—was bringing beauts and European royalty to Coconut Grove. The Super Bowl and perfect season–bound Miami Dolphins were drawing national press; all sorts of media and sports VIPs flocked to the Mutiny.

Best of all for Burton Goldberg: two massive commodity booms were about to pack Miami with free-spending horndogs.

For starters, the global oil shock of 1973 gave rise to the era of the *"Dame Dos"* (Spanish for "Give Me Twos")—rich Venezuelans who'd flock to Miami to strip shelves bare, spend big on fine food and wines and luxuriate at resorts. Also known as the Fat Cows of Caracas, these men would often fly in with their families in the morning, leave their planes at Miami International and send their wives and daughters to shop at Dadeland Mall—all while they relaxed, wined, dined and fornicated at the Mutiny. They'd all reunite in the evening at Miami International Airport to fly back to South America.

At the same time, thousands of Miami's Cuban exiles dived headlong into smuggling marijuana. After all, this was the 1970s. Everyone in America wanted good weed, and no one knew how to smuggle it into the country better than South Florida Cubans who had spent a decade and a half memorizing every nook and cranny of the state coastline, with help from the CIA.

Adding urgency to their career pivot: in 1975, the government of the Bahamas (free of British colonial rule for two years) banned US fishermen from its waters, on the justification that it needed to defend lobster from overexploitation by Florida trappers. This gave the nation's corrupt government more nationalistic cred—i.e., "Our seafood is our natural endowment, not to be plundered by the richest country on the planet."

Miami's seafood industry was overwhelmingly Cuban. Boat captains and laborers were at most a degree of separation from someone who had served at the Bay of Pigs, men who had by now sublimated their CIA training to storm Cuba into smuggling marijuana up and down the coast of Florida.

"Some of [these exiles] made over one hundred, two hundred, three hundred missions to Cuba . . . going in against the most heavily patrolled coast that I've ever heard of," explained a commando who had trained many of them. "These people came out knowing how you do it. . . . And they found it absolutely child's play when they started in [with drug smuggling] over here, because US law enforcement didn't have that kind of defense. They didn't even need most of their expertise."

Accordingly, one Jose Medardo Alvero-Cruz, a charismatic Brigade veteran, became known as "King of the River" for being connected to just about every Cuban fisherman and vessel docked along the Miami River. His value proposition to the men and their crews was straightforward: they no longer had to sully their hands on lobster traps, bycatch and fish guts; they could now become rich smuggling in neatly packed bales of marijuana—dubbed "square groupers"—off giant ships Alvero was anchoring miles off the coast.

The new thinking: Why just sit around and go poor when there were easy marijuana millions to be made? Look, *hermano*: Fidel Castro took your wealth, and Washington let him keep it. Bay of Pigs II wasn't happening anytime soon—surely not under a post-Watergate Democratic president, who would be in no mood to prioritize Havana. No, fuck that: it was time to get paid.

Not that Miami's reefer madness was solely supplied by Cuban smugglers. Mutiny waitress Deb Kendrick moonlighted as an unlikely smuggler for the Black Tunas, a marijuana gang run by two Jewish peddlers from Philadelphia.

Loaded padlocked sedans would get delivered to her, fresh off a barge on the Miami River, ready to be driven up the East Coast for delivery to various doormen on Manhattan's Upper East Side. "I was scared to death," said the Michigan native. "The cars stunk. I stunk. I was too terrified to stop."

But blond, 105 pounds, and five feet one, she didn't exactly fit the profile of a drug runner.

Chapter Three

SNOW IN MIAMI

SOMETIME IN 1976, a Venezuelan oil trader nicknamed the Sultan of Caracas summoned his Mutiny server to bring him a magnum of Château Lafite Rothschild 1827. When his waitress tried to gently remind him that the Mutiny only took cash, *"el Sultan"* asked for a phone, plugged it into his table, made one call and had thirty thousand dollars delivered right to the hotel.

"Everyone who'd come from Caracas, I'd put them up at the Mutiny," said Norman Canter, a Miami businessman who was dating a cocktail waitress who worked there. "You started seeing a lot of deals going down. Guy in a long ponytail and black suit walks in. Takes a drink at the bar. Looks around and takes a table for stone crabs. Always a lot of women around. It was like *Casablanca*. It had that aura. The mystery. The Venezuelans wanted women, and the women were at the Mutiny."

It was getting ever harder to score a table at the Mutiny Club. By 1976, its newsletter was showcasing three dozen "Mutiny girls," including a recently hired Playboy Club Bunny, a Doublemint twin and stunners from Hungary, Australia, Canada, Texas, Poland and Cuba:

> *Fresh, vibrant, aware. An international sampling of beauty. They come from all over the world with a variety of backgrounds. Actresses, top fashion models, singers and dancers. They're carefully screened and selected from a multitude of applicants.*

Silka, a Dominican brunette who spoke four languages, helped guests shop, land babysitters, replace lost passports and ship their loot back home. "Silka, soft as her name," read a brochure, "has become an invaluable friend to our international members."

Bo Crane, the Mutiny's first DJ, remembered Tom Jones, the international sex icon of "What's New Pussycat?" fame, walking in one night. "The dance floor was the size of a postage stamp," he said, "but the women went nuts. Barry White was fucking huge then. Seduction music. You'd get up and grind. It felt like the hottest place on the planet."

So big had the destination become that it was canonized by recording artists Crosby & Nash in the song "Mutiny" and in the Stills-Young Band's "Midnight on the Bay"—the latter penned by Neil Young on a Mutiny cocktail napkin in the bay-windowed booth atop the valet.

Both Crosby and Young had been mistaken for hobos by the hotel staff, which Burton Goldberg drilled to enforce a strict dress code (even if the owner himself sometimes sat naked at his penthouse desk overlooking the bay).

By 1977, the likes of Led Zeppelin, Cat Stevens, Prince Faisal of Jordan, the ex-president of Colombia, Joe DiMaggio, Rod Serling and Jackie Mason were turning up at the Mutiny. The place was so consistently mobbed by big spenders that Goldberg added a more exclusive level he called the Upper Deck.

The Mutiny Club's seafaring theme, which Goldberg had signed off on just six years earlier, now expanded to levels known as the Poop Deck and the Lower Deck. Also in the offing: a tiki bar above the pool that would be called the Gangplank.

Members could now rent the *Tonga*—a seventy-two-foot ketch once owned by Hollywood swashbuckler Errol Flynn—a six-seater, twin-engine Aerostar plane or a turbocharged Beechcraft B60.

"We can supply a Mutiny girl and ample provisions," touted an ad.

In 1978, Goldberg brought in San Francisco set designer Carolyn Robbins to complete the Mutiny's multiyear transformation into a hotel with 130 individually designed fantasy rooms. "You walked into the club and realized it was all about the seduction of the Latin male," she said. "Burton would always yell: 'We are a sexy place! Don't you know what a sexy place looks like? What do sexy people want?'"

The owner shuttled telenovela-grade beauties to Caracas, Bogotá and Panama City to sell memberships, wine and dine executives and extend reciprocity to exclusive South American clubs, such as Colombia's Unicorn Disco.

As the Mutiny's caliber of VIPs shot ever higher (Hollywood starlets, wealthy Latin families in the crosshairs of kidnappers), Goldberg hired Fernando Puig, a hulking Bay of Pigs veteran, to run security. During the botched 1961 invasion of Cuba, Puig was stationed by the CIA in Nicaragua, where he became best friends with Anastasio Somoza, next in line in a dynastic family to run the Central American country.

By the time Puig was hired at the Mutiny, Somoza was preparing to flee Nicaragua with billions and cronies in tow. Though the dictator was unwelcome in the US (he would later get assassinated in Paraguay), Somoza's cabinet and colonels flocked to Miami—to work for Fernando Puig's security firm. They all became active members of the Mutiny.

Norman Canter remembers all sorts of military types crowding into the Mutiny in the mid- to late 1970s. A pair of Venezuelan air force guys approached him to see what he thought about their smuggling in cocaine several times a week in their military planes. Could he help them cut and place the kilos in Miami? Did he know people?

Canter said using marijuana was as illicit as he would get. "I didn't know cocaine, and I didn't do cocaine," he said.

Perhaps he hadn't read the January 1975 issue of *Playboy* that was making the rounds up and down the Mutiny. In a lengthy feature titled "A Very Expensive High: The Truth About Cocaine," the magazine observed:

> *A blizzard of cocaine is blowing over us, little spoons hanging from our necks like crucifixes, snorting noises in the next room coming from people who don't have colds, people working twenty-hour days who used to work four. . . . Who, even as recently as five years ago, would have guessed that otherwise straight people, doctors, lawyers and merchant chiefs, would be snorting what many were calling "flake," "blow" and "lady"?*

Cocaine was being promoted as the Dom Pérignon of illegal narcotics: non–habit forming, mind opening, invigorating, high-class. No less than Thomas Edison thought best under its influence, and Sigmund Freud wrote poems about it. "That issue was everywhere," says Mutiny girl Joanna Christopher. "It was the topic of conversation not just at the club but at your dentist's office and at your exercise classes. Everyone wanted to try cocaine."

Mutiny member Nelson Aguilar recalled his first bump. In 1971, at age thirteen, he was the class president at Ada Merritt Junior High, where he won a trophy for his speech on the life of Martin Luther King Jr. He was doing so well that his aunt (his guardian) moved him to a school in a more well-to-do neighbourhood. To earn money on the side, Aguilar signed on as a door-to-door sales boy for the *Miami Herald*. "It was," he said, "the best thing. I was so awesome at selling subscriptions; I shattered fucking records. You would knock on the door and Cuban-Americans would shout back: 'What? The *Miami Herald*? It's Communist! Here's the money. But it's for *you*, okay? Just don't ever send the fucking paper!'"

Within a year, Aguilar was clearing one hundred dollars a week and eyeing a fat promotion that promised him five times as much in salary and commissions—a fortune for a teenager in the early 1970s. But his big cousin Jesús, a high school dropout, intervened with other plans. One night, while the boys were being chauffeured in Jesús's new Cutlass Supreme (he was sixteen and had his own driver), the older cousin stuck a knife under Nelson's nose. "Sniff!" he ordered from the front seat. "Come on, bro. Sniff!"

"When I did that hit," said Aguilar, "the whole world—anything, anything became possible. No doubt that you ever had meant anything anymore. It was euphoria—like heaven." Aguilar said his eyes felt like they had 360-degree vision. His heart raced, and he felt like running a marathon. And saving starving kids. And fucking for hours on end. And then doing more coke.

"You suddenly had all the answers to every problem the world ever had," he said. "*Bam!* Solved. The only problem is, no one woke up the next day to do all that solving. Reality sets in. And then you just feel dirty."

It took Aguilar little time to drop out of school. Aguilar remembered shooting up signs on the downtown expressway with his big cousin's .44 Magnum. He recalled Jesús somehow managing to shoot himself in the hand; he was so coked out that, bloodied left fist be damned, he just shot at everything else on the expressway while ordering his driver to go faster. Faster.

FASTER!

In 1975, a gregarious Peruvian named Pepe Negaro barnstormed the Mutiny with samples of his high-purity cocaine, which he had dyed light pink and spritzed to smell like bubble gum, ostensibly to razzle-dazzle the ladies. He was an absolute hit at the club, recalls then-manager Chuck Volpe. Liza Minnelli latched onto him, and he had little trouble bedding women who were mesmerized by his charm and nose candy.

Pepe the Peruvian had his cocaine smuggled into Miami International Airport from Lima in giant cored-out wood hangers, the kind that might hold a heavy fur or a knee-length leather coat. They'd then get driven over to the Mutiny in the trunk of limos he owned with a Miami heroin dealer.

When he wasn't boinking various women in his suite at the Mutiny, Negaro would carefully pry apart the hangers and portion out sample sizes in reclaimed Vicks inhalers.

There was a radio station on the fifth floor of the Mutiny. Its Sunday night DJ was so fond of Negaro's import that he would cue up especially long jazz LPs while he was downstairs mooching stuff to nose-binge. He sniffled so much that listeners across Miami assumed he had a permanent cold.

Cop Wayne Black wired an informant inside the Mutiny and attempted to listen in to Negaro from his surveillance van across the street from the hotel. But to little avail: "Liza Minnelli would not shut up for even a minute," he said. "She kept bugging Pepe for more blow."

Chapter Four

TABLE 14

IN FEBRUARY OF 1977, after months of being tailed by the DEA, a Mutiny girl was arrested when she tried to sell a pound of cocaine to undercover officers at the hotel's beauty salon. Three months later, a pair of Miami Dolphins players who frequented the club were arrested for trying to sell their own pound of cocaine.

But these busts were penny-ante compared to the volumes being moved by a couple of flamboyant Cuban drug lords who by 1977 were practically running the Mutiny.

Thirtysomethings Carlos "Carlene" Quesada and Rodolfo "Rudy Redbeard" Rodriguez Gallo held court on the Mutiny's Poop Deck, an elevated set of tables over the driveway that served as a landing of sorts between the club's two floors.

Redbeard, Quesada and their crew wedged their guns in their booths' giant leather cushions and sat steps from the back exit, ready to bolt, should wives or the cops suddenly arrive unannounced.

Redbeard dressed in white Italian suits and dyed his whiskers red, earning him his sobriquet. Quesada was partial to silk shirts and reptile-skin shoes. Even for a Miami Cuban, he spoke fast— faster than most gringos could ever understand—often having to repeat his order in slowly . . . enunciated . . . Spanglish.

At the Mutiny, these coke lords swilled Dom Pérignon, Perrier-Jouët and 1,300-dollar bottles of wine, preferably from years just prior to the Cuban Revolution. Flanked by hit men, Ricardo "Monkey" Morales and Bay of Pigs veterans the Villaverde brothers and Frank Castro, they ordered lavishly and tipped in the hundreds. Waitresses would angle and tussle for the privilege of serving them.

"When I got there," said Redbeard, "the Mutiny, it shot up in popularity. The manager knew how to take care of me, rotating the waitresses. I wanted to be fair to everyone with my tips."

"We bought the fucking place," said his son, Rudy Jr. "Dad rented a whole floor of rooms. Nobody gave a fuck anymore if you were Cuban. *We* had the connections. What else did you fucking need?"

Well, how about a giant yacht? Redbeard docked *Graciela*, his fifty-eight-foot Bertram, right in front of the Mutiny. It had a grand piano, a king-size bed and a sixty-four-inch projection TV. On board, guests could challenge Captain Rudy to arcade games for a kilo of cocaine.

At least, if the drug lord was feeling social.

On most evenings, "Uncle Rudy," as he was also known at the Mutiny, preferred to smoke his special cocaine mix in dark paranoid isolation. "Keep the squatters away!" he'd warn his waitress, Eugenia, a Miss Florida contestant.

Mollie Hampton was a churchgoing brunette from Tampa who took a job at the Mutiny in early 1978, having just left her fiancé to explore women. She was assigned to hostess for upstairs VIPs.

"It was overwhelming to walk into that place," she said. "You had all these gorgeous women—so confident—big shots at the bar and tables. You felt it. There I was: wearing my big Mutiny girl hat [a mandatory piece of attire, per Burton Goldberg's rules]. I had no idea what was going on."

"We said she wouldn't last a week under Burton," said another Mutiny girl, noting Mollie's Bible Belt drawl, unladylike guffaw and refusal to wear makeup and haute dresses. "But she was so funny and sweet that we hid her from him."

Goldberg was notorious for firing girls on the spot for a transgression as small as a dirty ashtray. Everyone also had to undergo monthly lie detector tests: Are you using drugs? Do you steal? Are you a prostitute? Have you ever taken home liquor from the hotel?

Staff knew that passing them was a joke; you just had to walk in stoned. One working girl who managed to land a waitressing job at the Mutiny popped downers before her test.

But it was cocaine that unleashed Mutiny Mollie. "After that first hit," she said, "I was hooked. I felt like fucking Superwoman. You felt empowered, invincible. Like you could solve all the world's problems."

She now thought nothing of showing up for work and ordering a prime rib and a bottle of fine vintage on Redbeard's or Quesada's tab. The Poop Deck tables would be covered with pricey bottles, with various women actually kneeling before Redbeard to kiss his ring and get a Quaalude. "What you want, baby?" he and Quesada would ask her, Dom getting popped left and right.

"I'd zip over there, do a hit, have a cocktail, go from table to table," recalled Mollie. "There was always cash thrown around; we'd snort out of hundred-dollar bills. It wasn't even like we were working; it was like we were hosting the party."

Word soon got out that Mollie was a lesbian, she said, and suddenly the most feared dopers and gunmen at the Mutiny were stuttering in her presence. "It fucking drove these guys nuts," she said. "They'd get all curious and serious, asking me about it."

Rudy Redbeard had her on his yacht, where she would enjoy other women. When they were alone, the drug lord would have Mollie individually empty out his cigarettes and reroll them with freebase cocaine. His manic side would last until about sundown. "People were definitely scared of him," she said. "Sometimes he'd be so happy. Sometimes you didn't know if he'd kill you."

In a suite at the Mutiny, Carlene Quesada called down to the club and asked Mollie to take a break and head upstairs. "Girl, whatchoo doing? Come over!" He introduced her to his mistress, Terecita, and asked if she'd initiate the shy, crucifix-wearing brunette into her sapphic ways. "I want you to be with her," he said, his rapid-fire voice slowing to a quiver. Quesada watched, seemingly traumatized, while Mollie undressed and made out with someone she'd literally just met—a woman who had never kissed a woman, no less.

Within a week, she said, it was Terecita who was calling her upstairs.

For Mollie's twenty-fourth birthday, Bernardo de Torres, a mysterious Bay of Pigs operative who practically lived at the Mutiny, ordered her eight escorts, including Colombian sisters who roughed her up in a bruising threesome. Mollie found herself enjoying the straddle between pleasure and pain.

"They thought I was a woman who had all the good parts of a man," she said. "Everyone was doing everyone. They loved watching me with other women."

Monkey Morales, the Redbeard-Quesada gang's de facto head

of intelligence, got off in a whole other way. One evening at the Mutiny, he threw Mollie the keys to his red Cadillac Seville and told her to meet him and Quesada by the valet. In the car, Morales handed her a gun and told her to be ready to drive fast. "I've never been so scared in my life," she said.

Mollie off-loaded Morales and Quesada in front of the famous Fontainebleau Hotel and waited for what seemed like way too long. She lost her nerve and went up to look for them. "I opened the door and saw guns everywhere," she said. "Screaming in Spanish. It felt like a rip-off or shoot-out."

The trio got out of the hotel alive, bumping hits of cocaine and laughing fiendishly across the causeway back to the Mutiny. The next day at the club, one of Quesada's associates handed Mollie an envelope stuffed with ten thousand dollars in cash.

The Mutiny was paying her one dollar and fifty cents an hour.

"I never thought about money at that job," she says. "All my food and drink was free. My ride. My rooms. The parties. Then you got gigs like this, and they'd throw you stacks of cash and say, 'Just take it.' Other times I'd help them count cash, and they'd hand me a stack for myself. I can't believe I lived that."

RUDY REDBEARD AND Carlene Quesada were childhood pals in the fishing port town of Batabanó, Cuba. In 1962, the teenage Quesada stole his father's gun and hijacked a shrimp boat, hell-bent on making it to Miami.

Redbeard had fled to Miami a year earlier when he paid his way out of La Cabaña, an infamous prison and torture chamber in Cuba supervised by Che Guevara. He had been part of the anti-Castro underground that lobbed grenades into police stations.

"The fucking Americans screwed us," said his son, Rudy Gallo Jr. "They just handed our country to Fidel."

Reunited in Miami, the duo lived a life of mostly petty crime. Gallo's legitimate line of work was a boatbuilding business that he says was felled by the 1973 oil shock. He then scraped together a living installing vinyl tops on Monte Carlos at a big Chevrolet dealership whose owner took long lunches at the Mutiny. Mafioso customers of the Chevy lot particularly liked Rudy Redbeard's landau roof work.

He developed a taste for cocaine, which was a delicacy for big shots in the old country—something you might see on a tiny gold saucer in a governor's country home. *Playboy*'s treatise on the drug reported that prerevolutionary Cuba had the world's highest per capita cocaine use. It made sense: cocaine paired perfectly with the era's bordellos, casinos and frenetic *cha-cha-chá*. Exiles who brought the habit to Miami looked at it as a nostalgic indulgence, something to turn to when the homesickness became unbearable. Some called it *postre*, pastry.

Rudy Redbeard was godfather to a child of Miami pot smuggler Juan Cid, who hooked him up with a guy who could provide quality blow. "Coke," said Cid, "was nonexistent here. It was rare, like a couple of mules coming into Miami International from South America or ten kilos in a banana boat in the Miami River. It was not yet the big gold rush."

As associates kept trying to mooch the stuff off Redbeard, he turned to dealing cocaine himself. "If there was any other merchandise with that profit," says Gallo, "I'd do that. There was so much money. Too much."

Juan Cid connected him with suppliers in Colombia. "I needed someone older," he said, "with a little more reputation. Rudy had the boat business. He liked cocaine. He had a warehouse. He partied all the time."

And so Redbeard and Quesada, the pals from Batabanó, Cuba, ran with Cid's hookup. They installed a chemist and lab in Colombia's southernmost city and experimented with the smuggling of cocaine in the bilgewater of Gallo's custom fast boats—the drying and desalination saved for South Florida, where Gallo built a nine-acre cocaine lab.

As more cocaine was smuggled into Miami, users—everyone from gangsters to dentists to depressed trophy wives—became discriminating connoisseurs. You could only command high prices if you could deliver consistently good stuff; too many upstarts were trying to cheat the market with heavily diluted or hastily cured batches.

For Rudy Redbeard, cocaine became a family business. Son Rudy Jr. stocked the big lab with drums of ether and acetone, sharkskin boards and Pyrex filters. He told everyone he was a chemist. "All I did was count cash, pack coke and go to school—in my Jaguar convertible," he said. He also got to drive Maseratis, Porsches and Ferraris. "I'd be carrying suitcases full of cash around. I was still in fucking high school!"

The Redbeard-Quesada syndicate was now riding one of the most lucrative commodity plays in history. Consider:

Cultivating a thousand cocoa leaves in Peru, an easy distance from their south Colombia hub, cost them 625 dollars. Converted into a kilogram of paste and cocaine base, it was now worth upward of 6,500 dollars. When the resulting kilo of high-purity cocaine hit South Florida, it would be cut, or diluted, to make two kilos of cocaine, worth a total of eighty thousand dollars. Finally, two or three middlemen cut their take—one kilo having been diluted into six to eight kilos—and sold the cocaine on the streets at seventy-five dollars a gram.

The upshot: a kilo of "pure" cocaine was actually somewhere between 92 and 96 percent cocaine hydrochloride. "Uncut" 96 percent cocaine could be cut all the way down to 12 percent potency, which was enough to satisfy most mom-and-pop palates. Pushed all the way through the transcontinental supply chain, spanning planes, boats, plastic baggies and baby laxative, an original 625-dollar investment could eventually turn into six hundred thousand dollars of street value.

Rudy Redbeard smoked *basuco*, the ashen base of cocaine that some drug lords craved for its mellowing, stamina-boosting attributes. Colombian processors would prepare it by larding up cocaine dregs with brick dust, chalk and even volcanic ash. Unrefined and unpurified, *basuco* contained varying amounts of lead, sulfuric acid, ether, chloroform, kerosene and sometimes gasoline.

Smoking it was asking for multiple layers of highs and lows—it was risky, unpredictable stuff.

Pepe Negaro, the Peruvian coke dealer, smoked way too much of his own product: by 1977, he was reduced to showing up across the street from the Mutiny in a banged-up Subaru with a propane tank tied to its roof. Like David Crosby with his blowtorch, Pepe was now so addicted to the stuff that he felt the need to travel everywhere with his freebasing fuel.

By 1978, Rudy Redbeard was smoking through a pound of *basuco* a week in his hollowed-out Marlboros, which gave off an antiseptic aroma, akin to an electrical fire in a dentist's office. "We'd smell him walk in from the back," said Jane Podowski, a Mutiny waitress. "We'd be like, 'Oh, my God, who's station was he going to sit at tonight?' He tipped like crazy."

Redbeard's estate in Miami's posh Banyan Drive neighborhood had roaming peacocks and Miami's biggest library of Betamax porn. His bedroom was the size of most houses, and featured a grand piano on a rotating stage.

"The party was ongoing with Rudy," said Mutiny girl Joanna Christopher. "It didn't start or finish. It just went on." She remembers the kingpin masterfully tickling the ivories in his bedroom. Dozens of party girls would shuttle between the mansion and the Mutiny. Rudy could screw for hours at a time when he was fully "based out."

Redbeard befriended Christopher's boyfriend and his pals in the Italian mob, who had been members of the Mutiny since the early seventies. The Cuban told them he lit a candle for Lucky Luciano, the Italian mobster who had owned swaths of pre-Castro Havana. He adored the film *The Godfather*, and took to buying Brioni suits from Miami's finest Italian tailor. "He saw himself in Don Corleone," said his son.

"The first era of cocaine in Miami," Redbeard insisted, "was me. When I started in the biz, the cocaine was very rare. The elite did it in Cuba—the vice president, doctors."

"We were young," said Quesada. "We didn't respect the law. The only thing we wanted was to be alive, party and go back to a Cuba without Fidel."

At the Mutiny, Rudy Redbeard's traveling pianist, Sunshine Sammy, lived in the 5,500-dollar-a-month Egyptian Suite, where he mixed vodka with 'ludes in a rickety blender and mined the room service boy for intel about his volatile boss.

A nocturnal creature, Sammy would sometimes commandeer the club's piano to play the theme to *The Godfather*.

Redbeard was also obsessed with the song "Life's Been Good," by Joe Walsh, which was recorded right next door to the Mutiny in 1978. He tipped the DJ two hundred dollars to play the crowd killer. (Mollie and other Mutiny girls got their playful revenge against Uncle Rudy by getting the DJ to spin anything by the Beach Boys, which, she said, "Cuban dopers hated. It was like Kryptonite to their ears. They cleared out of the joint in no time.")

"Redbeard and Quesada were gods to us," said Nelson Aguilar, the young dealer who caught a glimpse of the kingpins when he first snuck into the Mutiny at age sixteen. "They had made it. And if they could, anyone else here could."

Chapter Five

DMZ DISCO

RICARDO "MONKEY" MORALES, indentured to the FBI after his misadventures as a bomber and hit man, spent much of the mid-1970s in Venezuela, where he helped Washington monitor the activities of Cuban exiles linked to international terrorism. In Caracas, he also aided Israeli intelligence in its pursuit of terrorist Carlos the Jackal and Nazi fugitives hiding out in South America. Israeli prime minister Golda Meir awarded him a medal of gratitude.

Had Morales been unscrupulous enough, he could have milked the position, which handled airport and border security, for bribes. But he grew paranoid in Caracas—Carlos the Jackal was going to kill him, he swore—and asked his government handlers to let him come back to South Florida.

So, in late 1977, he returned to Miami. And he was very broke. The good news was, his skills and connections were apparently still in demand, only now in the world of international drug running. He hooked up with doper Carlene Quesada, who naturally brought him to the Mutiny.

Bellied up to the bar, nursing Johnnie Walker Black and smoking through packs of Benson & Hedges, was barrel-chested narcotics sergeant Raul Diaz, a ringer for Erik Estrada from the show *CHiPs*. "The Mutiny," Diaz said, "was like a DMZ, with cops on one side and bad guys on the other. You didn't fuck with each other. It was a bizarro world, but it's where the dopers went, and so that's where I went."

In July of 1961, when he was thirteen, Diaz and his seven-year-old brother were sent to Miami from Cuba by their parents in Operation Pedro Pan. The archdiocese of Miami sponsored the youth airlift to get children out of Cuba before the Castro regime indoctrinated them.

At the airport in Havana, Diaz and his kid brother were questioned by security forces about the purpose and duration of their "vacation." The boys knew their mother, a seamstress, had stitched gold chains into their clothing, which would be a dead giveaway to agents that they were being smuggled out for good (leaving Cuba also meant leaving your wealth behind; authorities at the airport confiscated all valuables—often while loyalists jeered and spit at you as you walked to your plane).

In this pressure cooker, the younger Diaz brother was so frightened that he got a nosebleed while repressing the urge to cry. To move them past the guards, Raul Diaz started whistling a Communist hymn.

At Miami International Airport, the brothers were warmly received by an aunt and uncle. Children who were not picked up that day were bused to youth camps. The lucky would be claimed by American friends or relatives. Others would filter through to the Catholic Church or adoption agencies.

The Diaz brothers were exceptionally fortunate. It took only until Christmas for their parents to flee Cuba and reunite with their children in Miami Beach, where they all thrived.

By 1967, police trainee Raul Diaz was making his first undercover marijuana buy for the Miami Beach Police Department. "I fell in love with law enforcement," he said. In 1971, he was a rookie in the Miami Police Department's organized crime bureau.

A year later, a fellow cop introduced Officer Diaz to Ricardo Morales, the on-and-off contract hit man who was now playing the field as a confidential police informant.

Morales had made a career out of toggling between breaking the law and helping law enforcement; in total, it kept him out of jail. In a show of braggadocio—i.e., "Look at what I did with my CIA explosives training"—Morales confessed to Diaz that he had once bombed the home of a bookie (the Playboy Bunny's husband).

It turned out that Raul Diaz's mother was the Playboy Bunny's visiting seamstress. Diaz says he was ready to reach across the table to deck the smug Morales. "That could have killed my mother, you fucker!"

"Well," the informant deadpanned, "accidents happen."

An intrigued, somewhat beguiled Diaz drove Morales around Miami. They shared stories about Cuba, where, it turned out, Diaz's father was once Morales's grade school gym coach. He taught Rafael Villaverde, the Bay of Pigs veteran, too.

Diaz's father-in-law, moreover, was an anti-Castro exile (who was coincidentally being recruited to break into the Watergate Hotel).

The men hit it off.

The cop had Morales read thirty-five license plates, which he jotted onto a pad. Three hours later, Morales recited all but one back. "Ricardo was an incredibly intelligent person," said Diaz. "I've never known anyone with a memory like his."

By the time the unlikely duo had circled back to the Mutiny in 1977, it was pretty much public information that Monkey Morales and Raul Diaz were in some sort of cahoots.

Not that this relationship discredited either man in his respective line of work—far from it. Cops in Miami did not just reflexively bust drug lords in their midst. More likely than not, they were willing to cut deals with smaller players to build cases against the majors. It was a fact of Miami doper life: you informed on one another to any of the *tres letras* ("three letters") of law enforcement: the FBI, DEA, IRS, CIA, MPD, etc. In his decade and a half in America, Morales had worked with all of them.

"Unlike *Cosa Nostra*, it was nothing personal with the Cubans," said Joanna Christopher, the Mafia sweetheart who worked at the Mutiny. "You did what you had to do. Sure, talking could get you killed. But it was not some act of cultural heresy. It was self-preservation."

Ultimately, as a criminal, you had to hope that your coconspirators were informing in patterns that gave you a force field of inoculation. Throw in some corruption and bureaucratic confusion and your crew might just live to see another haul.

"This group," said Miami cop Raul Martinez, "had no Italian code. People did what they had to do to get out of jail."

"Raul Diaz—this was his job," explained Rudy Jr. "We were doing our job. We were the mice, and the cat had to chase after us. Monkey Morales was our asset. He was counterintelligence, an insider within the enemy."

Even so, Quesada's bodyguard, Humberto "Super Papi" Becerra, was not thrilled about the risk-reward proposition of bringing Monkey Morales into their drug-smuggling operation as an intelligence chief, of sorts. After all, he pointed out, Monkey had in 1968 betrayed Cuban exiles to the Feds to save his own ass. "I never liked that motherfucker," he said. "I didn't trust him. If we had to sleep in the same place, I'd keep one eye open."

But Super Papi also did not trust "Mon" Perez Lamas, Rudy Redbeard's bodyguard and hit man. Knowing Mon was into voodoo worship, he always warned the superstitious Puerto Rican that he would come back to terrorize his dreams if he dared kill him.

"I'd sit at the Mutiny bar and would watch guys who often hated one another," said Raul Diaz. "Ricardo could not stand Rudy and Carlene. They were way below him, he thought, intellectually. He hated these guys—fucking *hated* working for them." But he needed the money; Morales calculated he could play the drug lords and law enforcement at the same time. Quesada and Redbeard figured running with Morales would buy them both intel and some modicum of protection from police and the Feds. Raul Diaz, the ambitious cop, needed Morales and his drug-running associates to give up big rivals. It was a marriage of necessity in cocaine Miami.

By 1978, Rudy Redbeard had six rooms at the Mutiny blocked off for both business and pleasure, some of them adorned with paper grocery bags stuffed with cash. One of the club's assistant managers kept the Redbeard-Quesada gang's machine guns stored in the wine cellar.

Redbeard was throwing around so much cash at the Mutiny that its cleaning ladies grew territorial about turning around his rooms. "You'd find bags of coke, fist-size chunks of hashish left in trash bins," recalled a room service boy. "I'd be digging through the carpet before they vacuumed and I'd find a giant rock of cocaine. You were finding shit all the time."

Kingpin Mario Tabraue discovered sixty grand in cash in a paper bag behind a curtain, proceeds of which he used to buy a smuggling boat and to bling out Caesar the chimp.

Miami police detective Raul Martinez, who was earning thirty thousand dollars a year, including overtime, resented the dopers' pornographically conspicuous consumption. "These guys were blowing more up their nose and out of their wallets in one night at the Mutiny than I was making in a year," he said.

Chapter Six

BUSTING BATABANÓ

In late 1977 and early 1978, Miami police were surveilling Carlene Quesada's heavily gated ranch house. Said Raul Diaz: "That place was a convention of informants."

They noticed an old familiar face drive up, look around in his aviator shades and knock on the front door. It was Monkey Morales.

The cops flipped on a wiretap. Quesada, the homeowner, was hardly oblivious to this possibility, having changed his phone number at least four times that winter (not that it made a difference; Southern Bell kept the wire going throughout). He assumed he was further covering his tracks by speaking in metaphorical code, as in this fishing-themed exchange about a marine cocaine shipment gone bad:

Carlene: How are you doing, Inspector?
Associate: J went fishing.

C: Yeah?

A: Yeah, and I arrived last night.

C: Ah, it doesn't matter. I went by there but I didn't see you.

A: We had an accident yesterday and we had to come back.

C: Ave Maria.

A: With Lulito.

C: Yeah?

A: Yeah. Perforated his hand with a kingfish hook.

C: Who?

A: Lulito.

C: There, at the kingfish store?

A: No, there fishing. Out there for kingfish.

C: Aha.

A: [Garbled]

C: Aha.

A: He perforated his hand with a big kingfish hook.

However, Quesada let himself slip in a February 1978 exchange with Morales:

"It's coming big and good," he said.

"Listen, man," replied Morales, "this is the year I'm going to get even in this fucking world."

To which Quesada boasted: "We're supplying everybody. We've taken care of almost everybody you know."

By late March, the cops figured they had enough incriminating audio from the wiretap and corroborating tips from informants to make their move on the gang from the Mutiny Poop Deck.

Police arrested Rudy Redbeard at twelve thirty a.m., as he was being chauffeured to the Mutiny in his new bronze Cadillac limo. Originally custom-ordered for the king of Spain but then remaindered at the last minute, the bulletproof vessel sported a television, a bar, a telephone and three-inch shag carpeting.

When he was cuffed, Redbeard was wearing a white hat, a suit and shoes, and he had 6,800 dollars in cash stuffed in his coat pocket. Behind him in the backseat of a white Rolls-Royce, practicing tunes on a keyboard, was his traveling pianist, Sunshine Sammy.

As Redbeard was driven to the station for processing, the cops stuck around to watch everything coming in and out of his compound. At three a.m., when the motion detector at Redbeard's manse went off, they moved in, sending several peacocks scurrying. "We know there's stuff here," Detective Raul Martinez told the woman at the door. "We can either tear it apart or . . ."

She gestured toward the master bedroom.

In a gold footlocker in the closet was just under one million dollars in large bills. Right next to it were fifty-six pounds of uncut cocaine bricked up in Christmas wrapping paper. Police also seized sophisticated testing equipment. The conservative street value of the blow was fourteen million dollars.

Carlene Quesada was busted at his home shortly after sunrise.

Posing heroically on the front page of the *Miami Herald*, cops compared the haul to "winning the Super Bowl!" One enthused: "It was like opening the right door on a TV game show." From the evidence, they estimated that the Mutiny gang ran a 200-million-dollar-a-year drug smuggling ring, easily Miami's largest ever.

Though he had been on probation for a weapons charge, Rudy Redbeard managed to get out on bond—which struck cops as odd. If you were arrested while on probation, you went to the slammer. "His attorney, we figured, was the best fucking fixer in Miami," said Raul Diaz. "Surely, he found a loophole or something."

Whatever the case, Rudy Redbeard went right back to his table on the Poop Deck, which police were still watching.

"Some of these people," said Raul Martinez, "all they know is the fast life at the Mutiny. I'm not sure Rudy took so much as a two-week break. He sure as hell wasn't going back to upholstering cars."

Chapter Seven

MONKEY IN THE CAGE

MONKEY MORALES MANAGED to get busted a little over a week later, when, thinking the wiretap was dead, he used Quesada's home line to arrange delivery of a truckful of marijuana. He needed the money, what with Carlene, his benefactor, now spending big on defense attorneys.

Cops promptly blocked the caravan of grass, which Morales was leading in a Buick.

Detective Bill Riley slapped cuffs on the stocky exile, who was caught with Venezuelan spy credentials and the highly confidential radio frequencies of the DEA, FBI, coast guard, highway patrol, Secret Service and the Miami and Miami Shores police departments.

Morales tried to remind Riley that he had well-placed friends in Miami and Washington. "He was one cocky SOB," said Riley, "telling me he had huge balls, that I had no idea. You had to be in his head, I guess. I didn't give a rat's ass about the CIA."

Cursing Morales from his patrol car, Raul Diaz rushed to the scene to try to negotiate with Riley. He would not hear any of it. His informant was going to jail, unable or unwilling to pay the 350-thousand-dollar bond the state slapped him with.

The next morning's *Miami Herald* unspooled: "The spy for all seasons, Ricardo 'Monkey' Morales, became the latest suspect" in the Quesada-Redbeard smuggling ring. "Friends say he favors Johnnie Walker Black on the rocks, spending sheaves of money at pricey clubs like the Mutiny. He reads every espionage book he can find and cries every time he sees the movie *Casablanca*."

But much as he did in the 1968 Polish tanker saga, Morales used his incarceration as leverage with the authorities—informing this time on the exiles who sat with him at the Mutiny.

Almost as soon as the cops pulled out their notepads, he divulged that Mon Perez Lamas, Rudy Redbeard's hit man, had to his knowledge already killed seven or eight people in Miami. He told the police the crazy-eyed Puerto Rican could be found walking around a South Miami mall, where he answered to *"Boricua."*

A detective asked Morales if he knew of any government officials tipping off drug dealers.

"Let me relate to you what happened," he answered. "I went to the Mutiny for lunch because you have to have the power and money to get into places. . . . [A city official] told me to send a message to Carlos Quesada that he would have no problem with the City of Miami Police Department. . . . I mean, you socialize with them and they spill the beans."

Word got out in Miami that Morales had "deduced" which low-level Gallo-Quesada associates had initially informed on the conspiracy, setting up the wiretap that led to the busts, including his own. Maybe the cops told him. Maybe he was bullshitting. Did it matter? Morales willed it to reality.

Bluff or no bluff, said Raul Diaz, "they were scared shitless." After all, Mon, Rudy's hit man, executed "rats"—actual or suspected—with zero hesitation.

The immediate upshot was that the informants now refused to testify against the Table 14 gang. Which made Ricardo Morales—part-time snitch, part-time doper, full-time untouchable—look indispensable to its ringleaders, Redbeard and Quesada.

A six-man jury promptly found Morales not guilty. The acquittal, wrote the *Miami Herald*, was "only the latest narrow escape in his varied and risky career."

Chapter Eight

"GOD BLESS AMERICA!"

MEANWHILE, BACK AT the Mutiny . . .

When the daughter of Rudy Redbeard's defense attorney graduated from college in 1978, the kingpin threw her a 35-thousand-dollar disco champagne bash, blocking off the club's upper deck for the party's thirty private guests.

Mutiny girl Joanna Christopher watched as Redbeard peeled off and handed out more than four thousand dollars in tips, his long pinkie nail pointing to recipients while his entourage ran upstairs to get more cash from all the stuffed grocery bags he left in his suites. "His guys went nuts in a room full of gorgeous college girls," she said. "Getting arrested didn't keep him from having a good time."

The drug lord's lawyer—the most expensive in Miami—was earning his keep. When he successfully claimed the cash seized at Redbeard's mansion was from his family fish business, the IRS took its cut and gave Redbeard the rest back. Paying 40 percent on a million bucks beat the shit out of losing all of it.

The night that decision came down, behind the haze of his Benson & Hedges, Raul Diaz watched as an elated Redbeard demanded waitresses put a bottle of Dom on every table of every floor of the Mutiny Club, with unlimited refills. "I don't want to see any empty glasses!" he barked. "God bless America! Only in America!" He tipped the DJ extra to spin every patriotic-sounding record he had.

In the summer of 1978, Detective Raul Martinez got a tip that Mon Perez Lamas, Redbeard's fugitive hit man, would be making a cameo that night at the Mutiny. Redbeard was apparently feeling invincible enough to let his notorious bodyguard come out of hiding.

Martinez and another officer rushed to the club in plain clothes, knowing that off-duty cops who worked security at the Mutiny would tip off managers if the police had something official in the works. The managers then told their hostesses, who either called in special warning codes to the dopers' pagers or had the men spirited out the back of the hotel, from where they'd be sped off into the chaos and anonymity of US 1. Membership had such privileges.

Martinez and a partner took a table, ordered drinks and watched as the hulking Mon and Rudy handed out five hundred bucks to a manager and hundred-dollar bills to several Mutiny girls. When Mon suddenly got up, Martinez, rail thin and 125 pounds, stood up and jabbed his gun into the giant Puerto Rican's side. He arrested the fugitive for several murders.

"It'll be OK," reassured Redbeard, looking none too flustered as the cops cuffed his bodyguard. "I'll make some calls."

Raul Martinez had finally apprehended the internationally wanted hit man. His partner called in news of the big haul to the Miami Police Department, which then notified the FBI and Interpol. A Puerto Rican magistrate was on his way to Miami to arrange for extradition.

In theory, at least.

Just hours later, Mon was mysteriously sprung from jail—he was let free and into downtown Miami—and immediately went back into hiding. The prison bureau explained that Mon's record had somehow been previously wiped clear off the system. When Martinez found out, he wanted to punch a wall.

As he fumed, the cop thought back to when he first showed up at court after the March bust only to get heckled and laughed at by codefendants Rudy Redbeard and Carlene Quesada—who you'd think would have been on their best behavior before the law.

He remembered Redbeard dodging a parole violation (and automatic time behind bars) when he was busted in the limo outside his mansion. A judge notorious for draconian sentences, nicknamed "Maximum," had, for reasons unclear, recused herself from the case.

In her stead, the terminally ill Judge Joseph Baker, known to be close to Gallo's defense attorney, was wheelchaired in and after little discussion removed Redbeard's probation tag. He'd be free on bail. "Only in America!" blurted Gallo from a back row. As prosecutors attempted to object, to no avail, the frail Judge Baker was wheeled back out of the courtroom.

None of it made sense. Until it did: Redbeard had bought off the court system.

"We wondered how Redbeard could always be so cocky, so self-assured," said Raul Diaz.

"You have to realize that everything and everyone in Havana before Castro was for sale," explained Sam Burstyn, a criminal defense attorney who kept a table at the Mutiny. "Cuba was corrupt. Bribery was how business was done. It was natural for exiles to bring that mind-set to Miami. Plus, many of them were convinced they would not stay here. Think about it: have you ever washed a rental car?"

Judge Baker died just before Christmas of 1978. His funeral was a who's who of both sides of South Florida law. After the burial, state prosecutor Janet Reno accosted Rudy Redbeard, who seemed half her height.

"Mr. Redbeard," she vowed, "we will get you."

The kingpin was unfazed. Just months later, in February, Ricardo Morales was still straddling the fence between doper and government witness. Now, for whatever reason, he wanted to resuscitate the state's fading case against the Table 14 gang that he helped sabotage from behind bars—by taking it to a federal prosecutor.

He informed US Assistant Attorney Jerry Sanford that Redbeard's hit man, Mon, was out killing again, pointing to the pair of government witnesses whose murders had just been reported in the *Miami Herald*. He also warned that Rudy Redbeard, smoking more cocaine *basuco* than ever, was feeling especially macho of late and was talking about maybe killing a cop. The volatile kingpin increasingly complained that it felt like rats were scratching his brain.

"The Mutiny," reported Morales, "was full of dope and weapons: M16s, Thompsons with silencers," and the like. Smugglers there, he said, were now calling cocaine *"yeyo"*—should that word come up in any wiretaps.

In June, more than a year after Redbeard and Quesada were first busted, a magistrate granted their defense's motion to suppress "the fruits of the wiretap . . . and evidence seized at [their] homes." With the state's case against the Mutiny Poop Deck now looking hopeless (the prosecutor even suffered a heart attack), federal prosecutor Sanford swooped in to try to appeal the ruling to a district judge.

Having been tipped off that there might now have been a bounty on his head, Sanford started carrying a Browning semiautomatic and wearing an FBI-issued bulletproof vest. His wife had to learn to live with threats and police watches on their house; their daughter would wake up sobbing after dreaming that Daddy was shot and killed.

"Constantly looking over my shoulder," wrote Sanford in his diary. "Watching for strange cars or vans, concerned for my family."

The prosecutor was so worried about getting blown up in his car that he would study the dust streaks on the doors and hood before getting in and turning the key.

"Will I live out the summer?" he wrote.

Chapter Nine

DADELAND

July 11, 1979, two p.m.

GERMAN JIMENEZ, A Colombian cocaine dealer, stopped at the Crown Liquors at the Dadeland Mall in South Miami, seeking a festive handle of Chivas. Flanked by his bodyguard, Jimenez left his loaded handgun beneath the front seat of his new white Benz. The men sauntered in and looked around.

Seconds behind them were two other Latin men. They kicked through the front door, pulled up their machine guns and wallpapered Jimenez and his bodyguard with bullets.

As Jimenez tried to bolt for the exit, he had part of his head blown off; his bodyguard flailed and crumpled to the floor. The clerk took a stray bullet to the shoulder, and the stock boy, who had been eating lunch in the back, ducked behind a counter, covered his head and rolled for the exit.

The gunmen emptied their clips, reloaded and surveyed the

scene. Splashes of blood and smoke from their guns mixed with the smell of gin and whiskey and vodka and mixers. Glass shards and spent bullets were everywhere.

Though their targets may have been very dead—the coroner compared the corpses to "Swiss cheese"—they still had unfinished business. To put the loudest possible exclamation on the double hit, the gunmen exited the liquor store and sprayed the mall's parking lot with bullets from their getaway van painted with the words HAPPY TIME COMPLETE SUPPLY PARTY on its side. The liquor store's stock boy, taking cover under a parked car, got shot in the feet.

Stunned cops arrived at the scene. Within a few minutes, they found the Happy Time van idling and abandoned behind the mall. Double-steel-plated, the "war wagon," as they called it, sported one-way reflective glass above shooting holes, six bulletproof vests and a veritable arsenal: a nine-millimeter Browning automatic, an Ingram submachine gun, a pair of revolvers, a .30-caliber carbine, a .45 automatic and a Beretta with a silencer.

It took days to identify the victims. "I started counting bullet holes in one of them," said the coroner, "and gave up."

This shoot-out would go down in Miami history as the Dade-land Massacre, the opening fireworks show to the city's coronation as the new murder capital of America. And what was the beef? Cops were almost certain that Griselda Blanco, the godmother of cocaine from Medellín, Colombia, wanted to get competitors in Miami out of her way and to send a loud warning shot in the process.

Blanco, thirty-six, went by many sobriquets, including the Godmother, *la Madrina* and the Black Widow. Like Rudy Redbeard, she could recite every line from *The Godfather*, having just named a son Michael Corleone.

The Godmother's syndicate was selling an estimated eighty million dollars of coke a month, much of it wholesaled to Miami. She got her start as a pickpocket and prostitute in Medellín, often just killing anyone she didn't want to pay. Or someone who gave her a bad glance. Or ex-lovers. She also infamously machine-gunned her ex-husband and his bodyguards.

In 1975, Blanco was named as a defendant in the first major federal cocaine-trafficking indictment—in New York, where there was a substantial Colombian community in Queens. Back in Medellín, she had an undergarment factory that specialized in making bras and corsets with special compartments for female smugglers.

She became a fugitive and took her act to Miami, just as Carlene Quesada and Rudy Redbeard were coating the city with cocaine. In 1976, the Godmother tried to smuggle cocaine in a tall ship that the government of Colombia had loaned to Miami for bicentennial festivities.

Now Dadeland was being viewed by police as the Colombians' shot across the bow: they wanted to remind all the dopers in Miami that Medellín, though 1,400 miles away, was ultimately in control of the cocaine trade. Not the Cubans all over the *Miami Herald* or the occasional Peruvian smuggler or even lesser Colombian syndicates like the poor kingpin who walked into that liquor store. Fuck with the Godmother at your own peril.

Shortly after the Dadeland Massacre, Griselda Blanco came to the Mutiny to chill.

Carlene Quesada knew Blanco and knew he had to worry: Rudy Redbeard, his longtime partner in crime, in full freebase-fueled braggadocio, now wanted the world to know that *he* was the godfather of cocaine in Miami—*Colombianos* be damned. Mon the hit man was on the loose again. Neither was feeling extra-rational these days.

And it wasn't like Quesada could talk sense into Redbeard. At the Mutiny, rumors swirled that he had recorded a sex tape with Quesada's ex-wife. And while, yes, everyone was sleeping around—Carlene Quesada included and especially—your childhood best friend doesn't just film himself in the act with a woman with whom you had exchanged Catholic vows. Unless you were somehow already dead to him.

Quesada, hearing less and less from his childhood pal and partner in crime, started demanding that "Super Papi" Becerra, his bodyguard and roommate, stay close.

One night at the Mutiny, both men were summoned upstairs to Griselda Blanco's suite. As they walked in, they were shown the Godmother herself. She asked them what they thought about her wide-brimmed hat—the kind Burton Goldberg insisted his girls wear (apparently, a Mutiny girl had given her one). Did they think she, too, could work at the club downstairs? For two seconds, Blanco looked dead serious. Then she laughed thunderously—as did the rest of her room—and urged her Cubans to help themselves to food and drink. She waved her long painted nails in the direction of the room service spread.

"She looked good, man," said Becerra. He started digging into lobster and pouring himself champagne; they had bottles and bottles of the stuff on ice around the suite. "You hungry?" asked one of Blanco's coterie, a shifty-eyed Colombian who went by "Cumbamba." The man was one of the Godmother's most prolific assassins, known for chain-sawing and chopping up his victims after draining them of blood in a bathtub. In his spare time, he painted watercolors.

He struck up a conversation with Becerra. "You happy with that guy?" he asked him, pointing his chin at Quesada. "Because, if you're not, you know, I can get you something with me."

"'Oh shit,' I thought," said Becerra. "What were they going to do with Carlene?" Meanwhile, the bodyguard kept noticing the Godmother locking eyes with him. Becerra said he caught her telling a handler, "I want that."

Quesada, maintaining a wan smile as the Colombians sized him up, walked up to Becerra and made small talk before whispering, "We need to get the fuck out of here."

The Cubans pretended to be paged away to urgent business. "We come back," they vowed. "OK, OK, we come back."

In the elevator back down to the club and lobby, Quesada jabbed at Super Papi Becerra's massive chest and got up in his face. "I just saved your life," he said.

He felt increasingly paranoid. Theories flew around, and Monkey Morales, purveyor of chaos, did his utmost to stoke them. Rudy Redbeard, smoking piles of freebase cocaine, was making overtures to Becerra to spend more time with him.

Morales was telling Mollie, Table 14's favorite Mutiny girl, that Quesada was broke and could no longer pay her. Others were sure Quesada would avenge Redbeard's cheating with his wife by offing Redbeard; Cuban honor (and machismo) demanded as much. A Mutiny waitress noticed Quesada was uncharacteristically starting to order hard liquor. One afternoon in his cups, he looked despondent as he mumbled, "I have to kill someone. I don't know. I have to kill someone. How I'm going to kill someone?"

"It was a crazy time," said Mollie. "I knew Rudy and Carlene as friends. Then all of a sudden you had to pick sides. You never knew if they'd open fire in the club. Things felt like they were just coming to a head between them."

On the night of October 17, 1979, Quesada and his fiancée were driving in her sports coupe when the driver's side was sprayed with M3 submachine gunfire. As he took bullets to his side and back, Quesada slammed into reverse and floored the car backward for six blocks.

A Mutiny girl paged Becerra and told him to rush to Carlene's house. The bodyguard saw Carlene's bullet-riddled car parked outside (cops later counted twenty-four holes).

"When I walked in," he said, "I see his fiancée crying. I could see blood coming out of Carlene's back. 'What the fuck happened?'"

"Someone tried to kill us," said Quesada.

Becerra found a pair of forceps and heated them with his lighter—"To sanitize, you know?"—and pulled out the .45-caliber slugs while Quesada howled and bled all over his bathtub.

Who shot him? Conventional wisdom pointed to Mon Perez Lamas, Rudy's hit man. "Please," said Redbeard, dismissively. "If I had wanted Carlene dead, he would not have survived."

But there were also whispers that Ricardo Morales himself shot up Quesada's car to drive a decisive wedge between the former partners—giving Quesada justification to testify against Redbeard. After all, the case against Redbeard & Co., which Morales was informing on, needed a blockbuster witness. Looking ahead, perhaps Morales surmised that he could continue enjoying both worlds—paid informant and protected drug dealer—if Quesada emerged from this trial with immunity. Quesada, for his part, could remain a free man. And stay alive. And maybe, just maybe, play cooperator long and well enough to resume the export/import biz before too long.

The next day at the courthouse, Quesada pulled Detective Raul Martinez into the men's room to show him his wounds. He asked to be taken to federal prosecutor Jerry Sanford, whom Ricardo Morales was simultaneously buttonholing.

"What would you do if Quesada flipped?" Morales asked Sanford.

He did. And he did not disappoint. For the next several months,

Carlene Quesada dished on the particulars of Redbeard's cocaine empire: the front companies, the hit men, the labs. The same Miami Police Department that had been bugging his house now issued him a round-the-clock bodyguard.

Maybe Quesada and Morales had figured out how to build the perfect cocaine business: one that was ignored by the authorities. You could mint millions a day and blow it all at the Mutiny, winking at the very cops who were until recently on your ass. You kept the Colombians happy by buying their kilos. No bullets or fugitive hit men. Lots of fucking. Make love, not war—right?

Or maybe Monkey Morales had something else in store for Miami.

Or maybe, just maybe, he was downright suicidal at this point.

In prosecutor Jerry Sanford's final 1979 briefing with the exile, he asked, "As far as you know, is your life in danger now?"

"Jerry," he responded, "it's been in danger for the last twenty years, so it's another day in the office."

In reality, Morales was sobbing his eyes out nightly on Mutiny Mollie's couch.

Morales confessed his tortured past: mowing down child soldiers in the Congo, shooting people in the face, surviving bombs.

"I saw a sweet, scared little boy," Mollie said. "I used to feel so bad for him. He didn't know who his friends were. He was wary of everyone. He couldn't sleep at night. The cocaine made him paranoid.

"It's like he had no place to go," she said. "His family left him and everyone wanted to kill him. I just let him open up."

They'd hug, and Mollie would beg Morales to try to get some sleep. He'd always close with the same utterance: "How am I still alive?"

Chapter Ten

ENTRAR: LOS MUCHACHOS

AT THE END of 1979, Monkey Morales, in an almost parenthetical aside, told prosecutors that he heard some Miami kid, Willie Falcon, had just moved one hundred kilos of cocaine, a monster-truck shitload for a newbie.

Morales didn't elaborate, and the Feds didn't much care to follow up. After all, who would have guessed that Falcon, now all of twenty-three, was incubating one of the largest cocaine operations in history? One that also kept office hours at the Mutiny.

By 1980, Augusto Guillermo "Willie" Falcon and his partner, Salvador "Sal" Magluta, pretty much controlled the Mutiny's Upper Deck, where they kept tables right by the DJ. "*Oye*: play it the Blondie. The *Dona Sommer*. No, no: 'Funkytown.'"

Unlike the CIA- and Bay of Pigs–hardened old guard downstairs in the Poop Deck, *los Muchachos* ("the Boys"), as they were called, came to Miami from Cuba as little kids in the early 1960s. Some, like Nelson Aguilar, were smuggled to Miami by relatives fearing indoctrination by the Communist Party. The most gung ho revolutionaries were shipping their children to Soviet academies. Aguilar's father, Nelson Sr., was a regional deputy to Castro's number two, Che Guevara. Nelson's aunt kidnapped the boy, renamed him and smuggled him into Miami.

Others, like Sal Magluta and Ralph Linero, were put on planes to South Florida by their parents in Operation Pedro Pan (recall Raul Diaz and his little brother at the airport in Havana).

Sal, Willie, Justo Jay, Bernie Gonzalez Jr. and several other exile youths emerged from this fraternal crucible as popular jocks at Miami Senior High. Though their blue-collar parents wanted them to study hard and chase the American dream—college, degrees, doctor, lawyer, etc.—most instead dropped out of high school and chased a life of speedboat racing, good weed and hot and loose women. "Death to Castro!"—sure. The Boys hated the bearded despot—detested him. They toasted every new year with hopes for a *Cuba libre*. It's just that the hedonism of 1970s Miami wasn't so bad in the meantime.

One of their rank, Orlando Begnino "Benny B" Lorenzo, did manage to graduate from Miami Senior High, where he was a star point guard on the basketball team and chick magnet who looked like the lost member of the Latin teen band Menudo. But when a motorcycling accident derailed his plans to play college ball, he signed up to smuggle with his old buddies Willie, Sal and crew.

If their fathers and uncles saved up for rickety shrimping vessels or for a loan to buy, say, bakery equipment, Los Muchachos coveted the millionaires' world of fiberglass hulls, precision building and national TV coverage. If you dealt cocaine, you dealt in speedboats—and so it behooved you to be involved in the race circuit. And there was no better way for immigrant kids to bed

Miami's hottest women than to show them off in million-dollar outboards.

Not that Willie and Sal's gang was just playboys. Indeed, by the turn of the decade, they mustered a resourcefulness and business savvy to capitalize on a business hookup for the ages: a direct wholesale line to Medellín's cocaine cartel.

For this bequest, the dropouts had to thank a star student named Jorge Valdes, a childhood friend of Sal Magluta's whose misfortune became their fortune.

Rewind to 1973. Not even eighteen, Valdes was the top accounting student at the University of Miami, which he was attending on a scholarship. The Cuban immigrant grew up poor. In Miami, Sal Magluta's baker father—a family friend from the old country—would bring his parents cake trimmings for Jorge and his brother, who were frequently hungry in grade school.

As an overachieving undergrad, Jorge Valdes landed himself a high-clearance analyst position at Miami's Federal Reserve Bank. To earn money on the side, Valdes set up dummy corporations in the Caribbean for just under two thousand dollars and turned around and charged Latin American businessmen in Miami upward of ten thousand dollars for those accounts.

Valdes first went to the Mutiny with an associate of member Melvyn Kessler, a lawyer who represented mobster Meyer Lansky and various Miami drug dealers. In the mid-1970s, Miami's most in-demand criminal defense attorneys—dubbed the "cocaine bar"—practically kept office hours at the Mutiny. Characters like Sam Burstyn, Pete "the Count" Baraban and "Diamond" Joel Hirschhorn would hold court at tables and exchange glances, bottles and business cards with prospective clients.

Kessler—"Mutiny Mel"—would even take dopers and their dates

out on his speedboat, which he kept in a marina down the street. "Hedonism combusted very well in the oxygen of cocaine and money," said Burstyn, who had a table on the first floor by the backgammon table. "You just knew you could come here and play."

Inside the club, Valdes, the young accountant, watched in awe as Cuban-American banker Ray Corona loudly threw around two-hundred-dollar tips at Table 3.

By 1977, word got out that the young Valdes was so adept at setting up offshore companies that wealthy South American businessmen reached out to enlist his help in setting up a banana boat company. One of these export/import guys was Colombian Manuel Garces, a former gem miner turned high-ranking Medellín drug lord.

Initially claiming to want to start a banana boat company, Garces admitted to the young Cuban-American that he actually wanted his help moving Colombia's real cash crop, cocaine. After giving it some thought, Valdes figured he'd do a load or two to help his parents buy a house. He liked Garces, a daily churchgoer who marked several kilos of every load with "for the nuns"—proceeds of those kilos would go to his sister, who was converting natives in the Amazon.

In short order, Valdes was raking in upward of one million dollars a month. No longer having any desire to stop at a load or two, he booked off rooms and tables at the Mutiny, where he invited friends. One was Sal Magluta, son of that baker who had looked out for Valdes's family when they first arrived penniless and hungry in Miami.

In 1978, Valdes asked Magluta if he and his Miami Senior High sidekick, Willie Falcon, were game to move thirty kilos of cocaine. A payment had fallen through—perhaps it was Redbeard's; he had just been busted—and Valdes was ready to go on a European vacation.

Sal hesitated. While his gang knew small bags and satchels of pot and blow, they had never moved anything close to that size. But Willie Falcon cut him off to tell Jorge Valdes, "We do it!"

When Valdes returned from his vacation, the boys had his 1.3 million dollars in cocaine proceeds and were raring to move even more.

As THE HAULS got bigger and bigger, Willie and Sal—Los Muchachos—themselves started annexing tables at the Mutiny, where they assembled a cocaine conglomerate of friends from the hood and the South Florida boat-racing circuit. There was Justo Jay, a ringer for NBA great Julius "Dr. J" Erving who in the Miami High gym went by Dr. J; Juan "Recotado" Barroso, short and stocky and perfect in the cockpit of a massive speedboat; George Morales, a cocky Colombian speed racer; and Bernardo Gonzalez Jr., a fellow Miami High dropout who was so fast on his feet at every sport (and with the women) that he earned the nickname "Venao" ("Deer"). You couldn't catch him.

The Mutiny, the boys would soon come to realize, offered them something akin to one-stop shopping for executive staffing. For legal representation, they naturally retained "Mutiny Mel" Kessler, a fellow speedboat aficionado who was Jorge Valdes's attorney. What the Boys lacked in financial acumen, they were able to outsource to one of the most connected and corruptible bankers in Miami: Table 3 fixture Ray Corona.

Corona, a prolific user of cocaine with a penchant for fur coats and watch fobs, was given to threatening managers and busboys with his gun. A mainstay at his table was Miami city manager

Howard Gary, who was on the board of his bank and good friends with Miami's chief of police. "He was Ray's puppet," observed Willy Gomez, the Mutiny security guy. Piss off Corona, he said, and Howard Gary would call in the fire department to cite the club for dangerous overcrowding—forcing Gomez to move one hundred members up to the building's roof, where they would be given complimentary Dom while the security guard pleaded with inspectors to leave.

Ray Corona had actually known Willie Falcon since the early 1970s. But the stars only aligned for a business relationship in 1978, when Falcon and Magluta first took those thirty kilos off Jorge Valdes's hands and needed a place to park their cash windfall.

It so happened that Corona had just assumed control of Sunshine State Bank with financing from a pot smuggler who needed wholesale laundering.

The Muchachos were dream clients for Ray Corona. Why screw around with everyday deposits and loans in a crap national economy when you could instead take cash deposits from coke dealers, legitimize them and scrape a thick vig off the top?

Corona's MO was critical to Muchachos Corp.: he could make jumbo "loans" to the boys that would be repaid with the dirty cash in the safes at Sunshine. Falcon and Magluta would then use the supposedly "clean" loan money to buy legitimate businesses and properties: horses, ranches, condos, houses, jewelry, gold bullion. Even the semen of prize bulls. They'd further throw off the authorities by putting these assets in the names of family members.

In 1979, Willie and Sal had gotten so good at moving their commodity that they showed up at Sunshine State Bank with twenty million dollars in bills.

Chapter Eleven

OUR MAN IN PANAMA

IN APRIL, JORGE Valdes flew down to Bolivia with Sal Magluta to look into fresh supplies of cocaine. The politically unstable country yelled opportunity to Miami: military figures linked to cocaine lords were reportedly keen to seize control in a coup and turn Bolivia into an outright narco-republic. Valdes and Magluta flew down with 300 hundred thousand dollars in cash strapped to their legs with rubber bands and kept in place by panty hose beneath their suit pants. When he was called away to a meeting in Nicaragua, Valdes asked Magluta to stay on in La Paz to handle negotiations.

But the small plane Valdes and three others flew off in crash-landed in Panama. Soldiers arrived to find the passengers—and their six suitcases of cocaine—unharmed.

As Valdes and his crew were arrested, he asked to negotiate a buyback of the contraband. The country's attorney general visited him in his cell to inform him that not only could he not have his cocaine back, but it would also cost 250 thousand dollars to get out of jail. Incidentally, he added, the DEA knew about the cocaine crash site.

The smugglers tried to keep poker faces, assuming the Panamanians were bluffing for a bigger payoff. But then a guard dragged in a local prisoner, stripped him naked, bent him over and sodomized the thrashing man with a broomstick. Blood squirted across the floor. Valdes felt stomach acid roar up his throat.

He and the smugglers were then dragged into a dark, rat-infested cell. Over several days, they were stripped, kicked in the ribs, burned with cattle prods and made to wait in terror while soaked in gasoline as guards smoked cigarettes.

Valdes awoke one morning to the presence of General Manuel Noriega, the country's small, acne-scarred strongman. Noriega was known in Miami as the CIA's man in Central America. He'd been visited by George Bush, spy chief under Gerald Ford, and in 1978, the DEA actually sent him a letter of thanks for his cooperation.

All that aside, Noriega informed Valdes that he now expected a 350-thousand-dollar payoff.

Pissing blood and not looking forward to more torture, the captive gave in. His plan was to take a quick flight to neighboring Costa Rica and play returning to Miami by ear, what with the DEA on his ass now.

Or maybe Noriega's men were just bullshitting. Everyone knew they were taking bribes from cocaine dealers. Why in the world would they involve Washington?

At the airport in Panama, Jorge Valdes realized he had actually been triple-crossed by Noriega. In a win-win-win for the strongman, not only did he seize all of Valdes's cocaine and shake him down for 350 thousand dollars in cash; he then won points with the White House for cashiering a major drug lord to the DEA.

"Welcome to the big leagues," quipped a smiling marshal to Valdes when the plane landed in Miami. DEA agents told Valdes they had surveillance footage of him brokering cocaine deals at the Mutiny.

Miami's most brilliant accountant—an alum of its cash-clogged Federal Reserve branch—was hauled off to jail.

Chapter Twelve

MUCHACHOS CORP.

IT WAS MAY 1979: Willie Falcon and Sal Magluta were now the biggest cocaine dealers in the biggest cocaine town in the world, having just inherited Jorge Valdes's direct supply line to Medellín. Not that this change of control had to be codified anywhere or reported to the Securities and Exchange Commission.

Succession planning in the growing enterprise necessarily boiled down to this: by now, Falcon and Magluta knew enough about the workings of Valdes's budding cocaine empire to keep the cash flooding in while he was off-line. Who knew how long their benefactor would be tied up in the courts or jail after his Panama imbroglio?

But this much was for sure: there was just too much product to move, too much supply and demand, too much money to bank, to just put it all on hold.

"Willie and Sal were local golden boys," recalled state drug agent Bill Riley. "They had a peerless reputation: they moved product; they moved it safely; they never stole, no rip-offs."

Plus, he says, they did it with charisma: "All the women were all over Willie. Sal was the businessman, the brains. Everyone wanted to smuggle for them, party with them when they rented out a whole floor at the Mutiny—the Dom, the girls, the coke binges."

"By 1980," concurred smuggler Juan Cid, "Willie and Sal were rock stars at the Mutiny. They were not feared. They were loved. There was brotherhood, fraternity."

It helped that they were munificent.

Gary James, a Mutiny valet, was tipped as much as three hundred dollars a pop by the Muchachos to park their Ferraris and Rollses out front. "Willie," he recalled, "was sharp and articulate. He carried himself as a businessman. Smiles. Handshakes."

Cindy Proietti, a blond fashion model and hostess at the Mutiny's Upper Deck, first learned of Willie and Sal in 1980. They liked to sit by her friend, the DJ Humberto Fleites, who would get big tips to play Willie's favorite song, disco chart-topper "Makin' It":

Goodbye, poverty.
The top of the ladder is waiting for me; I'm makin' it.

Proietti recalled the first time she walked up to the Boys' table to take a drink order. "One guy at their table stuck a spoon to my nose," she said, "like that was my tip. Then they tipped me a one-dollar bill folded around cocaine. I didn't know what it was or what to do with it."

"Baby, please breeeng me a ron and Coke, please" was Willie's standard drink order. Falcon had a speedboat named *Rum & Coke.* Singer Julio Iglesias, who also loved to hit on Proietti at the Mutiny, had a song called "Ron y Coca-Cola." But only Falcon would hand her a hundred-dollar bill for that four-dollar cocktail.

The boys called Cindy "Proietti the Prude" after she admitted to being freaked out the one and only time she'd smoked pot. They kept nudging her and fellow waitress Kim to try the white stuff, which they called *perico*—as in "parrot" (because it makes you yap all day).

One evening at the Mutiny, Proietti finally gave in and tried a bump.

She remembers a freeze and a flash. Then an all-enveloping euphoria.

"I loved it," she said. Falcon looked giddy and aroused as the model opened her eyes.

She and Kim were now inducted into the boys' "never-ending party" at the Mutiny: night after night of unlimited Dom, fine wines, hard coffees—prepared tableside by two fire-juggling baristas (guest Jackie Onassis loved them)—anything on the menu, big bashes up in their rooms, lines, lines, lines of cocaine. Keys to sports cars. Trips to the Florida Keys for televised boat races.

Muchachos pilot Ralph "Cabeza" Linero remembered Willie's all-night birthday party at the Mutiny. In addition to cordoning off the club's Upper Deck, his gang reserved an entire floor of suites. A drunken Falcon leaned over the balcony to invite up some Hare Krishnas selling flowers down on South Bayshore Drive. Wouldn't it be a blast for the Mutiny's biggest VIPs to wave these malodorous baldies past the big line outside? Upstairs, the boys egged on their robed guests as they tried Dom Pérignon and stone crab claws for the very first time.

Even off-duty cops were at the bash, wowing girls by snorting lines off their badges. "Every smuggler, distributor and dealer worth a grain of salt was there," said Linero.

At sunrise, the only revelers left standing had to put several dozen empty bottles of Dom down along both sides of the entire length of the hallway so that the room service guy could tally their bill. The Muchachos tipped the kid lavishly—cash and coke—lauding him for hustling across Miami the whole night to mooch Dom from other clubs.

"We'd party upstairs, get into the Rolls, you'd take them home," said Proietti. For six or seven months, she was "Willie's girl."

Romance at the Mutiny entailed a protocol: Fridays were for mistresses. Saturdays were for wives. Never cross-contaminate by accosting a wife or even another girlfriend.

Proietti and Kim now worked cocaine into their shifts. "I'd tap Kim on the shoulder and ask, 'Check your petticoat, miss?'"

(That was code for: "*Perico* in the ladies' room?")

Humberto Fleites the DJ would mix cassette tapes for customers at fifteen dollars a pop to help pay his tuition at the University of Miami. After he spun his last track, somewhat past three in the morning on Fridays and Saturdays, the Boys would invite him to eat stone crab claws and to drink Dom and whatever else he wanted at their tables. "I was doing drugs at every one of their parties," he said.

He said he once witnessed the volatile Ray Corona put a gun to someone's head. The same banker invited Fleites over to his mansion to fix his stereo. Soon afterward at the Mutiny, Corona pulled the DJ aside and handed him a four-thousand-dollar "loan" to complete his architecture degree.

Everyone at the Mutiny loved Ray Corona's personal "loans": Mollie the hostess said she never made a single payment on a Trans Am that Corona had leased for her for two years. Another girl used "Corona Credit" for a boob job.

He could more than afford this largesse. Whatever his personal-finance predilections, Corona's bank was processing and laundering ever larger amounts for the Boys.

Chapter Thirteen

COCAINE CAPITALISM

AT THE MUTINY, the Muchachos—free on bail while their attorney dragged out their appeals—were constantly striking new deals. "Willie and Sal were at heart capitalists," said Nelson Aguilar. "They handled their business like true Wall Street guys; they weren't deadly. Back then, if you fucked them out of a payment, you were exiled from what they had going on. But that was worse than death in Miami."

Case in point: Aguilar's cousin Tatico "Jackboy" Martinez was an armed robber who liked to go to the Mutiny to prospect for targets he could follow home and clean out. His uncle first took him there when he was a teenager, and he got a glimpse of Redbeard and Quesada living like the kings of the town. "Just walking in," he said, "the women—the way they were dressed. The money, you felt the money. I was a kid in a candy store. It was surreal."

He quicky realized the Mutiny was perfect for casing. "We'd hit the security guy with money, and go in," he recalled. "Mainly, I'd go to study the big boys—who they were, what they were wearing, what they were spending. The guys driving the really big cars were the big deals."

Word naturally got back to the Upper Deck that Tatico—built like Lou Ferrigno and fond of machine guns—posed a risk to Willie, Sal and their sprawling Upper Deck "corporation."

Tatico homed in on the flashy Ray Corona, who loomed over Table 3 with thousand-dollar tips in between long trips to the restroom for snorts of the white stuff. Corona would get out of his Rolls wearing fur coats (even in hot weather) and a J. Pierpont Morgan–like gold watch fob around his midsection.

If all that didn't bait a robbery enough, the rings on his fingers were the size of Christmas tree ornaments. One night, Corona bragged to a girl that just one of them was worth 250 thousand dollars.

Tatico stuck around at the bar and followed Corona out to the valet. "Me and my three boys," he said, "we carried heavy." They followed the Rolls and pulled up across from Corona's house. With machine guns in hand, they pounded open the front door and wrestled down Corona, the former boxer. The gunmen tied him up. The bodyguard offered zero resistance.

Corona swore he wouldn't give the robbers shit and would have them hunted down. Tatico heated an iron and held it to Corona's bare ass. "Ray," he recalled, "was shitting himself." The gunmen stripped off Corona's jewelry and looted the banker's home.

To further broadcast his badassery, Tatico had also recently tied up and cleaned out nine Colombians—Dadeland Massacre be damned.

Speaking of the Colombians, Willie and Sal could easily have had their suppliers put a contract out on Tatico. After all, they were now the Medellín cartel's guys in Miami; Pablo Escobar and Griselda Blanco eliminated people (and even their family members) for far milder affronts.

Instead, the Boys sent a delegate to sound out Tatico at the bar. "Look," he said, "don't hit us. Whatever you need, we'll hook you up, OK?"

The robber first played like he didn't know what the emissary was talking about. He shrugged acceptance. "OK, man," he mumbled. "Whatever, man. No problem."

Tatico almost immediately started getting huge amounts of tribute. "They gave me and all my crew money and merchandise," he said. "I became friends with Willie. I left them alone. He and Sal were very splendid and very good to everybody there."

Chapter Fourteen

MAKING LOVE, NOT WAR

Since their hotshot days at Miami Senior High, Willie Falcon and Sal Magluta had had a penchant for surrounding themselves with fellow good-looking jocks.

Not only were they speedboating and pickup basketball aficionados, but Sal and Willie hired professional ringers for the Mutiny's softball team, spending upward of 250 thousand dollars a year on the squad, including 50 thousand dollars and a lease on a red Porsche for a star Canadian pitcher. Hot jocks attracted hot women and their hot friends. And they often played in the diamond just across the street from the hotel.

Always with the Muchachos at the Mutiny was fellow Miami High dropout Bernardo "Venao" Gonzalez Jr.—the Deer. A six-foot-tall jet-setter with a perfectly sculpted beard, he earned his nickname by being hard to catch in any sport, especially in offshore boat racing. Venao was out of central casting for the rogue who steals your wife in a telenovela.

"He was so hot," recalled Kim Bacardi, a Mutiny regular who dated one of his friends. "There was something smooth, really sexy about him." When the transmission died on her car, Venao demanded that she let him pay the mechanic. The Muchachos teased Kim about staying in school. They called her "Princess," and treated her like one.

For other women, straight-up sex for blow was the Mutiny's standing exchange rate. Show up at the line; get waved in; drink, eat and toot to your heart's delight and end up on top of or beneath some doper until sunrise (in a suite, on a yacht, in some mansion or condo on Biscayne Bay). Many went home (or straight to their day jobs) tipped with cash, jewelry, Quaaludes or more blow in a velvet Crown Royal pouch.

"If you had the look the Cuban traffickers wanted—a tall, thin blonde who did coke—you were going places," said Vicky, an escort whose friend with said features was the recipient of a heavy gold bracelet with the letters "W-I-L-L-I-E" embedded in diamonds. "It was normal for someone to hand you at least a thousand dollars for four hours at the Mutiny, even if some dopers just wanted pretty girls to do blow with them."

One New Year's Eve, she said she got thirty thousand dollars just to talk to a Cuban smuggler. "People do weird stuff when they're doing coke," she said. Erections were hard to maintain and macho Latin dopers did not want to be caught flaccid. "But time flies and money is no object."

Owen Band, a small-time dealer with a ripped physique, was once invited to a Mutiny orgy this way: in the elevator, a midlevel cocaine dealer took fifteen thousand dollars out of his man purse, handed it and the keys to the Emerald Isle Suite to a deputy, and told both him and Band to knock themselves out.

Fast-forward to eleven p.m. In that suite, they splayed out stacks of cash and baggies full of blow. Owen Band started working the phones to the Moonflower Escort Company, a call girl ring that put up a giant billboard north of the Mutiny on US-1 and kept a twenty-four-hour dispatch office in a yacht in the marina in front of the hotel.

"We wanted four girls for the three of us," said Band. "But we wanted to interview many more." So Moonflower agreed to send more than a dozen of differing body types, ethnicities and hair colors.

As the hookers came upstairs to the two-room suite, the dopers asked them to line up against the wall. Band pulled out the desk and judged them, tipping those who didn't make the cut forty dollars and cab fare.

Band said he didn't think this was particularly exploitative. "They were there to party—all of them—coming and going," he said. "They wanted coke and they did not want to be waiting tables somewhere. You'd see them in the club the next night."

For other Mutiny women, however, sex for cash was more of a wink-wink, "soft dollar" arrangement. "You'd always have girls who you were inviting to parties complaining about having to work more hours to make rent and car payments," said Band. "Or about needing money to send to family in Latin America."

That, he says, was how they would telegraph that they were down to party for payment.

Chapter Fifteen

SUMMA CUM LAUDE

NO ONE IN this hedonistic fantasyland knew or cared that the twenty-two-year-old small-time dealer Owen Band had an older brother working drug cases in the state prosecutor's office.

Few in this lair of high school dropouts that was the Mutiny knew that he was the 1977 salutatorian at Boston University, where he gave a speech titled "The Value of an Education":

> We have seen countless examples today of unfulfilled lives devoid of ethics and an understanding of basic moral principles. We are surrounded and led by men with encyclopedic knowledge, but without a capacity to tell right from wrong.

Band turned down Georgetown to attend BU on a scholarship. He was a star wrestler and debater at North Miami Beach High, and was bar mitzvahed nearby at Beth Torah Synagogue.

So, how in the world could a nice Jewish salutatorian end up dealing and debauching at the Mutiny? This is the long and short of it: so big and sprawling was Muchachos Corp., so voracious were the demands of its supply chain, that it was bound to suck in the peculiar résumé of someone like Owen Band.

Rewind back to 1977. Salutatorian Owen Band thought he'd be giving his BU commencement address with an acceptance letter to Harvard Law School in tow. So confident was he of getting in that it was the only program he applied to, having spent hours across the river in Cambridge buttonholing professors and deans about his application. He even had a recommendation from his internship for Florida governor Bob Graham, an antidrug crusader.

But when Band was wait-listed by Harvard, he suffered an attack of Crohn's disease and had a nervous breakdown. He ended up depressed and back at his parents' house in North Miami Beach.

Band's parents, always doting on his older brother, an assistant state prosecutor in Miami, pushed the graduate to get out of the house and look for work. He settled on a bartending gig at a downtown Miami discotheque, where patrons such as Rafael Villaverde and Jose Alvero-Cruz would tip him in hundred-dollar bills and pinches of quality Peruvian cocaine.

About the first time he tried blow, Band recalled: "I took the guy's hundred-dollar bill, bent over and inhaled deeply. Immediately, my head snapped back, and I felt a rush—like all my senses were heightened."

"Whoo! Fuck!" he screamed. First, the stuff smelled like bubble gum. But then he couldn't feel his nose, and his heart felt like it was going to bore a hole out of his chest. Band saw his bright red face reflected in the table's glass layer. The sound track to *Saturday Night Fever* blasted in the background and he could discern the smallest notes. The agony of getting hosed by Harvard Law and having a nervous breakdown dissolved into irrevelevance. "I could do anything," he said.

In 1979, when the disco was shut down in a cocaine sting operation, Band went to the Mutiny to catch up with ex-coworkers who had just been hired there. He saw Fernando Puig, the club's gargantuan head of security, handling a Colt .45. "It looked like a toy in his hand," he said.

Band ordered a drink and took in the scene. The bartender pointed out *Deep Throat* star Linda Lovelace, a porn legend who shot most of her famous scenes a few blocks away. He traded glances with Bernardo de Torres, head of intelligence for Brigade 2506 at the Bay of Pigs, who was sitting by himself, dressed in jeans and a black Members Only jacket. The tall, lanky man's idea of a comb-over was tying up what was left of his longish hair in a bun.

One of Band's former coworkers, now a Mutiny hostess, filled him in. Bernie, she explained, "was like a godfather" to the girls who worked at the Mutiny. He always had coke and always hugged and kissed on both cheeks. He was a historical figure—something about Kennedy and Castro—and was enough of a big deal at the club that he somehow never, ever paid for anything.

Had Owen Band researched a bit more about de Torres, he would have learned that he was one of the last Bay of Pigs prisoners sprung by Fidel Castro. He took a bayonet to the shoulder while attempting to fight his jailers.

After John F. Kennedy was killed in 1963, the exile showed up in New Orleans, claiming to want to help prosecutor Jim Garrison, the assassination's chief investigator, with his case. Some politicos had been fingering Castro agents; others implicated the CIA and Cuban exiles. De Torres, invoking his patriotic duty, insisted he was so well sourced in both worlds that he would be an invaluable asset for Garrison.

The prosecutor agreed to the exile's offer, only to cut ties with de Torres when he realized he was depleting his budget with dead leads and unreliable information—and probably reporting back to his handlers in the CIA. In 1978, de Torres was ordered to appear before the House Select Committee on Assassinations, but was not questioned about the period leading up to Kennedy's death. The CIA instructed the committee on what it could and could not ask him.

At the Mutiny, Band walked over to the older man's table. They made small talk and Band told him about his unconventional route back down to Miami from New England's ivory tower. He dropped Rafael Villaverde's name; Bernie said they had fought together at the Bay of Pigs.

"He showed me a huge rock of coke," recalled Band. "Like three or four ounces. And he said he didn't just want to 'give it away to all the girls with long pinkie nails.'"

De Torres invited Band upstairs. In the elevator, he admitted he hadn't paid a cent for his dinner. No, he had "bartered" his quality blow with Chef Manny in the kitchen, who was happy to grill him up anything he craved, from a huge steak to lobster tails to any fish he could think of. "There's a lot going on like that here," he explained.

They entered the Mutiny's expansive Emerald Isle Room, overlooking the bay. Bernie, it turned out, had also traded cocaine for the keys (the weeknight front desk guy had a nose for it). Band and de Torres took a toot together. It was powerful, mind-fucking stuff, the kind that made you feel immortal and indefatigable. Said Band: "I had never tried anything like it. I didn't even know it could be that good."

He made some calls—"Hey, Mandy, what you doing? You down to party? Yup. Yeah, bring her, too. No, she doesn't have to be a member. I'll leave your name at the front"—and what ensued was an Emerald Isle all-nighter with five girls. The Brigadesman, lapsed honor student and coke whores multitasked, snorting lines, drinking champagne and boinking one another. On the bed. On the floor. On the balcony. In the hot tub, which they anointed with aromatic Vitabath.

At five a.m., Bernie abruptly got up and said he had to leave, warning his guests (those who weren't coked out of consciousness) not to use the room phone, and to be out by eleven a.m. at the latest, when the maid would show up to clean the five-hundred-dollar-a-night suite.

When he left, one of the girls who had been to this kind of rodeo before explained a thing or two about the mysterious Bernie: he kept a low profile outside the Mutiny and didn't want anyone to know where he lived. Endowed with an enormous cock and uncommon stamina—even when coked out—he had an insatiable appetite for younger women; one remembered him slapping his manhood against the side of their room's TV.

Bernie always kept a gun in his boot. He once pointed it at the head of some guy who dared beat him at arm wrestling. And the old spook often repaired upstairs to an always-booked suite whose balcony was equipped with a shortwave radio. He was receiving messages from Biscayne Bay and beyond—from dealers, spooks, gunrunners. Why? Who knew? Point was, the girls told Band, people at the Mutiny knew not to ask.

As for the legend that he was somehow involved in the Kennedy assassination, Bernie would only smile when a clubgoer dared ask if it was true that he had photos from Dallas's Dealey Plaza.

After the all-nighter, Owen Band drove home. His head spinning, heart pounding and mouth dry from all the cocaine and alcohol, he proceeded to sleep until ten at night.

Then he sped back downtown to the Mutiny. Only, through the back this time, and straight to Bernie's table. The old man greeted him with a big Cuban hug and a rascally grin—as in: Shall we do it again?

It was the middle of the week.

"Fuck me," said Band, "if I was ever going to go back to law school."

Bernie took him around the club. He introduced the well-spoken Jewish kid—"this is my smart nephew"—to Carlene Quesada on the Poop Deck. When Quesada got up to hug Bernie, the anti-Castro hero, he extended his hand to Band, who refused to shake. He thought of Quesada as a rat, remembering him in the pages of the *Miami Herald*. Nevertheless, Band took a seat at the doper's table and hit on his groupies.

Later in the men's room, Bert "Super Papi" Becerra, Quesada's bodyguard, walked up behind Band at a urinal. "You know," he said, "you'd be dead right now in a ditch covered with lime if you weren't with Bernie."

Band apologized and swore he didn't intend disrespect. He could explain. He followed Super Papi out to the valet and convinced him to let him ride shotgun in his black Benz, which sported a steering wheel covered in fifty thousand dollars' worth of diamonds that spelled "H-U-M-B-E-R-T-O."

Flying through stoplights on Biscayne Boulevard at eighty miles per hour while reaching into his glove compartment for cocaine, Super Papi remarked, "Hey, if you're going to be a criminal, be a criminal 100 percent of the time. You know?"

One night, while Band was having a drink at Bernie de Torres's table, none other than Willie Falcon sent over a bottle of Dom and gestured for him to come over. They shared some wine. No words exchanged. Just nods and heads bouncing to the DJ's latest spin. It was a body language check. Band glanced back at Bernie, who nodded back approvingly—as in, just roll with it.

Falcon's deputy, Venao, later materialized. He invited Band to a hallway connecting the Upper Deck to the hotel, where the Muchachos kept several suites.

"You cool?" he asked Band. "You cool, *meng*, to . . ." The dashing Cuban pinched the tip of his nose twice, pointing upstairs. They rode the elevator up to an especially large suite that practically covered a whole floor of the hotel.

Venao shut the door and opened the curtains to a gorgeous view of the bay. There were maybe 150 sailboats speckling the water. Venao cracked open a kilo of shiny blow. It was scaly and translucently pink—hallmarks of high quality, someone had told Band.

Venao gestured thumbs-up and pinched some into an indentation he was able to make in the fleshy area that connected his thumb and forefinger—the anatomical snuff pouch, it was called at the Mutiny. "Try it," he said. "It's good, *jes*?"

Band realized he was being recruited. It would be shrewd diversification on Willie and Venao's part: enlist an educated, well-spoken white kid to move the stuff among spoiled pals up north. Surely Bernie had filled in the Muchachos. "There was just so much cocaine coming in," reasoned Band, "that you couldn't find distributors fast enough."

But Band also knew he was a guppy. He could probably traffic in grams, not kilos. He crunched the risk-reward scenarios in his head as Venao tooted more of the pink stuff and licked powder up into his gums. If Band took on more than he could deal, he'd lose any goodwill or rep he had built up at the Mutiny, however inadvertently. If he took on grams, he'd be laughed at.

Or, he said, "It would be, 'I told you: Bernie's cheap Jewish nephew, Owen Band, wanted free blow.' No. No."

After another toot, Band mustered the courage to ask Venao for a special arrangement. The Deer shrugged an OK. "At the beginning," recalled Band, "they'd throw me a kilo and say, 'Go help yourself.' You'd put away seven or eight ounces at the table, using a ladle and baggies."

He learned that even when he cut Venao's blow with powdered baby laxative, his stuff sold like mad up north. Band had a pal in Atlantic City who would gratefully pay 2,200 dollars an ounce. Then there were old acquaintances from Boston University, spread all across the most moneyed parts of Long Island, who would pay top dollar for "good shit" to powder up with before hopping the evening train into Manhattan.

One was the son of Pittsburgh steel money who partied hard at New York's Studio 54. He introduced Band to co-owner Steve Rubell and his head of security at the mobbed disco. "I had carte blanche there," Band said. "I'd be partying with all the celebrities. Liza Minnelli. Morgan Fairchild. The 'disco dust' that all these 54 people were so used to was so fucking stepped on—so cut, abused and watered down. It might have been 20 percent pure."

Band's stuff, by comparison, was 50 percent pure. And, validating the gambit made by Venao, he was white, well-spoken and nonthreatening, compared with the stereotypical Cuban or Colombian cocaine cowboy. Band was summoned to Steve Rubell's mansion at least three times to deliver his product.

He was flying up from Miami four or five times a month now.

"The airports," he said, "were a joke back then." Band knew a coke-crazed stewardess named Candy and a dozen other employees at Miami-based Eastern Air Lines who were happy to mule suitcases for him and run interference with gate agents and security guards.

The seven a.m. from Miami to New York was his favorite flight: "The screeners," he explained, "were not awake." Walk straight through at a brisk pace. Always buy round-trips, even if you were only going to use one leg.

Band would walk into Miami International with three ounces of his cocaine in each boot. The rest was packed into seven hidden compartments in his jacket. "I never flew wearing the Rolex," he added. "I dressed down. I was Anglo. Just don't look nervous."

Back at the Mutiny, Band was now being extended several lines of supply, like so many credit card applications in the mail. "I could now go to eight different guys at three different tables to take product of any quality," he said.

"How many k's?" they'd ask.

"You mean, *kilos*? Kilos?! I'm talking ounces. I need, like, fifty ounces, man," he'd say.

"I'd be told to go up to a suite in the hotel to a walk-in closet. 'Here's the key. Help yourself, man.' Like it was a favor."

Band noticed that his suppliers weren't even counting his cash anymore. "Why disrespect a guy doing good business with you?" he reasoned. "And then you'd see each other at the Mutiny and just smile at one another. You felt connected," he said. "I felt like a little Meyer Lansky."

As he started raking it in, Band felt emboldened enough to approach Ray Corona at Table 3—the Mutiny's and Muchachos' de facto chief financial officer—for some lockable Kevlar Sunshine

State Bank money bags, mandatory fashion accessories for any serious Miami cocaine dealer.

On Passover, he pulled up to his parents' house in his new Mercedes two-seater, wearing a twenty-thousand-dollar diamond-studded Rolex and a gold coke spoon around his neck. His older brother, the state prosecutor pursuing dopers, barely made eye contact. Owen Band played up the tension by asking to read the parts of the Jewish seder that involved participation by the "wicked son."

His parents acted like they could hardly recognize their sniffling salutatorian; decked out in loud bling, he clearly was not studying for the LSAT.

In Band's childhood bedroom was the Perry Mason legal briefcase his father had bought him before his senior year of college, back when his manifest destiny was an acceptance letter from Harvard Law. "Work hard enough and you can go anywhere you want," read the card inside.

Bullshit, he thought, suppressing the urge to cry.

"To be able to get away with this," he said, "fucking the system that fucked me. Well, it was great comeuppance."

Chapter Sixteen

RECRUITING RALPHIE

In 1978, Ralph Linero, a speedboat aficionado, raced a twenty-four-footer 1,275 miles from Miami to New York in a record fifty-eight hours and thirteen minutes, and without the help of radar. That bested the old record by more than forty-four hours.

It was a treacherous ride up the Atlantic. Linero and his racing partner ran aground in shallow water and had to wait six hours for the tide to rise. Off the coast of Georgia, they were chased by armed conservation officials trying to nail poachers.

To keep from nodding off, Linero took his first-ever bump of cocaine. The toot had him fiendishly awake and focused for the balance of the race, which culminated with a triumphant Linero getting pushed into the water by his partner at Manhattan's South Street Seaport.

Linero was also a gifted pilot. He paid for flight school by giving tourists hang gliding lessons in Key Biscayne. There, he befriended a Colombian rancher and exporter, José Rafael Abello Silva, who dined at the Mutiny and kept a condo next door.

"At the time," he said, "José was a small fish and I was not aware of what he was doing." It turned out the Colombian was one of the top ten most powerful players in Pablo Escobar's Medellín cocaine cartel.

They struck up a friendship and the rancher hired Linero to fly him to Medellín, Colombia, in a rented Cesna. Upon landing, Abello nonchalantly handed him five thousand dollars in cash. Said Linero, "I had never seen that much money in my life."

Linero was a square. In 1963, as a twelve-year-old, he had come to Miami alone from Cuba in the Pedro Pan youth airlift, living with an aunt until his parents and sister could make it to Miami four years later.

In 1968, when he was a high school senior, he was featured in a front-page *Miami News* spread entitled "We Don't Want to Play Hooky." Linero told the reporter that his windshield was smashed in because he refused to stay away from classes during a teachers' strike. "I want to graduate and go on to college," he said, donning an NYU T-shirt. Striking teachers taunted attending students, warning them that their diplomas would be no good. "I am going to keep going," he vowed, "as long as they have teachers."

Sal Magluta, a fellow Pedro Pan, was a few years behind him at Miami Senior High. "I met Willie and Sal in the hood," Linero said, "back when they were just a couple of streetwise kids."

Linero went on to community college to pursue a degree in police science and criminology. But he lost interest when he flunked a test for color blindness and was told he could not become a police officer. Just six credits short of an associate's degree, he dropped out and sought part-time work to pay for flying school.

A decade later, Abello the Colombian convinced Linero to fly both pot and cocaine for him. There were, he explained, infinite amounts of the stuff to get to the States. From what he reconnoitered on their maiden flight down to Medellín, they could easily load four hundred kilos onto Linero's craft.

The twelve-hour flight down to a landing strip near Pablo Escobar's sprawling ranch was no pleasure trip. As Linero made his approach onto the narrow runway, he saw crosses in the grass where people who hadn't made it were buried. High on coke, he'd sweat profusely when thinking how he and he alone was responsible for each of his four hundred kilos. "If I crashed," he explained, "I would not be taken to a hospital. I'd be killed."

Ground pirates had a knack for waving at drug pilots with flashlights to trick them into landing at the wrong place, where they'd be robbed and likely killed.

But Cabeza was such an expert flight throttler—and the money was so good—that he kept agreeing to more sorties.

In June 1980, Colombian authorities arrested Linero in the city of Barranquilla and seized his plane. They found that he was traveling without a valid flight plan and discovered marijuana seeds in the cabin. Troops threw him in prison.

His girlfriend back in Miami tipped off Willie and Sal. Miami then called Medellín, where cartel overlord Pablo Escobar had a seventy-thousand-dollar bribe delivered to the mayor of Barranquilla.

Cabeza and his copilot were sprung loose, only to get nabbed again by soldiers who wanted their own cut. The mayor had not sufficiently spread the spoils.

Escobar described his approach to doing business as *"plata o plomo"*—"silver or lead." You could either accept his munificence or suffer a gruesome death. Accordingly, Escobar had the mayor's entire family kidnapped and got word back that he'd execute them one by one until the guys from Miami were sprung.

In no time at all, a prison guard showed up, unlocked their cell and looked the other way as a car waited outside for Linero and his partner. A private jet flew the men to Medellín, where for two weeks they partied with the hottest women and enjoyed the finest cocaine and accommodations, courtesy of their savior:

Don Pablo
El Mágico ("the Magician")
El Padrino ("the Godfather")
El Patrón ("the Boss")
El Señor ("the Lord")
El Zar de la Cocaína ("the Czar of Cocaine")
Pablo Escobar

Linero and his copilot were then flown to the Bahamas, where the Medellín cartel controlled entire islands through its head of Caribbean operations, Carlos Lehder. Land on Lehder's private Norman's Cay, and you would be picked up in a Jeep stocked with completely naked women.

This time, however, the men were met by Gustavo "Taby" Falcon—the younger brother of Willie Falcon—who accompanied them back to Miami.

Within a month, Linero was flying loads for the Muchachos. He now had a chair at their tables upstairs at the Mutiny, where everything was always paid for. Cabeza would sometimes helicopter Willie and Sal to their softball games literally right across the street in Peacock Park.

"They were not 'drug dealers,'" he insisted. "They were more like smugglers who were diplomats, salesmen and CEOs. It was like they were overseeing a conglomerate."

Willie & Sal Corp., he explained, invested good money and time in the best boats, planes, trucks, attorneys, accountants, bodyguards, mules and corruptible politicians and cops.

"One of the most interesting parts of the Mutiny for me," he recalled, "was when coke smuggling groups would come to the Upper Deck for what we called a 'coronation party'—all night long, the bosses held court while the various distributors and subdealers took turns wheeling and dealing for a piece of the action."

"Tension was high," he said. "Guys were trying to get an audience with Willie and Sal before all the available kilos were gone."

Linero says everyone carried what they called leather "fag bags" holding at least ten thousand dollars in cash "and, of course, a .380 Walther PPK semiautomatic"—the sidearm of choice for the discriminating 1980s cocaine dealer. "Everyone's uniform," he said, "was at least a Rolex, beeper and cowboy boots."

The opening ceremony to the tourney: at just before midnight, "Edwin and Maryann," a young couple Burton Goldberg hired from France's Crazy Horse, wrapped their lithe, nearly nude bodies around a stripper pole on the Upper Deck. "It was tasteful," said Goldberg. "It was erotic and it drew the crowds." And the animal spirit of sex drove revenue.

"You'd show up and we'd close off the Upper Deck," said cosmuggler Juan "Recotado" Barroso. "Steak. Lobster thermidor. Dom. Rosé. Perrier-Jouët. What do you want?"

The gang was now bringing in one thousand kilos of the finest stuff a week. "At the Mutiny," Barroso said, "everyone called us the Boys. I'd sit next to Willie and mooch on his girls. He was good to everyone."

Reco insisted he was mostly in it for the competitive thrill. "I liked the rush of doing something illegal," he said. "Every load I brought in and not getting caught. We were the ones dealing with bad weather, the ocean, Bahamian defense. If I was going to do this, I was going to do it good."

Carlos Ruiz was a Little Havana street gangster turned ocean smuggler (a *marimbero*) who shared notes at the Mutiny with Falcon and Magluta on logistics and evasion. He says this was like continuing education for the Cuban exiles. Little fourteen-karat-gold saucers topped with cocaine were placed out on the tables. "We were the ones who knew the waters, the landing points, the buyers here," he said. "The Colombians needed Willie and Sal. They had all the boats, planes and racers and would not rip them off."

Plus, he said, they always paid on time. What good was all the cocaine in the Andes if you didn't have people to count on in Miami, the world's cocaine hub?

Paying a "consultant" like Carlos Ruiz on time was a whole other ritual. When Ruiz was driving to the Mutiny one night in his new 'seventy-nine Corvette pace car, he stopped at a light and turned his head to see Willie Falcon smiling at him. With a flick of his wrist, he tossed Ruiz a bag stuffed with fifteen thousand dollars. "Go have fun!" he yelled, and sped off.

"It was unreal," said Ruiz. "I re-cycle it in my mind and can't believe it."

Similarly, Chuck Volpe, the Mutiny's general manager in the early eighties, remembers Willie Falcon just flipping him a thick stack of bills after an all-nighter.

Contrast this largesse with the recollection of a Mutiny girl who first met Willie and Sal at the club in 1976. "They were nobodies who were casing the place," she said. "I'd give them free drinks. They didn't have any money."

Four years later, the Boys were pulling in upward of 25 million dollars a month. "Mutiny Mel" Kessler, their attorney, and Ray Corona, their de facto CFO at Table 3, introduced them to Miami attorney Juan Acosta, who, with the help of Panamanian lawyer Guillermo "Porky" Endara, could set up offshore front companies that cycled cocaine cash into property and businesses in Florida.

For logistics, up in Florida horse country the Boys kept a ranch and airstrip that Jorge Valdes had procured before he was nabbed. Rednecks did not see Cubans often up in those parts. But rednecks also didn't see suitcases full of hundred-dollar bills.

The Muchachos bribed the county sheriff to look the other way when they'd bring in planes full of cocaine. When he died in 1980, his son, the town's narcotics chief, rolled over the old man's agreement with the drug lords from down in *"Miamuh."*

Chapter Seventeen

SPRING OF 'EIGHTY

IT WOULD SEEM like Willie and Sal's crazy streak of luck ran out at the turn of the decade, when the state nabbed them alongside dozens of other small-time dealers in a wholesale South Florida drug sweep called Video Canary.

But the case went nowhere.

On April 15, 1980, Willie and Sal pleaded no contest to cocaine charges. Attorney Mel Kessler contritely presented them to the judge as youthful offenders, immigrant children and paragons of Cuban-American citizenry who had never broken any law. They were free on bond while Kessler appealed their fourteen-month jail sentences.

Maybe the authorities would have paid more attention to sentencing them if Miami hadn't been about to slide into chaos.

Two hundred twenty-eight miles away, Havana was about to blow up. Fidel Castro was locked in a showdown with the Peruvian embassy, where on April 1, six Cubans drove through the perimeter fence in a bus and demanded asylum. A guard was killed in the cross fire and Castro demanded the raiders be handed over to face trial.

When Peru balked and the government withdrew the guards, word fanned out and at least ten thousand Cubans poured into the embassy on Easter Sunday. The embassies of Costa Rica and Spain also started taking on defectors.

On April 20, Fidel Castro countered with a bombshell: all Cubans wanting to flee to the US were now free to jump boats at the port of Mariel. "If they don't have the heart and the blood of the revolution," he thundered, "we don't want them. We don't need them!"

Suddenly, exiles up in South Florida were scrambling to get relatives picked up. Fishing crews and pot smugglers repurposed their fleets. Anyone with a boat in Miami was in clover.

At the Mutiny, Mollie the hostess rode down to the Keys with a pot smuggler she served to pick up family he had coming in. The ten-hour ride—double the normal time—down to the archipelago that ended Florida was bumper-to-bumper with trucks, vans, boats, campers, even horse wagons. Motels were packed. Gas stations were sold out.

As Cuba was collapsing, the story went, its population was bound to flee for America. So this was how Castro, in power for twenty years, would fall.

At the docks in Monroe County, Mollie witnessed thousands upon thousands of single young men emerging from rickety boats. Most, she said, looked sickly and malnourished. The boatlifters had splotchy skin and concave postures. The stench of sweat and bodily fluids was overwhelming.

Upstairs at the Mutiny, a doper nicknamed Kojak spent 100 thousand dollars on getting passage for Mariel relatives of his big syndicate of Miami pot runners. Jose Rotger, the hotel's Cuban-born engineer and handyman, desperately asked around for the keys to a boat he could use to retrieve his family. Reunion was a dream come true for the thousands of Cubans who had settled in Miami over three decades.

Amid this deluge of humanity into South Florida, however, exiles were increasingly observing ominous signs: dozens of the refugees getting off the boats wore boots they recognized from Cuba's infamous penitentiaries. Others were in hospital bands and gowns, and there were a significant number of transvestites on the flotilla.

It started dawning on everyone that Castro, the wily bastard, was emptying his jails and mental institutions onto Miami.

A sizable minority of the 125 thousand refugees who poured in over the following six months were hardened assassins with weapons tattooed on the insides of their lips. Others were rapists, many more convicted thieves.

It took little time for the authorities to realize that Marielitos were ending up the victims of homicides at a rate five times higher than the general population. In fact, the ninety rafters killed in the first year since the exodus commenced outnumbered all murders in Orlando, Fort Lauderdale and Saint Petersburg combined. The director of the Federal Bureau of Prisons remarked that he was seeing some of the hardest, baddest criminals come from Cuba in his twenty-five years of work in the system.

On May 8, 1980, Miami International Airport teemed with relatives of Marielitos flying in from places such as New Jersey and California. For reasons unclear, a young Latin male walked up to a gate and calmly fired five shots into a passenger exiting the vestibule. It was a hit job done by a rafter who was glad to trade time in Castro's jail for the three meals and humanity of a US jail sentence.

A Cuban gas station owner in Little Havana confessed he was now instructing employees, "If a black comes in here asking for money, give it to him. If an Anglo comes to rob us, give it to him. But if a Marielito comes here, kill him. I will pay for everything," so disdainful was he of what Castro's rejects were doing to Miami's exile reputation.

If only Miami could focus on Mariel alone.

LESS THAN A month after Castro "flushed his toilets" onto South Florida, a jury acquitted four Miami police officers of killing an unarmed black motorcycle rider after an eight-minute high-speed chase in December.

When the not-guilty verdict came down on May 17, Miami erupted into anarchy. A five-thousand-strong protest near the Metro Justice Building morphed into an outright riot by sundown. The violence—looting, torching, Molotov cocktails, sniper fire, motorists being dragged out and lynched—fanned out from downtown and into the Black Grove, the historically segregated ward just yards from the Mutiny.

Bullets ricocheted off the balconies at the Mutiny and the antennae on the roof, fuzzing up the reception for all those glued to their sets watching Mount Saint Helens erupt, the northwestern and southeastern United States convulsing in tandem.

The club's manager prohibited female staff from leaving the building. Coconut Grove was all but cordoned off by police, and the Mutiny's doors were blocked with kegs and tables.

Stir-crazy, Mollie the hostess and Bernie de Torres led a handful of club members and staffers in a manic coke-snorting binge. They grabbed machine guns and took to the roof of the Mutiny, where, laughing hysterically, they sprayed bullets up into the Coconut Grove air. "We shot at everything and nothing," said Mollie. "You could see plumes of smoke across the air. Sirens blazing. But somehow we felt above it."

By June, more Cubans—ninety thousand—had arrived in the United States than in any year since Castro rose to power. It took just six weeks for forty thousand of them to get settled in Miami, the balance held in military camps across the country, awaiting processing and clearance. Most would end up in South Florida.

All of which had Fernando Puig, the Mutiny's three-hundred-pound head of security, on edge. "Where my *gon*?" he would always be yelling, running through the club. "Where is my *gon*?!" (All the while, his Colt would be hanging out the back of his pants.)

Security monitored every angle outside the hotel for robbers, rapists, pickpockets and cat burglars—pretty much everything the Mariel disaster was coming to represent in Miami. One doper's on-and-off mistress was kidnapped off a bench and fought her way out of a car as she was groped.

A sense of foreboding wafted in and out of the club, the eruption taking shape on the afternoon of June 23. And while it wasn't the Marielito showdown everyone was dreading, it became a metaphor for a city collectively losing its mind.

A pair of white guys, Charles Pfeifer and Michael Borkin, were staying in the Mutiny's Bordello Suite, where they freebased cocaine. Suddenly terrified and screaming, they set fire to cash and threw it into their hot tub and across the room. Some fixtures caught fire.

The barefoot men, one of them shirtless and tattooed, then climbed down the front of the hotel from their tenth-floor balcony, pants still wet from their hot tub. Constantly looking over their shoulders at something beyond the marina that was terrifying them, they gripped balcony after balcony, swinging like monkeys, until they came to a stop at the bay window looking into the Mutiny Club.

Their eyes seemed lemurlike to a *Miami Herald* photographer. Police officers reached out from the window of the Poop Deck and pleaded with the men to get back into the building.

One of the "freebase jumpers," as waitresses were calling them, then punched a cop, sending cocaine flying out of his pocket and onto the striped awning above the hotel's doorman. That's when the rest of the police officers jumped the screaming men and tied their hands. "Just a couple of our regular cuckoos down here," explained a cop to a newswoman, as one of the freebasers banged his head against the inside of his squad car.

Luckily, the guests had left a loaded chrome-plated .44 Magnum back up in room 1020.

In case you're wondering what any of this has to do with Los Muchachos, Willie Falcon and Sal Magluta: they had the incredible fortune of ramping up their cocaine empire in this chaos. Miami had a desperate shortage of police officers. Its morgue was overrun. Who in the world was going to prioritize prosecuting a handful of largely nonviolent smugglers? April 1980 was maybe the most opportune time in history to get busted for dealing cocaine in Miami.

Too bad their old pal Jorge Valdes had been snagged a year earlier. Cashed in by Manuel Noriega, ruler of Panama, where Falcon and Magluta were now funneling tens of millions of dollars—he had just been sentenced to fifteen years in prison.

Adding insult, one of Noriega's torturers showed up to testify against him wearing Valdes's old Rolex.

Chapter Eighteen

REHEATING THE COLD WAR

BACK INSIDE THE Mutiny Club, the Poop Deck was shorn of its old patron saint, Rudy Redbeard, who had also just been sentenced to fifteen years in prison, thanks to Monkey Morales's machinations and Carlene Quesada's testimony. Mon, Redbeard's fugitive Puerto Rican hit man, was still on the lam.

Now Quesada, Morales, the Villaverde brothers and Frank Castro drank together at Table 14. They shared the Poop Deck with arms dealer Sarkis Soghanalian, who was known around the world as the "Merchant of Death." The rotund Armenian enthused about how much money he was going to make selling arms to whichever Arab nation decided to take the lead against now-rogue Iran, which was holding American hostages.

The Cold War was hot again at the Mutiny. Soghanalian, for example, hung out with the retinue of former Nicaraguan dictator Anastasio Somoza, who had been best friends with Mutiny security head, Fernando Puig, ever since they met at the Bay of Pigs. In addition to his job at the Mutiny, Puig oversaw Somoza's massive Miami funeral in September. The former Nicaraguan leader was refused entry to Miami by Jimmy Carter and had to settle in Paraguay, where a hit team killed him. There was no love lost in Miami for the Democratic incumbent.

Republicans, on the other hand, were amenable to the idea of arming those who would take on Nicaragua's leftist regime. Nominee Ronald Reagan was running with George H. W. Bush, former CIA director under Gerald Ford. Two Bush sons ate at the Mutiny. Jeb, a Spanish speaker married to a Mexican woman, had just moved to Miami from Houston and was working with prominent exile millionaires who kept tables at the club.

Bay of Pigs veterans such as Frank Castro and the Villaverdes were increasingly eyeing a retake of Nicaragua as the Cold War's next big Latin American front. Somoza's old guards and army officers were reconstituting into a guerrilla force called *Contrarrevolución* (Contras). The CIA had an asset in John Hull, a rancher who owned eight thousand acres in Costa Rica, right on the border with Nicaragua. At the Mutiny, Hull, Frank Castro, Soghanalian and the Villaverdes had plenty to talk about.

As usual, stuff was complicated with Ricardo "Monkey" Morales. He was on the outs with Rafael Villaverde, who had agreed to testify against his friend, rogue ex–CIA guy Edwin Wilson, who was doing political hits for Libya's Muammar Gaddafi. One night at the Mutiny, Morales got in a loud argument with Villaverde about the matter and threw butter pats at him.

By 1980, the Monkey, self-medicating with a constant regimen of cocaine, alcohol and downers, was above all else paranoid. Surely, he reasoned, Fidel Castro had dispatched his own assassins to Miami in the deluge of humanity that was the Mariel boatlift.

Thus, every Cuban exile who had participated in clandestine raids—especially a turncoat like Morales, who had first worked for Castro—was now a target.

Seeking to calm his nerves with a walk on the beach, Morales reached for his gun when he saw a dark Latin male walking toward him with a machete. But he was just a parks employee trimming bushes on a sand dune.

Authorities in upstate Florida heard Morales had strangled a Latin man with a piano wire, and in front of as many as twenty witnesses. Perhaps that show of force was a refresh of the way he pumped seventeen rounds into a guy in broad daylight in Little Havana.

As tens of thousands of Mariel refugees poured into South Florida, and the area's homicide rate featured on President Jimmy Carter's daily briefing, Ricardo Morales started carrying a gag grenade on his belt. Translation: "Threaten me, challenge me, etc., and I will blow us both to bits. I'm crazier than you are."

Chapter Nineteen

MARIEL & CO.

THE MARIELITOS' INITIATION into the world of the Mutiny, says member Laura Costanzo, "was like a round-robin to get picked up by dealers," whether Willie and Sal, Colombians or the various smaller Cuban enterprises that smuggled in the shadow of the Upper Deck.

Not that the welcome was unanimous.

"Cabeza" Linero, the Muchachos' pilot, was skeptical of rafters who snuck into the Mutiny to genuflect before his bosses. "I didn't need to socialize with these hangers-ons," he said.

He and Willie Falcon's brother, Gustavo ("Taby"), took in the nightly spectacle from another table, remarking under their breath about this guy's strut, or the way that other *maricón* mixed a St. Pauli Girl with cranberry juice or laughed at every other word out of the mouths of established kingpins. Said Linero: "They would kiss Sal and Willie's ass to get a handout or a few kilos to sell."

Down in the Poop Deck, Super Papi Becerra took a shining to José "Coca-Cola" Yero, a twenty-year-old Mariel refugee who was Cuba's former national cycling champ. He was sprung loose into the boatlift after attempting to break his way into an embassy three years earlier.

At the Mutiny, Yero was called Coca-Cola because he always proudly turned down members' offers to buy him a hard drink. *"Solo un Coca-Cola,"* he'd say.

"That fucker had class," said Becerra. "He looked American. Green eyes." When he had learned Coca-Cola was the national cycling champ of Cuba who had run afoul of Castro and ended up in jail, Becerra, Cuba's former judo champ (he defected in 1971), felt compelled to introduce himself.

Sometime in early 1981, he bumped into Coca-Cola in the elevator with a sexy, well-dressed South American woman. A nervous-looking Coca-Cola pinched the tip of his nose to gesture to Super Papi to hook him up with a little something.

Established dopers at the Mutiny usually kept two grades of blow in their coat pockets: one "stepped on" (diluted with baby laxative or powdered milk) for coke whores and staff tips, and the other a highly pure, blow-your-mind batch for business development with discriminating dealers or prospective clients. It was like Johnnie Walker versus Jim Beam. (In fact, some would quip: "Fuck the Jim Beam, bro. I want El Walker.")

That night in the elevator, Becerra accidentally handed the Marielito his vial of good cocaine.

He next saw Coca-Cola the following morning at the Mutiny's breakfast spread. *"Oye,"* said Coca-Cola. "Come sit with me." The Marielito bought breakfast for Becerra, charging it to his date's room. She was upstairs passed out in bed. "That shit you gave me last night, *hermano*? It was the fucking *best*!"

Good for him, figured Becerra. Best-case scenario: the kid comes into some money and starts buying his blow from me.

Two months later, however, Becerra pulled up to a nearby bar-bershop that was big with Cuban dopers to find a Lamborghini and a Ferrari parked out front.

"Hey, Gavi," he asked the barber, "whose cars?"

"Coca-Cola's," he answered, pointing an elbow to the dandy walking out of the bathroom. *"Heyyyyy!"* yelled Coca-Cola Yero. *"Oye!* I need to talk to you."

Becerra and Coca-Cola then sped off to the Mutiny, where the latter flashed his membership card. They took a table. "You remember that night you went up the elevator with me?" Coca-Cola asked him. He leaned in and guffawed. "That was Pablo Escobar's niece!"

Escobar, the head of Medellín's cocaine cartel, was by now the most powerful and feared man in South America and well on his way to becoming the wealthiest person the continent had ever seen. He kept a pink mansion in Miami Beach that relatives and affiliates often used, speedboats and yachts docked out back.

Coca-Cola explained that the visiting niece had promised to put in a good word with her uncle, a currency that he says he then bluff-parlayed into boat-smuggling deals that had made him hun-dreds of thousands of dollars.

"That's how small the world was at the Mutiny at that time," Becerra later reflected. "Your life could change in a Miami minute."

Actually, the cocaine baptism of Coca-Cola Yero was a tad more complicated.

Fresh off his big night with the Colombian niece, the refugee did indeed boast to everyone at the club that he was a man with a connection.

"Now's the time to hire me: I'll run your loads good and cheap. I'm Cuba's national cycling champ. Castro—*hijo de puta*—threw me in jail but, look, I'm here at the Mutiny."

"Coca-Cola tried to be something he wasn't," said Lourdes Castellon, Willie Falcon's girlfriend in the early 1980s. "He played a front. Everything was too flashy, too Mariel-over-the-top. He was fishy."

By 1981, Miami was laced with Mariel rip-off artists and hucksters who would advertise their willingness to smuggle fifty thousand pounds of marijuana for twenty thousand dollars, or a fifth the going rate. Some Marielitos did what they advertised. But several others absconded with merchandise and/or cash.

All of which infuriated incumbent exile smugglers, who had spent years (and time behind bars) refining their craft and carving their territory. Many established Cubans were even co-opting Fidel Castro's own epithet, *escoria* ("scum"), to refer to Marielitos.

Anti-Castro solidarity was only so strong an adhesive: like the aforementioned gas station owner who OK'd shooting and killing Marielito robbers, Cuban drug lords would not think twice about wasting wetfoots who stole from them. Coca-Cola himself faced this reckoning when he somehow managed to run afoul of Rene "Raspao" Rodriguez, a master smuggler who moved huge volume to and from the Bahamas with his girlfriend and partner in crime, blond babe Nancy "La Rubia"/"Big Blonde" Mira.

The Cuban-born Raspao (Spanish for "Snow Cone"—he was bald) worked in construction and marine repairs until 1978, when, like many South Florida exiles working in fishing and boatbuilding, he was recruited to captain boatloads of marijuana. "It was quick money," he said. "I was very familiar with the water and the inlets."

He had since traded up to the more lucrative and less bulky business of smuggling cocaine. Nancy and Raspao were working with Venao (the Deer), Falcon and Magluta's chief of Bahamas operations.

Raspao was convinced that Coca-Cola, acting as a subcontractor for one of his captains, ripped him off of 200 thousand dollars in a 500-thousand-dollar smuggle.

"A lot of these Marielitos," he said, "would fuck the wrong people. At least three times a week, they would get wrapped in barbed wire and left in trucks. Or they'd get handcuffed to telephone poles. They were really out of hand."

Raspao had Coca-Cola tied up and driven to a farm out in the boonies.

Yero, trembling, swore there had been a misunderstanding. He had seen Raspao and his girl at the Mutiny. Upstairs. He begged for his life.

"You tried to rip me off!" yelled Raspao. "You want to die?"

Histrionics aside, Raspao and La Rubia were actually not much for murder. They were in this for the rush—the thrill of the chase. Evasion. Partying. Great food and massive boats and cars.

Nancy, eighteen and a bit of a tomboy, was thrilled that she could do smuggling sorties in her bikini and then walk into Dadeland Mall with cash to buy Swiss army knives and a camera.

La Rubia was one of the only female smugglers in a sea of macho men. Her parents assumed she had dropped out of high school to turn tricks. "We'd bring in a load and laugh. 'You wanna go again? Shit, yeah!' It was so easy," she said.

She and Raspao were regulars upstairs at the Mutiny, where they would bump into friend and fellow smuggler Carlos Ruiz. "The bouquets of flowers," she recalled. "The money. The power. The Muchachos were my friends—they liked how I was around boats. I felt like one of the guys."

"That place for us," said Ruiz, "was like stepping into what a Havana disco would have been—like the American answer to the Tropicana" (the legendary nightclub and cabaret seized by Castro).

"You felt important, wearing the Brioni suits and ostrich-skin belts and shoes," Ruiz said. "You'd snort the best coke."

Nancy said she appreciated how intoxicating this must all have been to the recently penniless Coca-Cola. She actually admired his audacity: in 1977, he had snuck into an ambulance in order to make it past the gate of an embassy in Havana. He was caught and imprisoned. Castro let him out into the Mariel boatlift. Exiles in Miami loved seeing star athletes abandon Castro.

Raspao figured he'd give Coca-Cola a second chance: he could work off his debt. The deal: run these two loads of cocaine, pay us and we'll talk.

Coca-Cola came through—on time to every last buck—and asked for more cocaine sorties. The couple agreed to continue working with the new refugee.

Super Papi Becerra was proud of his fellow exile athlete. After he'd defected to the US in 1971, it took Becerra five years, spanning dead-end wage work, to finally hook up with his big break, Carlene Quesada.

It took Coca-Cola less than a year to become a cocaine kingpin.

Months after Coca-Cola begged for his life, Tatico, the armed robber who liked to case the Mutiny, spotted the Marielito driving up in his Lamborghini and strutting into the club in a twenty-thousand-dollar Rolex and matching suit. The bartender told Tatico that this was the second Rolex and matching wardrobe he saw Coca-Cola wearing in as many days.

Impressed, Tatico resolved to leave Coca-Cola (an easy target) alone. "To come here, on the streets, and then get a ranchero to hire you to bring in lots of cocaine," he said. "Then to be drinking Dom in this joint. 'Fucking Coca-Cola!' I remember thinking. He was the ultimate Mutiny Mariel."

Chapter Twenty

THE MARLBORO *MENG*

A MARIEL REFUGEE who immediately made a name for himself at the Mutiny was twenty-seven-year-old Luis "Weetchie" Escobedo, a chiseled, mustached ringer for the star of *Magnum, P.I.*, Tom Selleck.

Guard Willy Gomez recalled none other than Willie Falcon and Sal Magluta personally introducing Weetchie to him at the entrance to the club in late 1980 or early 1981. "They were so happy when they brought him in," he said, "beaming like they had just acquired the best player in the draft."

Weetchie cut an unusual swath for a boatlifter. "He was very nice, well-dressed, soft-spoken," said Gomez. "He was built like a brick shithouse. He looked like he was eating steak in Cuba and living the high life there. I am telling you, nobody washing up in Miami looked that big and healthy." Gomez was reminded of this every morning on his drive to work, when he passed by a refugee tent city whose inhabitants looked like concentration camp survivors.

At the Mutiny, members and staff wondered if this unusually hale-looking Weetchie was a spy for Fidel Castro. They started referring to the mustached Marielito, variously, as Tom Selleck (*"Tone Selley"* was how Cubans pronounced it), Magnum P.I., Marlboro Man and Brawny Man.

But Super Papi was creeped out by Weetchie. "He was a piece of shit," he said. "Weetchie had no money. He used to go from table to table, stealing drinks and tips from people who left to go to the dance floor. He was just a fucking scumbag walking around. I'd never let him sit at my table. I don't know how Willie gave him a chance."

It turns out, Weetchie's big break in Miami came with the ardor of a former-beauty-queen attorney who was representing the family of the black motorist whose killing set off the 1980 race riots.

She was into coke and partying all night at the Mutiny, and, it seems, the exotic thrill of bedding a statuesque, well-hung Marielito. The attorney gave Weetchie cash and the keys to her black Corvette. She would get him into the Mutiny and he would linger when she left, swiping tips off tables.

Mutiny hostess Bonnie Tolentino was one of Escobedo's early love interests. "When I tell you he was beautiful," she said, "he was *beautiful*. Tall. His jewelry. The way he smoked. He didn't speak a word of English, but he had women left and right. I was in love with him. He'd have me, then not have me."

Owen Band recalls Bernie de Torres wagging tongues with Weetchie in the Mutiny's Gangplank, the tiki bar overlooking the pool. "Bernie thought he could help get him laid," he said. "And Weetchie being seen with Bay of Pigs—well, that only helped his standing with the Upper Deck."

Band came into the Mutiny one early weeknight to find Weetchie and some other Marielitos checking out the Upper Deck before Willie and Sal's crew started taking their tables. "They all stood out," he said. Their pants, worn too big, were invariably rolled up at the bottoms—not cuffed or hemmed. This was the hallmark of a hand-me-down from the Little Havana Activities Center, the massive charity and anti-Castro nerve center run by Rafael Villaverde, the Bay of Pigs hero who held court on the Mutiny's Poop Deck.

Band went to the bathroom to do a bump of coke. As the frost shot up his sinuses, he looked in the mirror to see a chubby Marielito staring at him. The guy smiled and longingly put his thumb up to his nostril.

Alberto Bover introduced himself in solid English, explaining that he was a civil engineer in Cuba who left for Miami on the 1980 boatlift. He had studied French in Havana. His wife was an economist in the Castro regime. His brother Jesus was close with the guys who stormed the Peruvian embassy. Alberto and his three brothers took their chances on the Mariel exodus, hoping to hook up with relatives in Miami who owned a jewelry store.

When he got off the boat in Key West, Bover was put on a plane to an INS refugee camp up in Pennsylvania that had a disproportionate number of gay and transgender refugees, many of whom relished the chance to finally be queer out in the open.

He said he won points with the camp's army captain, a devout Christian, when he stood atop a boulder to admonish the homosexuals for their flamboyance. "We're in America!" he said. "Show some respect!" He was pelted with rocks and yells of *"Infiltrador!"*

"You immediately noticed that Alberto was more intelligent than most of the guys," recalled Band. "His English was not half-bad, and he could talk French. He was college educated."

On July 4, 1980, Bover, cleared by Immigration, was put on a plane to Miami, where his relatives had just vouched for him. Fireworks were going off as he landed. The refugee immediately searched for his uncle Ignacio, the Little Havana jeweler. "In reality," he told Owen Band, in between bumps of cocaine, "that guy just showed up at homes and fixed broken chains. My aunt? She was cleaning hotel rooms."

Alberto's younger brothers, Kiki, Jesus and Miguel, subsequently made it to Miami. Kiki had had a close call when the shrimp boat he hitched a ride on at Mariel capsized and he had to be rescued by a Navy helicopter.

A handsome bridge player who liked to croon salsa and merengue, Kiki took English night classes at Miami Senior High, where he heard about legendary dropouts Los Muchachos.

When a Cuban exile initiated the Bovers into the world of credit card fraud, the brothers pounced. Kiki—"Kiki Disco" they called him at the Mutiny—opened a pair of record stores, which were used as fronts for an operation that replicated Visas and MasterCards. The Bovers recruited other Marielitos to dig credit card receipts out of trash bins and from employees on the take. The brothers used the numbers to buy televisions, VCRs and other hardware and sell them on the cash black market.

It wasn't such a leap for them to pivot into dealing drugs; after all, if you dealt cocaine, you were also in the market for money laundering. The bet was that white-collar crime would hold little priority in a Miami criminal justice system overburdened with homicides.

The next thing Owen Band knew, he was driving with Bover to a cocaine stash house, kilos of product just moving around in the Marielito's backseat. Band invited the refugee up on one of his smuggles to LaGuardia Airport—the well-spoken scholars breezing past security at Miami International in not one but *two* smartly stuffed jackets.

Bover reciprocated by offering to bring Band into a Queens, New York, credit card fencing operation. When Bover had him over to his new apartment, Band noticed crates of Coca-Cola bottles stacked literally floor to ceiling in his kitchen. "He couldn't drink enough of the stuff," Band said. "It was like a metaphor for how hungry many of these guys were for everything after twenty years of deprivation."

"I liked the Bovers," said Super Papi Becerra. "They had class. College educated."

"The Mariels got up quickly and made money quickly," said Lourdes Castellon, Willie Falcon's on-and-off girlfriend, whom they took pains to charm. "They took risks."

She called Weetchie the "Marlboro Man." "He had a presence, an arrogance," she said. Like in *The Godfather*, the refugees made no shortage of appeals to Falcon, who had sent his boats and chartered others to ferry relatives of friends in the boatlift. Legend had it he scanned the morning paper for fellow exiles that needed bail money or legal help.

The velocity of the Marielitos' assimilation, Castellon says, was impressive. "They liked the nightlife and the hustle," she said. She remembers the boatlifters throwing one of their guys a twenty-thousand-dollar birthday bash at the Mutiny. They hired local salsa artists and rented out a whole floor at the hotel, complete with Dom and hookers.

Other Marielitos, however, were getting up in the face of the Mutiny's membership sales director, who checked for cards and confiscated stolen IDs. They called her a whore for not seating them. A growing number would show up with brothers and sisters and try to sneak into the club through the hotel. She said she was now afraid to walk to her car.

"You started having incidents almost nightly," said Willy Gomez, the security guard. "People started snorting in the open. A lot of lowlifes didn't even rent rooms to do their shit. That wasn't right. I said this will get us shut down."

When Burton Goldberg did drop in to survey the club, he lately had a habit of saying, "Get those ice suckers off my tables." Translation: "Buy drinks or leave."

"There were guys who'd pass out at their table," said a membership sales girl. "We'd wheel them up to a room in their chair, take out their gun and wallet and leave it on the table with a note."

Mariel refugees were on their way to being murdered at a rate that was five times more than that of the county's general population. "If we didn't have them," remarked a Miami homicide sergeant, "our murder rate would be down by one-third."

After months of reading headlines about corpses and bullets, Ralph Renick, the legendary Miami TV anchor, looked tired and defeated. He was drinking more than ever at the Mutiny's bar before heading off to do the evening news.

One night in December 1980, his trademark monologue sounded more like a cry for help:

Jimmy Carter has six more weeks to serve as president. He has been big on human rights. To protect the human rights of the people of Miami, he still has time to arrange an exodus back to Cuba. For these undesirable Cubans, airlift them to our naval base in Guantánamo. Open the gate and let these Cubans be returned. Good night, and may the good news be yours.

Chapter Twenty-one

RICARDO'S MORALS

THAT SAME WEEK, a hush-hush meeting was taking place just up the street from the Mutiny, in the parking lot of a waterfront restaurant.

In a police car with Raul Martinez and D. C. Diaz was Monkey Morales, a little more than a month after nearly getting his brains blown out by bouncer Willy Gomez.

Morales had a news flash he wanted to share: Carlene Quesada, the Villaverde brothers, Frank Castro and the rest of Mutiny Table 14 had now diversified into heroin. Which, he solemnly swore, "goes against, you know, my own belief and religion, and, you know, I . . . flatly refuse to go along in this new kind of business." (Much of which was patently bullshit; it's not like the Vatican approved of Morales's cocaine dealing and contract hits. And heroin was not a Table 14 thing. But the cops still gave Monkey a hearing.)

They all repaired to a nearby Holiday Inn, where Morales offered to sit for a fifty-page deposition. He handed Raul Martinez his semiautomatic and they discussed the topic of witness protection.

"You have to ask yourself," said Martinez, "why is he telling me this? He was used by many people. And he used us."

Martinez had Morales repeat over the phone everything he had divulged in the cop car, to see if his claims matched up. They did.

Morales then called his sister and asked if he could come over.

He sobbed and screamed in her kitchen, tearing out a column that connected the counter to the wall. His niece watched him from the living room, ignoring her mother's demand that she go outside.

This would not be one of those nights when "*Tío* Richard" would throw her up in the air and playfully bite her ear. "I've given my fucking life to this country," he yelled, riding out a panic attack. "Sons of bitches!"

When Morales finally calmed down enough to eat some warm pudding—an infantilization of sorts; his mother used to make it for her children back in Havana—he still kept his right hand on his gun, beneath a hat on his lap, and his back to the kitchen wall, both doors of the house within his line of vision.

Chapter Twenty-two

ALIASES

IT IS QUITE possible that, by early 1981, Raul Diaz, the Miami Police Department's rising homicide star, had bumped into a Mutiny regular who went by the name Michael Keller.

Keller was a high roller, thinking nothing of blowing 750 dollars on a bottle of twenty-year-old French wine. He sat with pugnacious banker Ray Corona at Table 3, where they'd both throw money around and draw in women with hungry noses.

What Raul Diaz had no way of knowing at the time was that this Michael Keller, a prolific doper, was also a serial killer. Since the turn of the decade, the man had killed at least ten people with his own hands—some to rip off in cocaine deals, others as blood sacrifices, others for no apparent reason at all. In any case, Miami's variously crisscrossing law enforcement bodies seemed Inspector Clouseau–like in their inability to nab him since he had been first arrested, in 1972.

In 1981 Keller found himself at the Mutiny, sitting conspicuously with Corona, the loud member who liked to wear mink coats and drove up in a Rolls that he demanded be parked on the curb.

Club manager Chuck Volpe had frequent showdowns with Corona, who was always armed and always coked out. Despite repeated warnings and complaints about Table 3, the Mutiny's head of security, Fernando Puig, refused to do anything about Corona, who had already pulled a gun on Volpe several times.

He was just too profitable and too connected; the club would risk alienating Willie and Sal, whose money Corona handled, as well as City Manager Howard Gary, who sat with the banker and held a seat on his board. Gary could make Burton Goldberg's life a hell of surprise health and fire inspections and code violations.

So Volpe tried another tack. When Corona threatened him for refusing to allow a couple of Mutiny girls off their shifts early, he warned, "If you're going for your gun, Ray, I will shoot you dead."

To which Corona's tablemate Mr. Keller interjected: "Do you know who I am? I will fucking hunt you down!"

Volpe had no way of knowing that Keller had killed a dozen other people for far lesser affronts.

Michael Keller's real name was Miguel Miranda, and he was known in coke-dealing circles as Miguelito, a shady, gravel-voiced kingpin who owned a nearby nightclub. He lived in a former mango grove that he had converted into a five-acre walled compound where he decapitated animals, carved bone talismans and stockpiled machine guns.

Miranda was into Santeria, the Afro-Caribbean religion that featured animal sacrifices. He loved the jet-set lifestyle, often flying to Vegas and the Bahamas and getting big-spender photo ops with the likes of Frank Sinatra and Paul Anka. He had at least four wives but spent prolifically on prostitutes.

Miranda had last been in jail in May of 1980, but he was sprung free less than an hour and a half later after no one could identify him. Law enforcement in Miami was so dysfunctional that it took fully two months for the FBI to even realize it had let a killer walk, and less than two weeks for Miranda to murder yet again—this time a Santeria statue maker who had had the temerity to invoice him. After hog-tying the man, Miranda shot him at least twenty times from toes to scalp and dumped him in a garbage bag by the road.

In August, Miranda hog-tied, executed and garbage-bagged a pair of cocktail waitresses and left their bodies in the trunk of a Cadillac. Was it over cocaine? Was it a voodoo offering? Deviant sexual rush? The cops racked their brains for answers.

Two months later, a man named Frank Crawford, who liked to party at the Mutiny with his neighbor, Miami Dolphins star Mercury Morris, was found shot to death with the same bullet profile as the above murders. This victim was also garbage-bagged, his body discovered sticking out of a fifty-five-gallon drum bobbing in the bay just north of the Mutiny.

The cops incorrectly tallied the find as a "janitor in a drum." It took them weeks to identify the body as Crawford's. Miranda had tried to use the man to shake down Mercury Morris for ransom money.

Miguel Miranda—aka Michael Keller, aka Jose Fernandez Velasquez Cruz, aka Mike Cosme, aka Douglas Daxx, Wilfredo Cuevas and multiple other names—had been on the run from the law since 1972, when he was first arrested for cocaine dealing but was allowed to remain free on a fifteen-thousand-dollar bond.

As the authorities vacillated and bungled, he bought a false passport and traveled the globe under various names. In June of

1978, acting on a wiretap of a Coconut Grove apartment they linked to a double homicide, police traced a call to a room at the Mutiny. But they got there too late to apprehend this Jose Velasquez.

As the stars aligned, in early 1981 Miranda crossed paths with Margarita Eilenberg, a twenty-three-year-old Dominican-born hostess who had recently started working at the Mutiny.

In a club full of blond European male fantasies, this mocha-skinned catalog model fit the stereotype of exotic mulatta, often appealing to white businessmen who'd otherwise never get the time of day from such a bird of paradise.

Margarita capitalized on this fantasy. She had a four-year-old daughter and an ex-husband in jail and desperately needed to send money to family back in the Dominican Republic. At the Mutiny, she'd be in front of everyone from *Playboy* scouts to Hollywood types to everyday sugar daddies.

Mutiny girl Karen Landsberger remembers training Eilenberg. "She had no interest in methods or the craft of customer service," she said. "It was all 'Who's that?' and 'Who do I need to know?'" as her eyes were constantly scanning the big tables.

Which played right into Miguel Miranda's arms. On the night of March 27, the big-tipping Mr. Keller introduced himself to Margarita as a movie and fashion-industry heavy. Mutiny girls were encouraged to chat with guests and allow them to buy them drinks. Keller seemed intent on offering more; he could break Margarita into television and film.

Margarita was no stranger to cocaine or VIP parties where lots of cash would be handed out. This one guest's party invite could be her big ticket.

She asked to take the rest of her shift off.

Margarita Eilenberg was last spotted drinking three martinis in the bar overlooking the pool, and then fumbling around with a bottle of champagne outside a hotel suite.

The following morning, her housekeeper and babysitter called the Mutiny to check in on her. The shift manager reported that Margarita hadn't yet shown up for work.

Days later, on March 30, police found her fully clothed body on the side of the road in Key Largo. Wrapped in a pink Mutiny blanket, Eilenberg had been injected at least five times with massive amounts of cocaine: twice in the jugular, twice in her arm and another shot in her leg.

The Mutiny Club remained closed as police swarmed the place to gather evidence and interview staff. Every floor and nook of the place echoed with the screams, wails and frantic *Oh my God!*s of girls who showed up for work and were blindsided by the news.

"It shook everybody," recalled Carolyn Robbins, the designer of the hotel's fantasy suites. "It was terrible. That's when I knew things were out of control."

"Fuck, but for the grace of God," said Mollie, "that could have been me."

The cops interrogated Mollie. Nicknamed "Smalley's Mollie," she had the keys to Miami Dolphins co-owner Earl Smalley's poolside suite, where it was thought that Margarita had partied with Miranda.

Authorites grilled security guy Willy Gomez and demanded an inventory of hotel linens. "The police were around for days," he recalled.

The Mutiny became an echo chamber of conspiracy theories. Was Margarita an informant who was killed while cooperating with authorities to get her husband's sentence reduced? Why had she turned up hours away in a hotel blanket?

Robbins said all of her staff were instructed not to talk to anyone about Margarita. "Fernando Puig," she said, "was hush-hush, but he for sure knew who got her out of the building."

"If I had to bet," said Chuck Volpe, "Puig moved the body."

Though Burton Goldberg was hardly ever at the Mutiny, he rarely missed the chance to dial in after big nights to grill club managers on liquor sales and big spenders.

He said he'd never heard of Margarita.

Chapter Twenty-three

MURDER CITY, USA

HOMICIDE LIEUTENANT RAUL Diaz was now completely immersed in all the unsolved "Juan Doe" murders that were clogging the county morgue. The cop's pager would go off endlessly when he was at the bar of the Mutiny. Diaz was being bombarded with interview requests from national reporters who were being sent to Miami to cover the bloodshed.

"Counting Casualties from One Miami Weekend," read one Associated Press news investigation. A highlighted crime: a Mutiny waitress, Camille, was in Mercy Hospital, just north of the hotel, with her boyfriend, Frank Marrero, a small-time cocaine dealer. He was recovering from a gunshot wound in his stomach that he'd suffered in the parking lot of his nearby condominium complex.

At twelve thirty a.m. a few days after the botched hit, a gunman snuck through the emergency room entrance and up to Marrero's fourth-floor bed. He finished off the patient with one shot to the forehead. An hour later, the assailant called the hospital to make sure Marrero was dead.

The same Associated Press article told of a husband, his pregnant wife and two small children found executed in a torched car and a deadly shoot-out between Mariel refugees who had run afoul of one another in one of Castro's prisons.

It was just barely March and Dade County had already tallied 110 homicides, compared with 580 for all of 1980.

"The police felt utterly hopeless," said Diaz. "The case backlog had never been so long. No one knew the names or identities of all the Latin guys turning up in the morgue."

The papers dwelled on official incompetence, miscommunication and blown opportunities to stop the tide of cocaine-related killings plaguing Miami.

It emerged that Miguel Miranda, Margarita's killer, was a freebasing junkie who had slipped out of various arrest warrants and brief visits to jail. He was so cocky in his ability to avoid capture that he even gave a cop his real address. "I think the names are what got everybody screwed up," confessed a police spokesman to the *Miami Herald*.

The US Marshals tasked with finding federal fugitives similarly punted on Miranda: "I don't know why we didn't go out there," said a spokesman when asked why marshals hadn't simply checked Metro-Dade's arrest sheet.

Though Miguel Miranda had been linked to the Mutiny for at least three years, no one in law enforcement bothered to leave his mug shot with security or hotel management. "Miranda killed for nothing," lamented a detective, fatalistically, after cops found Margarita's body. "It was like getting up in the morning and eating breakfast."

In April, a month after Margarita's murder, Frank White, a DEA sharpshooter and Vietnam Purple Heart, was mapping out Miranda's enormous compound. He was tipped off that the elusive doper would be at his supper club not far from the University of Miami. White showed up, parked and watched men who fit the description of Miranda and his brother in cowboy hats, getting into a tinted Cadillac.

He called in help. Several DEA trucks and at least one police car raced to the scene. When Miranda sensed he was being boxed in, he floored his Cadillac in reverse and attempted to run over an agent and smash through the cordon of vehicles. What ensued was a wild shoot-out, car chase and, finally, two bullets to the back of Miranda's head courtesy of Frank White, nicknamed "Dirty Harry" by fellow DEA agents. Miranda's brother, a Mariel refugee, emerged from the front seat yelling in Spanish, "You don't want me! It's my brother you want."

On Miranda's five-acre compound, authorities discovered an arsenal of machine guns and silencers in a room with a plaque that read: HEAVY EQUIPMENT OF THE COCAINE COWBOYS. Evidence of animal sacrifices and blood drinking abounded beneath the many fruit trees behind the tall barbed wire fence. Despite countless complaints from Miranda's freaked-out neighbors over the years, no one in Miami law enforcement ever pursued a warrant to check out the site. Miranda's victim count was in the teens.

When State Attorney Janet Reno's office rebuked White for using excessive force in the shoot-out, he was defiant: "Somebody had to do something," he said. "I have no badge of shame about what happened. How do you arrest a guy like that?"

Chapter Twenty-four

TICK-TALKS

WHILE ALL THIS went down, prosecutor Janet Reno had her hands full with a whole other operation: the wiretapping and bugging of the Table 14 gang that Ricardo "Monkey" Morales had kicked off with his sworn deposition in December.

Morales had not been to the Mutiny since his Halloween-week run-in with security man Willy Gomez, who'd come within a heartbeat of plugging him when Rafael Villaverde emerged from the elevator to talk his tablemate off the ledge.

Now Morales was returning this favor by swearing under oath that Villaverde and his two brothers were part of a dangerous and massive drug conspiracy.

Carlene Quesada's bodyguard, Bert "Super Papi" Becerra, had dropped out of the gang, warning his boss that Morales could not be trusted. Morales had shot up Super Papi's Corvette, accusing him of hitting on Mollie the Mutiny girl; Morales was livid when Quesada intervened and forced him to pay for the repairs. Said Becerra: "I told Carlene Quesada, 'Monkey is going to fuck you up. He was a snitch. I'm walking. I'm leaving you. I'm not going to do time for this prick.'"

In March of 1981, investigators noticed that Quesada and the Table 14 gang had all but stopped talking over the phone. The Miami police showed up at Quesada's home, claiming to want to talk to him about recent drug-related hits and kidnappings. A cop walked around inside the ranch house. It was devoid of furniture, presumably to prevent informants or the police from planting bugs.

Later that week, while Quesada and his men were away, officers arranged to have his house servant stopped for a bullshit traffic offense. While he was waylaid, they raced to make a copy of the servant's house key, which an electronics specialist then used to get into the house. He installed bugs in a light socket and in Quesada's mirrored wall clock.

The Miami police and state prosecutor Reno called this operation Tick-Talks. In the first month that the bug in the wall was on, cops noticed that a bad bearing in the clock's motor was obstructing the feed, which they listened to in a landscaping van parked down the block.

Cops scrambled to find the exact same clock in a Miami store. They broke in and swapped the new version in.

Fifteen days after that caper, Detective Raul Martinez could not sleep, as it suddenly occurred to him that the suspects in the house would surely find the bug when they opened up the clock to reset it for daylight saving time, which would kill the cops' now-unobstructed feed.

Police dispatched an informant back to the house. The servant recognized the man and let him in to make a phone call to his boss.

"Hey," said the guest, while making a call *to the police*, "you didn't set your clock ahead. I'll take care of it."

That maneuver bought the Miami police and Reno's team two weeks of quality bugging. The caretaker finally discovered the bug on May 14.

All told, the gang's conversations revealed they had placed a pair of three-hundred-kilo cocaine shipments valued at sixty-six million dollars wholesale, thanks to a new smuggling route involving Paraguay and Argentina.

The dopers talked about how to jury-rig a gun silencer and how to convert a legal semiautomatic into an illegal submachine gun. Raul Martinez remembers the voice of Monkey Morales throwing some braggadocio at Quesada in a drunken stupor: "You screwed me. I screw you."

The night before the Miami police handed Morales to witness protection marshals, he called to ask Martinez and D. C. Diaz to come and see him at a motel by the airport.

Morales gave Martinez his Uzi and shrugged.

Operation Tick-Talks (the bug in the ticking clock tells all—get it?) had recorded the habitués of Mutiny Table 14 dishing more than a thousand hours of criminal chatter, interspersed with the sounds of clips being loaded into guns.

Dynamite stuff
Long planes
Pregnant mares
Ponies
Rocks
Cars
Smiles

All code words, the police charged, for cocaine. "Half a smile," for example, was half a kilo.

There was banter about someone in US Customs the gang had on their payroll, raucous drinking games and fights at the Mutiny.

Frank Castro shared best practices for attaching a silencer and shooting a victim in the skull.

The gang referred to the Miami police narcotics squad eyeballing them at the Mutiny as "those four damn little Cubans."

Cops finally pounced in August. A posse of thirty officers, some in plain clothes, spread out across Miami to haul in the fifty-one suspects, including Quesada and the three Villaverde brothers.

Mollie, their Poop Deck hostess and sometime coconspirator, had luckily been tipped off by a Miami cop months earlier. She had since avoided Table 14.

The same officer was trying to prevail upon her to give up cocaine and enter the taxi business, where he had a good connection out in Miami Beach. Mollie was using heavily and mourning Margarita—thinking back to all her close calls. There was a hole in her septum, and her gums were so red and swollen that she had to get them excised. When she tried to lay off the powder, she overrelied on alcohol. Sleep was elusive.

She called her mother in Tampa, sobbing. "I can't do this anymore."

Chapter Twenty-five

THE BIG HAUL

"Time Runs Out on Suspected Coke Ring," blasted the front page of the *Miami News*. "The plot is an intricate blend of international narcotics intrigue flavored with *Mission: Impossible* daring by Miami police."

The two-page spread showed Bay of Pigs hero Rafael Villaverde, director of the esteemed Little Havana Activities Center, being perp-walked out in handcuffs in a sloppy Izod polo shirt. So, too, were his brother Jorge, Carlene Quesada and Frank Castro.

Rafael Villaverde met with four hundred weeping supporters at his Little Havana Activities Center, where he showed up to resign his executive director position. "I tell you that I am innocent," he told the defiant crowd.

As this dragnet was happening, a young law school student named John Mattes was enjoying his first night in Miami. Reading the Tick-Talks headlines at a café in the Mutiny's shadow, he took in

Coconut Grove's bohemian sights and sounds. Head shops. Hippies. The occasional feral parrot flying past a moped. Mattes was told he could well bump into David Crosby or Joni Mitchell in these parts.

He looked up from his coffee mug to see some guy in tie-dye spinning around in the middle of the street. The man was apparently so drunk that he tripped and fell on the curb.

Mattes rose to help the guy—figuring he'd prop up the poor bastard and put him in a taxi.

But as he walked up to the man, he saw blood gushing from his slit throat and cascading down onto what was actually just a white T-shirt.

John Mattes had picked quite a time to commence law school in Miami, which by his matriculation was the murder capital of America. In 1978, there were 243 murders in Dade County. In 1979, the year of the Dadeland Massacre and turnpike shoot-out, there were 320. In 1980, the number shot up to 515.

Already in the first seven months and change of 1981, Dade had seen 380 murders and was en route to reaching 621 by year's end.

Chapter Twenty-six

INVESTMENTS

WHEN CARLENE QUESADA appeared in court to face a state prosecutor, he wore a subdued blue suit and a well-knotted red tie. His mustache and hair seemed bankerlike. His shoes, however, were blue lizard skin. Quesada gave his interrogator the look of death.

"What exactly do you do for a living?" she asked him.

"I told you," he snapped. "I have investments. I sell jewelry."

"What was your income last year?"

Quesada shrugged and said he owned a stake in an electronics company. Thing is, he couldn't remember its address.

The judge was "not completely happy with the answers to the questions." Quesada, after all, had just boasted to the cops raiding his parents' house that—"So what?! Help yourself."—he had five more boxes of money. Police seized an Uzi, ten handguns and two rifles.

Quesada was asked if he had ever threatened to kill an under-cover Miami cop, as prosecutors had been briefed.

"Did you ever hear a Cuban who didn't talk shit?" he sniffed.

Carlene Quesada was taken to jail, where he traded in his Brioni suit and lizard-skin shoes for a prison jumpsuit.

Chapter Twenty-seven

SHOOTING TO KILL

LIEUTENANT RAUL DIAZ had no idea why Monkey Morales was doing this to Quesada, Villaverde & Co.—and *now*, when he most needed the informant's help finding and taking out assassins and murderers such as Miguel Miranda. This was 1981 Miami—Murder City; Morguetown, USA; Beirut, Florida: you could afford to countenance mostly nonviolent drug smuggling if doing so gave you intel on killers. "Ricardo was paranoid," said Diaz. "He was always drunk and using. I think he told me he was seeing little green men. I did not know him anymore."

Only a year had passed since Raul Diaz had accepted his transfer to homicide from narcotics. Out of the gate, he'd had big plans for Morales. In Diaz's first week on the job, two associates accosted him to ask if he could get them to his star informant; word on the street was he knew about a recent murder.

The three cops went to the Mutiny and headed upstairs past the bar. Morales was sitting by himself at Table 14, his back to the wall, nursing a Walker Black. He flashed a wan smile and the cops sat on the giant cushioned chairs.

"I'm surprised you don't have a gun here, Ricardo," said Diaz, playing dumb.

"Jenny," said Morales, summoning his waitress, a gorgeous Italian brunette. "Hey, *mi amor*, can we have some bread?" She nonchalantly brought a bread basket to the table. This was a standard scene at the Mutiny; Burton Goldberg insisted that his girls constantly toast fresh little sourdough rolls at their stations.

As Morales thanked her, he unfolded the cloth napkin to show the cops his Browning semiautomatic.

"Thank you," he said, leaving the covered bread basket at the corner of the table. Jenny took it back and left it in a shelf beneath her toaster. Morales gave the cops a "so, what next?" look.

In 1981, the ascendant Raul Diaz was lobbying the Justice Department to let him establish a Central Tactical Unit (CENTAC), an elite joint task force of federal and state homicide and narcotics officials to tackle Miami's cocaine-related murder crisis.

The status quo of official infighting and interdepartmental politics was a disaster. So many murders, so many unresolved cases that it felt "like we were pushing sand against the tide," said Diaz's deputy, Al Singleton.

Said Diaz: "Departments were shorthanded; overtime was limited, or nonexistent; officers and detectives were overworked and overburdened; there was so much frustration in the ranks—with no time to dedicate to a homicide call, even one with great leads. You'd clear one call and had ten more waiting. Morale was never worse."

Cuban refugees suspected of scamming criminals or ratting them out were showing up chopped up in cardboard boxes by the side of the road, or in trunks of cars, secreting maggots and bodily fluids that had the neighbors calling 911. "We have been invaded by aliens from outer space," lamented Miami's chief medical examiner on the evening news. "I will not apologize for feeling very deeply that [Mariel refugees and Colombian dealers] have engaged in an orgy of killing, the likes of the old roving bands of pirates and corsairs."

"They are psychologically, totally, not even human," exclaimed the coroner. "They're animals. Not even animals; that's an insult to the animal kingdom."

Raul Diaz was of the emerging school of thought that the only effective response for law enforcement was reciprocating with the same cold blood. Like what DEA sharpshooter Frank White had just done to Miguel Miranda, who had vowed never to get taken alive. "I wasn't surprised that he took out Miranda," said Diaz. "Frank was a go-getter. Proactive. I've always admired him."

As Lieutenant Diaz went headlong into his homicide assignment, Morales was increasingly using and abusing uppers and downers. He drank a ton and gained weight. At night, he'd sob for hours in the arms of Mollie, the departing Mutiny hostess, who took him in as a roommate.

A sense of learned helplessness enveloped Miami; a columnist in the *Miami Herald* urged readers to beg President Ronald Reagan—he of Morning in America fame—for some sort of lifeline.

It all came to a head the week of Thanksgiving 1981, when *Time* magazine indicted Miami on its cover as "Paradise Lost."

TROUBLE IN PARADISE
South Florida Is Hit by a Hurricane of Crime, Drugs and Refugees

Washington immediately gave Diaz's CENTAC-26 the green light.

Chapter Twenty-eight

THE CARTEL WHISPERER

IF YOU WALKED into the Mutiny and felt compelled to blow thousands of dollars on a champagne bath, or a castle of glasses cascading with the bubbly, Baruch Vega, Burton Goldberg's son-in-law, was the man to see.

Vega, then a New York–based fashion photographer, first checked in to the hotel in 1978 for a magazine shoot. Since coming to the US from Colombia in 1972, he had photographed everyone from Cheryl Tiegs to Lauren Hutton to up-and-coming blonde Christie Brinkley—and had romanced countless models.

But Vega said he'd never been as turned on as when he first walked into the Mutiny, this boutique hotel in Miami that couture pals in Saint Barts, New York and Paris would not shut up about. Touring the halls with his models in tow—all of them sipping Dom as they walked in and out of the nooks and suites—Vega succumbed to the property's seductive charm.

One of his models jumped onto a bed and declared she never

wanted to leave. Vega changed his flight plans, and they stayed at the Mutiny for a week of fine food, dancing, entertainment and passionate lovemaking.

Vega took a shine to Burton Goldberg's daughter. Channeling a bit of Pepé Le Pew, he managed to convince her to pose for a poolside photo shoot. They fell in love and got married at the turn of the decade. Baruch Vega was now living in Miami and enjoying the insider high life at the Mutiny.

His life of hedonism was a long shot. One of eleven children born to a poor trumpet player in Bogotá, Colombia, he grew up in Bucaramanga, where at the age of fifteen he won a twenty-thousand-dollar amateur photography contest sponsored by Kodak.

He became known as a local playboy—the charmer who seduced women into gorgeous photo shoots and hopefully more. At Bucaramanga University, Vega also made a name for himself as an antileftist. The Cold War was raging, and Fidel Castro had Cuba and every other country in Latin America convulsing ideologically.

"As a student leader," he recalled, "immediately you become the target of revolutionary groups and bad cops. We were extremely nationalistic. We did not want to import foreign ideologies. Communism was the worst thing that anyone could be part of."

One morning in 1969, the undergraduate was snatched by the local police and thrown into an unmarked car. Instead of taking him to the police station, however, his captors took him to a secluded farm. The men marched Vega into an abandoned barn, where they pummeled him and commenced an interrogation. "I thought I was being roughed up for messing with some cop's wife," he said.

What did he know? they asked.

Who was he working for?

Who was he reporting to?

Vega had no idea what the men were talking about. This was not about a woman. From the questions, he deduced that these police were in the employ of leftist guerrillas and had fingered Vega, the student nationalist, as a government snitch.

The beating and torture went on for hours, and Vega lost consciousness, believing he was about to be killed. The men roused him to continue their regimen. "It went on for many, many days," he said.

Vega begged them to just kill him. They again bludgeoned him. This time, however, he awoke late one night to the sound of gunshots.

Vega summoned all of his energy to yell for help. What next woke him up was an elderly woman peering into the barn with a lantern. Vega rose to his knees to beg her to help him. His hands and feet were bound and he had wet and soiled his pants.

As a thunderstorm raged, the woman returned with a small boy who untied Vega. As they walked him out, Vega stuck out his tongue and took ravenous slurps of the rainfall. The woman and boy pointed him to a road. Vega walked for as long as he could, his clothes soaked and skin chafed, until he came to a pond. He collapsed at its bank.

When Vega woke up at dawn, he took off his bloody and soiled clothes and went for a swim. He then limped down the road until he saw a farm. He walked toward the main house. Two barking dogs were about to jump him until their owner called them off. At the farm, Vega finally made it to a phone, where he dialed an American official whose number had been given to him by his roommate—to call in case of emergency.

The next thing he recalled was being spirited across the border to Venezuela by American agents. That was when it dawned on Vega that his roommate was a spotter for US intelligence. These people who had just rescued him would want to recruit him to their side in the Cold War, in which Latin America was a critical battleground.

Grateful to have his life saved, Vega agreed to go to Chile to help the CIA destabilize leftist ruler Salvador Allende, who in 1970 was the first Marxist to be elected president in an open Latin American election. Allende lasted until a 1973 military coup.

The agency transitioned the educated Vega into one of its multinational front companies—a halfway house, of sorts, to full civilian life. By 1976, having completed his CIA tour, Vega was formally employed as a structural engineer in Manhattan. On the side, he started a modeling agency and took law school classes.

Around this time, one of his models came sobbing to him about her husband's arrest for dealing drugs. He needed a good attorney. What could Baruch Vega, the part-time law student, suggest? Vega called an old CIA friend at the FBI and asked if he could check on the impending charges against the husband, a Colombian national. The agent told him the government had no case.

"I had great news to present to his wife," said Vega. "He would be released shortly." Before returning to Colombia, the man came to Vega's studio to personally thank him for his "intervention."

Turns out that he was a member of one of Colombia's biggest cocaine families.

"That," said Vega, "was the beginning of something that was huge." The Bogotá cocaine cartel flew Vega down and thanked him for getting their guy released. "They offered me an incredible amount of money as a reward."

Vega took the money and a list of names of other people the drug lords thought he might be able to help. Soon, he was being flown in, wined, dined and hosted in the homes of some of the most infamous Colombian kingpins in Medellín.

By 1978, Baruch Vega was a full-time fashion photographer who was moonlighting as a fixer for the wealthiest cocaine families of South America. The CIA, he figured, was indifferent to his free-lancing.

At the Mutiny, Vega, Burton Goldberg's new son-in-law, be-came famous for setting up cascading champagne glasses for big hitters who wanted to impress women. Cabeza Linero's pal "Mono" Abello, the number four guy in the Medellín cocaine cartel, liked to party at the hotel with Vega. "Everyone who had major amounts of money had to go here," said Vega. "The highest levels of every group would be at the Mutiny."

Sometime in 1979, a friend of Vega's was partying at the club after closing a forty-million-dollar oil deal with Arab investors. He giddily asked Vega to come up with the most extravagant stunt he could pull off at the hotel, which was swarming with celebs and party girls.

Vega improvised. "By any chance," he asked, "have you ever bathed in champagne?"

"I just made it up," Vega admitted later. "I didn't know." The guest snapped his fingers and summoned room service to fill up his tub with Dom—bottles and bottles. And when that wasn't enough, whole cases. "The bathtub was just a quarter filled," said Vega. "We needed more."

"I was the first sucker to jump in and burn my ass off," he said.

After about four hundred bottles, he says, everyone in the guy's suite stripped down and jumped in. So began the Mutiny's famous champagne bath, the most ostentatious way to pour thousands of dollars down the drain—stinging private parts be damned.

In Miami, Vega bought a two-acre, twelve-bedroom estate once owned by gangster Al Capone and the Busch brewing family. He was making upward of fifty thousand dollars per photo shoot and consorting with the likes of Miss Universe and multibillionaire Saudi arms dealer Adnan Khashoggi.

This was all barely a decade after Vega was left for dead in that barn in Colombia.

"I don't believe I was ever happier," he said. "I was so in love that I didn't want to see other women, not even to shoot photos." His new wife, Burton Goldberg's daughter, wanted him to leave photography altogether to concentrate on international deal making and business development at the Mutiny, which was raking it in.

Indeed, some of Latin America's biggest developers and industrial scions were approaching Vega to expand the Mutiny concept to places like Panama and Cartagena, where its famous gold license plate adorned armor-plated sedans.

One day after lunch, Vega was accosted by a burly gringo at the club's entrance. "Don't you remember me?" the man asked, furrowing his brow. Vega was suddenly overwhelmed with a mix of guilt and paranoia: "It was a thunderous shock," he said.

The guest was Agent "Ben Hur," a CIA asset who had worked alongside Vega in Chile. "I hadn't seen him in years," Vega said. "He was smiling and had put on thirty pounds and a beard."

Ben Hur flashed a grin and they exchanged small talk about Vega's travels and how beautiful the Mutiny was. He then asked that Vega please join him and his colleagues at their table upstairs. Were they coming after the Colombian for something? he wanted to know. Vega had been off the grid for years and hadn't broken any law.

Ben Hur introduced the startled Vega to his tablemates. He explained that he and his old CIA crew had since taken their talents to the Drug Enforcement Agency. The men confessed to having tailed Baruch Vega in Miami. Not to worry, however; he was clean, as far as they were concerned.

But they now needed him: Could he help them set up a major surveillance operation at the Mutiny?

Vega felt utterly blindsided. He knew the Feds (the "*tres letras*" or the cheaply dressed "JC Penneys") were notoriously half-assed in their Mutiny operations. After all, these were the guys who managed to nab a Mutiny girl with a kilo in the hairstyling salon while Carlene Quesada and Rudy Redbeard moved one hundred times as much in a week. And they were anything but discreet. "The girls could tell you who the cops were by their bad tips," Vega said. "Plus, cocaine dealers never asked for a receipt."

Vega knew he had a ton to lose by helping the DEA. His life, for one thing. He had the confidence of the very biggest cartel families in Colombia, who plied him with money and luxuries whenever he was back in the homeland. His wife was pregnant.

But he also thought about Margarita, the slain model and Mutiny girl he used to photograph for the Burdines catalog. "My God, was she beautiful," he said. "Her hair and skin. And she was kind and loving. She only wanted to help her mother and daughter."

Now Vega had a baby girl on the way while Margarita's four-year-old daughter was orphaned by a cocaine psychopath. He knew he'd had intel that could have helped the bumbling authorities nab Miranda before he murdered so many.

So he agreed to help the Feds.

And immediately came to regret it.

The DEA asked Vega to start by doing "gram deals" for cocaine at the Mutiny. "This was an insult to me," he said. "To my education. I didn't even do drugs."

Agents asked him to sign documents vowing to testify against major traffickers. "Are you kidding?" he shot back.

"I worked with the CIA," said Vega, "where everything was meticulously and carefully planned. There was staging, budget and discretion; there was a tradecraft. I was a PhD and engineer. But these agents, they did not have a clue. They were the cheapest at the Mutiny. I told them, 'Really, you're not fooling anyone. You fit the perfect profile for heat.'"

Vega was prepared to cut the cord completely until he was summoned downtown by homicide detective June Hawkins, who was now working with Lieutenant Raul Diaz in CENTAC-26. "I liked Raul," Vega said. "He was a familiar face from the club."

Hawkins and Diaz could sometimes be seen at the Mutiny, having drinks and agonizing over scribbles on cocktail napkins. They were trying to crack the coded phone numbers they were finding in the address books and wallets of Latin homicide victims. "All the movers and shakers of the underworld were at the Mutiny," recalled Hawkins. "It was just their hangout. Maybe like the mob's favorite restaurant in New York, that's what the Mutiny was to Miami. That aura and undertone—that undercurrent of criminality. It was understood. I'm sure they knew who we were. But it was neutral territory, like 'We all know what we're doing here, but we're not going to attack one another, OK?' It was an unwritten code."

Speaking of code . . .

"We were sitting up at the Mutiny and playing all these different combinations," she said. The encrypted phone numbers they were finding would have an area code—say, 305, for Miami—followed by letters in a pattern that never repeated.

One night over drinks, Hawkins and Diaz had a breakthrough. "Son of a bitch!" she yelled. They had finally deciphered three code words: *WaltDisney, Murciélago* (Spanish for "Bat") and *HijoDePuta* ("Son of a Bitch"). Each letter corresponded to a number from zero to nine.

So, if:

W-A-L-T-D-I -S-N-E-Y = 0-1-2-3-4-5-6-7-8-9, then 305YWESNTA meant phone number (305) 908-6731.

Diaz and Hawkins referred to this legend when they found code scribbled on a valet ticket near the body of a man killed not far from the Mutiny. It was Baruch Vega's phone number. They called Vega in to police headquarters and proceeded to show him the photos of several victims and suspects. He identified a majority.

"Have you heard of this Rafael? *El Loco?*" asked Detective Hawkins.

"You mean, of course, *Amilcar*," he responded.

The room went silent.

"Yes," Vega continued into the dead air, "I do. I know him very well. He is close to me."

Vega explained his unusual connection to the Venezuelan. In the mid-1970s, Amilcar was introduced to Vega in New York as a millionaire developer who wanted to invest in his modeling agency. As they became friends, Amilcar confessed to being a cocaine trafficker who was in love with one of Vega's models. "If one day something were to happen to me," he said to the photographer, solemnly, "just help my family."

Shortly after, Vega was tipped off to Amilcar getting machine-gunned at a disco. Goons were about to dump the Venezuelan into the East River before Vega arrived to intercept the body, which was wrapped in a Persian rug.

He felt Amilcar's bloodied neck and wrist. There was a pulse.

Vega called a doctor friend and carried the bleeding Amilcar up from the service entrance of his building. In Vega's studio, the doctor and Vega sliced down Amilcar's back and removed several bullets. They sutured him up and pumped his veins with morphine. Amilcar stayed at Vega's place for two weeks.

He lived. And was now doubly grateful to the fashion photographer.

Naturally, at the turn of the decade, cocaine took Amilcar to Miami, where he bumped into his old friend at the Mutiny. The drug lord, now addicted to crack cocaine, was in the middle of a major war with other drug lords. He carried a nickel-plated .357 Magnum.

Amilcar was killing anyone who owed him money—and even subcontractors whom he owed. And totally innocent associates and family members of anyone on his shit list. He had the son, daughter and babysitter of a couple who had crossed him raped, sodomized and left to freeze to death in the basement of an old post office.

Still, perhaps not realizing the full extent of Amilcar's bloodthirst, Baruch Vega held out hope that he could prevail upon the father to put down his guns and go to jail. His family would be relocated and prison would protect him from all the people who wanted money from him or wanted him dead. "I tried to ask him to surrender to authorities," says Vega, "hopefully to serve a long-term sentence and escape his debts."

Amilcar's habit was to call Vega at home from an unidentified pay phone and ask him to meet him at his "office" at a certain time. The office was a pay phone by Vega's house. It was in that conversation that the men would agree on a meeting place.

Amilcar would come to the Mutiny through the back of the hotel. Vega would send the number of the room he had reserved to his pager and Amilcar would head straight up and knock.

"The whole story was just incredible," said June Hawkins. "It was the kind of stuff you read in spy movies. Miami was such a Casablanca and we were in it. I just tried to soak it up."

This Amilcar, they learned, was very unusual for a murderous Latino. "He was not your run-of-the-mill Miami thug," said Hawkins. "He was rather well educated and soft-spoken. He was, like most sociopaths, charming. But he never wanted to tangle with the cops. He didn't want to kill cops."

And so there was more than a small chance they could utilize Vega to go good-cop on the murderer before CENTAC-26 had to draw its guns.

"He was seriously considering 'cooperating,'" said Vega, "but would always say, 'I'm in the middle of something. Let me sleep on it.'"

Not that any of his many enemies were going to give him the luxury of easy sleep.

The killings would not stop. A hit man named Winston whom Amilcar had recently ripped off had him machine-gunned while he was in a swimming pool. This time, Amilcar recuperated in an area hospital—not Baruch Vega's studio—and was back on the street, smoking more crack and raring to kill in less than a week.

Paranoid, armed, coked, delusional, vengeful. The most dangerous breed of cocaine cowboy. He was a textbook first trophy for Raul Diaz's CENTAC-26.

Chapter Twenty-nine

HUNTING "EL LOCO"

WINSTON, THE GUY who tried to kill Amilcar in his pool, was now frequenting the Hotel Mutiny's pool. He wore a thick beard to disguise an ominous scar across his cheek—legend had it he was slashed as he was offing a victim—and had his neck weighed down by pounds of jewelry, including crucifixes, pendants of the Virgin Mary and interlocking chains.

Winston exchanged menacing glances with Baruch Vega, who he knew was close to his rival. He got word to him that he would give him at least 500 thousand dollars in cash for any tip that led him to the little Venezuelan.

Indeed, Vega was also getting offers from Colombia. A handful of friends flew in and paid for a quiet corner table at the Mutiny. They explained that Medellín had issued another half-million-dollar bounty on Amilcar's head.

Vega knew that the crack-addled Amilcar had torched so many bridges that he had lately resorted to hiring Mutiny Marielitos.

ABOVE: Burton Goldberg, founder and owner of the Mutiny until he sold it in 1984.

Courtesy of Burton Goldberg

LEFT: Member and cocaine kingpin Mario Tabraue, owner of Caesar the chimp and a reputed inspiration for Tony Montana.

Courtesy of Mario Tabraue

Summer 1976: the Mutiny girls.

Courtesy of Burton Goldberg

Rudy Redbeard, photographed by his limo, which was built for the king of Spain.

The famous gold-plated matchboxes and key chain.

Miami cops posing with their haul from the 1978 bust of Rudy Redbeard and Carlene Quesada.

Courtesy of Raul Diaz

ABOVE: The Fourth Dimension and Nautical suites at the Hotel Mutiny.   © *Dan Forer*

LEFT: Mutiny girls Pammy and Mollie, circa 1979.

Courtesy of Mollie Hampton

RIGHT: Owen Band's party invitation. *Courtesy of Owen Band*

BELOW: Mutiny girl Cindy Proietti. *Courtesy of Cindy Proietti*

Sal Magluta. *Courtesy of T. Rafael Cimino*

Willie Falcon. *Courtesy of T. Rafael Cimino*

Luis "Weetchie" Escobedo, cooperating codefendant shot dead by a Colombian hit squad.

The smuggler known as Nancy the "Big Blonde" or "La Rubia."

Courtesy of Nancy Meneses

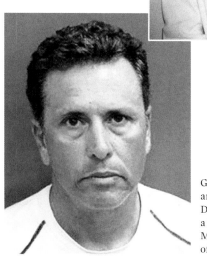

Gustavo "Taby" Falcon, arrested in April 2017 near Disney World after being a fugitive since 1991. US Marshals called him "the last of the Cocaine Cowboys."

Aguilar's gold membership card.
Courtesy of Nelson Aguilar

Kingpin Nelson Aguilar with Rick James, 1983.
Courtesy of Nelson Aguilar

ABOVE: Amilcar "El Loco" Leon, assassin and CENTAC target.
Courtesy of the Lynn and Louis Wolfson II Moving Image Archives

LEFT: Mutiny "freebase jumpers."
Courtesy of Tim Chapman/ HistoryMiami Museum

TOP LEFT: Mutiny girl Margarita at a staff softball game.   *Courtesy of Anonymous*

TOP RIGHT: Margarita's murderer, Miguel Miranda.   *Courtesy of HistoryMiami Museum*

BOTTOM LEFT: Baruch Vega in 1980.   *Courtesy of Baruch Vega*

BOTTOM RIGHT: Carlene Quesada in court for his Tick-Talks arraignment.
Courtesy of Miami News

Recotado Barroso in 2015. (Note his scar—he was machine-gunned in a 1992 witness shooting.) *Courtesy of Roben Farzad*

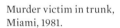

Murder victim in trunk, Miami, 1981.

Courtesy of Tim Chapman/ HistoryMiami Museum

Ricardo "Monkey" Morales makes the cover of *Newsday* magazine, June 1982.

Courtesy of Newsday LLC

Though he didn't necessarily trust these new Cubans, they were eager for dope and enforcement work and could presumably be disposed of with less grief, heat and risk of retribution. "We called them Dixie cups," said Detective Hawkins. "They'd get paid three hundred dollars or four hundred dollars to do a hit, not even knowing or caring for who. 'Put me in prison—go ahead,' they told us. 'I'll be with my buddies.' It was like they were disposable. We had no leverage."

"There were rumors everywhere," said Vega. "In Miami, in South America, in New York—that 'El Loco' Amilcar was on a killing rampage to retire his cocaine debts. He was practically bankrupt. What was his way out?"

"Amilcar had the instincts of a snake," said Lieutenant Raul Diaz. "And if you looked into his eyes in his mug shot, you saw the gaze of a reptile."

Vega said the final straw for him was when a friend's pregnant wife came knocking at his door, hysterical that her husband hadn't called for two days. The police found the man's car across the street from the Mutiny.

She explained her husband merely wanted to collect money Amilcar owed him from two years earlier, to tidy up affairs before becoming a father. He was now working for a medical supplies company, having rediscovered Christ and repenting two years after flying a cocaine load for Amilcar.

Amilcar never paid the man for piloting that load, which he managed to deliver in full even after his plane ran out of fuel and crashed.

Vega agonized. He was loving life as a married man and father-to-be. He was about to sell his modeling business to a major agency. He had a mansion on an exclusive gated island in Miami

Beach, where he docked his seventy-eight-foot yacht, *Abbey Sue*. He lived large at the Mutiny.

All of which would fade to black if Amilcar "El Loco" Rodriguez just decided to off him right then and there. Said Vega: "I thought I was going to be next."

What cemented the decision for Vega was Amilcar sending a hit-man bodyguard to escort Vega to a supposed meeting with the kingpin. The guy had a bloodied hand and bragged that he and his boss had just dumped a body out at sea. Vega said he intuited that the victim was his friend, the former pilot.

"I felt sick," said Vega. "They just killed, like that, a friend who had made one mistake. He was a noble person. He wasn't a criminal. He never stole. He did the opposite. No way did he deserve that."

Vega frantically begged out of the meeting, claiming that his wife was about to give birth. The thug reluctantly left. Amilcar then phoned Vega, saying that he had spied the *tres letras* in and around the Mutiny. "I believe those were your friends, the ugly Feds," he said. "I am going to send a friend to give you a message in person."

That threat sealed Amilcar's fate. On Monday, December 14, Baruch Vega called Raul Diaz to inform him that CENTAC's number one target was at the Mutiny.

Diaz immediately ordered 360-degree surveillance of the Mutiny and personally monitored the hotel's notorious rear entrance with binoculars.

"We had a fucking airplane and ten units on him," said Diaz. "This guy was an incredible speedster. Was it the crack? I don't know. But I do know he was above all a survivor. Adaptable."

Amilcar and his bodyguard emerged from the Mutiny. They hopped into a sports car and into the bedlam of US-1, where they then veered into one of the busiest intersections in Miami.

Diaz trailed him west. He saw Amilcar and his guard walk across Miracle Mile, a pedestrian-heavy row of shops and restaurants; the men had parked their car and mixed into the crowd. "These guys fucking stopped for a soup? Or coffee?" Diaz swears he saw Amilcar wink at him. "He was that crazy," he said. Diaz called in for support.

Amilcar and his driver got back in their getaway car. Diaz and his support circled back to encounter them at a busy intersection. The ensuing shoot-out, he said, "was like nothing any of us had been trained to expect." Blocked at a stoplight in front of a Burger King, Amilcar and his driver shot at two of Diaz's officers from inside their tinted car. The bullets exited their rear window and shattered the cops' windshield. They rolled out and took cover.

Amilcar's driver then bolted on foot, holding his gun, before getting hit by another cop car. He lived. Amilcar, meanwhile, ran to an opposite corner, stopped a vehicle, pushed the driver into the passenger seat and floored the gas pedal.

He later dropped the man off in North Miami and handed him his Rolex, "for his troubles." Amilcar dumped the car nearby.

Two days later, Amilcar was cornered behind the washers and dryers of a residential laundry room. Courtesy of CENTAC-26's extraordinary powers, Diaz and his partners were packing steel-tipped bullets that could easily pierce through the machines and make a fricassee of the Venezuelan.

When he heard the cops talking about these bullets on their walkie-talkies—and Diaz instructing them to shoot to kill—Amilcar promptly surrendered. "You caught me," he shouted, emerging with his hands up. "Your job was to catch me," he told the cops as they cuffed him. "My job was to get away."

As Raul Diaz sped to the scene, he imagined what Amilcar's

lifeless sociopathic gaze would look like in person (he had only seen photos). "There was no soul in those eyes," he said.

But when the lieutenant arrived, his target, a man who had murdered at least a dozen people—including three mutilated children—poured on the charm, smiling graciously and congratulating his pursuer on a job well-done.

Chapter Thirty

YOU FIND YOURSELF IN 'EIGHTY-TWO

FOR MIAMI, WHICH in its ninth decade of existence had managed to become the hemisphere's murder capital, 1981's chaos drew in everyone from the National Guard to Ronald Reagan's cabinet. And unwanted attention from just about every publication on the planet.

The cover of January 1982's issue of *Harper's*, the venerable national magazine, read:

MIAMI DOES BUSINESS

Drugs and Terrorism in America's Casablanca

Turn to the article "The Informant," and its subtitle teased, "Meet the Biggest Dealer in Miami's Biggest Industry." The subject of this feature was none other than Ricardo "Monkey" Morales. Mocked up on the cover in a tropical shirt and Cuban hat and speaking into a telephone, he was by date of publication well into the process of taking down dozens of cocaine dealers, including his mates at Mutiny Table 14, in Operation Tick-Talks (it involved a bugged wall clock, *Harper's* said). The issue hit the stands just as the Zelig-like Cuban exile was about to take the stand as the make-or-break witness in Miami's most publicized drug bust.

John Rothchild, the author, wrote:

> *The Mutiny is to the après-deal what Sardi's is to the après-theater, and Quesada was a familiar patron with a big bankroll and lizard-skin shoes. The tables are surrounded by wide-leaved plants and venal waitresses in leotards. There are phone jacks at the tables so people can do business in these junglelike surroundings. . . . One can imagine that Morales felt right at home . . .*

One can also imagine that Morales reveled in this kind of coverage, which drew the ardor of big literary and Hollywood agents who had never even been to Little Havana. He toggled in and out of witness protection (offered to him by the US Marshals for informing on other dealers), and also cooperated for a splashy cover article in New York's *Newsday* magazine.

It was the beginning of the end for the first kings of the Mutiny, a vacuum that would be filled by the next generation of dopers.

By now, homicide cop Raul Diaz, Morales's main handler in law enforcement, had no idea what his star informant was trying to do. Diaz had his hands full with a whole other operation, CENTAC-26, where he was putting in grueling hours finding and flipping killers to deliver a big follow-up catch to Amilcar, who was in jail and law-yering up. Rumor was CENTAC was close to nabbing the gunmen who shot up Dadeland Mall. "At that point in my life," he said,

"Tick-Talks was inconsequential; I had bigger problems and bigger fishes. I mean, I assisted Tick-Talks when and if I could, but it wasn't often."

The stakes were especially high for Diaz. President Reagan deputized George Bush, his vice president, to run the South Florida Drug Task Force, the administration's big response to Miami's narco-murder emergency. What could look more badass than a Hispanic shoot-to-kill sheriff type like Raul Diaz running the FBI? Or becoming mayor of Miami or governor of Florida? Hollywood, after all, had created Ronald Reagan. His less alpha-seeming right-hand man, Bush, could do lots worse than a photo op with a triumphant Lieutenant Diaz, who resembled "Ponch" Poncherello on *CHiPs*.

The fact that Bush was America's top guy in the new War on Drugs struck Mutiny playboy and photographer Baruch Vega as a bit weird. When he was CIA director in the mid-1970s, Bush had visited and praised Manuel Noriega in Panama. He was one of the strongman's biggest champions.

By 1982, after the mysterious death of Panamanian dictator Omar Torrijos, Noriega started consolidating control of the levers of power. The CIA hiked Noriega's monthly retainer, demonstrating his value to the Reagan administration, as a foil to both Castro's Cuba and the leftist regime in nearby Nicaragua. Plus, that canal.

Who could possibly have been a more geostrategically vital ally in the War on Drugs than our man in Panama?

None of which squared with what Vega was hearing on the ground with respect to the cocaine trade. He said this epiphany came to him during a business meeting at the Mutiny. The sons of Panama's new nominal ruler, General Rubén Darío Paredes, flew up to Miami to ask Vega about opening a Mutiny in the isthmus.

Reciprocity with the club was already a perk enjoyed by rich Colombians and Venezuelans—the product of Vega's father-in-law Burton Goldberg's aggressive promotion of the Mutiny brand in Bogotá and Caracas. So why not offer the continent's "Fat Cows" a place to wine, dine, fuck and waste obscene amounts of money at the gateway between the Pacific and the Atlantic? Panama City could conceivably become as corrupt and debauched as prerevolutionary Havana. Imagine the profits.

Vega, intrigued, brought up the subject of Manuel Noriega. The brothers responded that the general would have nothing to do with this hotel venture—"unless," one of them asked, "are you looking to move product?"

They then matter-of-factly explained what they said was by now common knowledge across Latin America: Noriega was almost openly accepting payoffs to allow tons of cocaine from points south—Colombia, Peru, Bolivia—to be flown and shipped through Panama.

Vega, still skeptical, wanted to see for himself. After tipping off one of the Colombian families he consulted for, he arranged to personally deliver 500 thousand dollars in cash to Noriega as a down payment for clearance to run kilos through neighboring Panama. When the general accepted the tribute, Vega assumed that the CIA had to be authorizing these transactions (or at least looking the other way), ostensibly in some sort of swap with Noriega to fund or enable some operation vital to Washington. Salutary neglect, they called it in intelligence circles. "As far as I was always told," he said, "Noriega was the head of the CIA in Latin America."

This all reverbed back to the main intrigue at the Mutiny: the fate of Table 14, which, thanks to Monkey Morales, was now snagged in Operation Tick-Talks. If the CIA was willing to countenance Manuel Noriega's wholesale cocaine racket, how in the world was it going to let a state drug rap fell Rafael Villaverde, one of its top exile assets from the Bay of Pigs? Washington, after all, paid Fidel Castro to free this guy (among other star captive Brigadesmen) from prison and fly him to Miami after the botched operation.

In April, just as the marathon Tick-Talks depositions were set to begin, Villaverde skipped on the terms of his bail to go on a deep-sea fishing trip with three codefendants, including fellow Bay of Pigs fighter Frank Castro. Though the four pals had logged countless hours at sea—the CIA trained Villaverde and Castro to invade Cuba, and marine raids continued into the mid-1960s—three of them returned to shore claiming that they were fishing off a cay in the Bahamas when their craft caught fire and sank along with Villaverde. They said he was the only one not to get rescued. "When I say, 'apparently he has drowned,'" said the judge overseeing Tick-Talks, "there is absolutely no proof of that."

Was it an elaborate April Fools' Day prank? An arranged disappearance? Conspiracy theories wafted across Dade County. Word in Little Havana was, Villaverde, the CIA-trained exile fighter and community leader, had been reabsorbed by the agency into Central or South America. There were whispers at the Mutiny that the freedom fighter from Table 14 had been spirited to Cuba—that his whole Miami anti-Castro persona was just a front for drug running that he accomplished with the *help* of Havana.

The surreal developments compounded. Behind the scenes, star witness Monkey Morales was calling as many journalists as he could—not to underscore his testimony, but to dump on his own credibility. What was the logic in doing that? Everyone in Miami had a theory. Perhaps he wanted to flex his clout to fellow exiles—i.e., "Hey, look what I single-handedly orchestrated and took down.

I own this town. I run the courts." Maybe he just wanted a book deal.

It is also very possible that years of cocaine, downers, drink and PTSD from his tour in the Belgian Congo rendered him outright delusional. "His state of mind was not stable," says Jerry Sanford, the ex–federal prosecutor who worked with Morales to nail Rudy Redbeard. "I'm convinced he did Tick-Talks purposely, and with a plan. I'm certain he knew and planned that the case would fail."

Three days after major codefendant Villaverde supposedly died at sea, the Tick-Talks depositions finally got started. At long last, Monkey Morales got to be *the* star witness of a high-profile case steeped in international intrigue, and all of Miami (and even erudite readers of *Harper's* across the land) took in the spectacle.

Tick-Talks boiled down to Morales's word against that of more than four dozen defendants. If the defense, composed of Miami's highest-paid lawyers, could make Morales look unreliable, the judge could well throw out the one thousand hours of clock recordings that underpinned the state's cocaine sweep.

Out of the gate there were three weeks of nonstop grilling—chiefly by defense attorney Douglas Williams—in a ninth-floor office of the Metro Justice Building. Morales let it all hang out. Under oath and granted immunity by the state prosecutor, he calmly admitted to various bombings, shootings and dope deals here and abroad, on top of a 1973 murder of a Miami exile that Williams himself had unsuccessfully tried when he was a state prosecutor.

Three weeks into the depositions, on April 29, newswires flickered with the Associated Press headline "Informant Admits Jet Blast Role." The papers were abuzz when Morales admitted he had helped detonate a Cuban jetliner with seventy-three passengers in 1976, when he was working for Venezuela's spy agency. "The historic responsibility," he declared (malapropism mixed with an attempt at hyperbole), "was on my shoulders."

"Informer Spins Web of Murder, Terror," blasted the front page of the *Miami Herald*, to which Morales granted a wide-ranging, ask-me-anything interview. The story read:

> *He regrets nothing, he told the* Herald. *Morales said he would gladly bomb the Cubana Airlines DC-8 again if he thought it was necessary. "I don't repent doing it, despite the 73 that died. Just as if there had been 273 . . . if I had to, I would do it over again."*

Translation: the Machiavellian end of finishing suspected Castro agents justified the gruesome means of killing civilians. That might well have endeared him to Miami's most hardened anticommunists. But why would anyone confess to an act of international terrorism right as he was taking the stand as the star witness in Miami's biggest drug trial (especially if there wasn't even solid evidence that placed him as the bomber)?

At this point, it was not so much the Table 14 cocaine conspiracy on trial as it was the credibility of Monkey Morales and his backers in law enforcement. And the star witness only egged on his own reputational demise. In the evenings, he dialed reporters, including John Rothchild, his *Harper's* profiler, to boast about his many crimes, from bombings to hits to wholesale drug dealing. The joke in Little Havana was that Monkey must have shot J.R., too.

Rothchild said he struggled to interpret the informant's real motivations. Raul Diaz said Morales told him he was increasingly seeing little green men—that he was drunk and coked out beyond rationality.

Building a case this big around someone as unpredictable as

Morales became a nightmare for prosecutors. "For several days," Rothchild wrote, "the state of Florida struggled to defend Morales against his own evidence, planted in the morning editions. What absurd theater it was. To support Morales and save the wiretaps, a Miami policeman testified under oath that blowing up a Cuban airliner was not such a bad thing to do."

In late June, as eight weeks of testimony and legal positioning drew to a close, lead defense attorney Douglas Williams declared before the judge: "One feels like a great white shark running into a batch of seals. Everything looks so fleshy, I don't know which one to go after."

That same month, Monkey Morales made the cover of *Newsday* magazine:

MORALES THE INFORMER
A License to Kill

The feature sported a vivid illustration of Morales whispering in Uncle Sam's ear. The reflection on his sunglasses showed Uncle Sam reassuring Morales, who held a machine gun and wore belts of bullets around his neck. Sartorially, the Monkey looked like a cross between Sylvester Stallone's Rambo and Vegas-era Elvis.

Like the *Harper's* cover story that ran in January, this story delved into how Morales, a man who had confessed to murders, bombings and even the blowing up of a Cuban jetliner over Barbados in 1976, essentially held office hours at this otherworldy joint called the Mutiny.

The author expounded upon Morales's spat with Villaverde at the club—he chucked pats of butter at the Bay of Pigs hero—and wondered whether Villaverde was now up to something covert in Nicaragua or even Cuba after his supposed drowning in the spring.

Going by the headlines, Operation Tick-Talks was now officially a farce. Monkey Morales was working all hours to sully his credibility in the court of public opinion, flaunting the blanket immunity the state had granted him for his many killings and bombings in the twenty years since he arrived in Miami.

"The police must have been beguiled by Monkey Morales," argued Douglas Williams to the judge. "He's capable of being cordial, affable, charming, persuasive—all of those things. He's also capable of blowing people out of the sky at thirty thousand feet. He's capable of doing anything and everything else to create murder, mayhem and destruction."

"Douglas and Ricardo, their two egos were so huge that you couldn't walk into that courtroom," recalled Raul Diaz. "It was a Mensa war: Ricardo was completely fucking with Douglas's mind and Douglas got into a mind war with Ricardo."

On the stand, Morales took no pains to conceal the fact that his brain was marinating in cocaine. "I had a normal childhood," he insisted. "I believe in Santa Claus."

As Williams relentlessly questioned him, a typical exchange went like this:

Q: All you wanted is to go out and bomb someplace, and here somebody had to come down behind you and mess up the whole place? They have no respect.

A: No respect at all for the professionals.

Q: You told me that you bombed Mr. Calloway's house for free?

A: Yes, that was a free ride.

Q: Were there any other episodes that followed in which you reverted to your more familiar role of the perpetrator—bombings, explosions, that sort?

A: You know, *perpetrator*, I will take it as a derogatory remark about my person. . . . To me, it matters. I've got my values, you know.

Chapter Thirty-one

A FAREWELL SALUTE

RAUL DIAZ WAS not in much of a position to enjoy the Morales-Williams show. His wife was filing for a divorce and a federal parole officer had reported Diaz for overstepping the law in his use of two key CENTAC informants. The FBI, he heard, was about to look into the affair. Speaking of affairs, Diaz had been hooking up with Nancy Cid, ex-wife of Juan Cid, the prolific pot dealer. Juan Cid's attorney was none other than Douglas Williams. Douglas Williams was also representing the bodyguard of Amilcar, Raul Diaz's prize catch, when he wasn't busy grilling Ricardo Morales, Raul Diaz's star asset. (No use drawing a Venn diagram.)

Throw in seventy-two-hour work benders, and Diaz was drinking and chain-smoking like never before. In mid-1982, as Morales dished sensational testimony in Tick-Talks, Diaz went to his doctor complaining of debilitating pain in his insides: he had an ulcer running down the length of his digestive tract, all the way down to the bleeding exit. Depressed, paranoid and full of whiskey, he kept dialing Internal Affairs and the FBI to see what, if anything, they had in store for him. At best, the Feds might curtail CENTAC's extraordinary powers. In a worst-case scenario: Raul Diaz's fifteen-year career as a cop would end—just as it was about to catapult him to great heights.

Operation Tick-Talks arrived at its hyperabsurd climax when Morales finally appeared to face his old pals from Mutiny Table 14. Under heavy security, in a courtroom filled with airport-grade metal detectors and stacks of deposition transcripts, the visibly heavier informant walked in wearing jeans and a loose-fitting velour shirt, with sunglasses hanging on his V-neck collar.

Taking it all in from a back bench, author John Rothchild was struck by the sheer *anti*climax of the moment: Morales had once talked of cross-continental heroin routes and silencer-equipped guns; more than four dozen people had been nabbed in Tick-Talks; newspapers and magazines across the map were all over this trial.

But now its star witness walked in—the grand entrance for a role he had coveted—dressed like a bum.

Before Morales took the stand, he blindsided everyone in attendance by detouring to approach the accused, including and especially Mutineers Carlene Quesada, Frank Castro and Jorge Villaverde. He faced the men, brought himself to attention and saluted them, Bay of Pigs Brigade–style. The fellow exiles, blushing, reciprocated. "Twenty years of anti-Castro heroics," observed Rothchild, "were caught up in that gesture."

The codefendants reached across the wooden railing to hug Morales and pat him on the back. The prosecutor, looking disgusted, decided she had nothing to ask her star witness, Morales.

"No questions?" asked the judge, annoyed. "So why do we need Mr. Morales?"

"The prosecutor made an effort to appear impassive," Rothchild recalled. "But any doubt about the future of Tick-Talks was now removed; we all knew the case was over. It made no sense for the state to rely on him now."

Finally, in September, the judge overseeing Tick-Talks suppressed the thousand hours of Poop Deck gang recordings that underpinned the case. He blasted State Attorney Janet Reno and the Miami police for depending on the unreliable likes of Monkey Morales in the first place. And so unraveled the state of Florida's largest drug case and two years of effort.

Mutiny Table 14 was officially over, even if Frank Castro and an occasional Villaverde brother stuck around.

Back in February, free on bond and awaiting trial, headline defendant Carlene Quesada was home with his wife and their two-year-old son when someone shot up his house with a semiautomatic. One of the seven rounds broke through a window of the boy's bedroom and came within inches of his bed. This was less than three years after Quesada himself was machine-gunned and nearly killed in his sports coupe. Said Quesada: "I stayed home. I left town. No way I was going back to the Mutiny."

When film scouts called to see if the famous doper from Table 14 wanted to advise a huge Miami movie production—something about a Cuban immigrant and the cocaine trade and the American dream—Quesada thought he was being pranked.

"You fucking *keeding* me?"

Chapter Thirty-two

MIAMI VERSUS MONTANA

As THE MIAMI Monkey Trial dominated the local headlines in mid-1982, the city's exile leadership was fighting what it perceived to be a parallel insult to its reputation: Hollywood was coming to town to film a Cubanized remake of the fifty-year-old mob classic *Scarface*. After two years of race riots and refugee robberies and a record Latino-on-Latino body count, the Magic City needed this flick like it needed another shoot-out at its biggest mall.

The 1932 movie (also known as *Scarface: The Shame of the Nation*), which followed the rise and fall of Italian-American gangster Tony Camonte, was being updated to take place in Miami and would star a murderous Mariel refugee coke dealer named Tony Montana. Miami's own Steven Bauer (born in Havana as Esteban Ernesto Echevarría Samson) would be playing Montana's sidekick, Manny. Screenwriter Oliver Stone and director Brian De Palma had been staying at the Mutiny ahead of filming.

Miami Herald columnists and editors swiftly urged the city to turn down the expensive production. City commissioner Demetrio Perez Jr. introduced a resolution to deny the use of city facilities to any project that might portray Cuban-Americans in unfavorable ways. But Florida governor Bob Graham and the Greater Miami Chamber of Commerce pleaded with coproducer Martin Bregman, maker of such hit films as *Serpico* and *Dog Day Afternoon*, not to follow through on his threat to re-create 1980 Miami elsewhere—probably in Southern California. The Magic City desperately needed the millions in hotel, restaurant and freelancer revenue that something as ambitious as *Scarface* would bring to town. Tourism was way off.

Shooting for *Scarface* was supposed to start in mid-October of 1982. Bits from Oliver Stone's screenplay were leaking out:

> *[Tony Montana's corrupt lawyer] smoking yet another cigarette, his voice a hoarse, graveled croak, the eyes— with their deadpan stare—always pausing before they speak. He doesn't get up from his desk. His hair is flaming red. We saw him before, at the Mutiny Club.*

(The Mutiny was referenced by accident here. The makers of *Scarface* erected the Babylon Club, its simulacrum, back in LA's Universal City.)

Coproducer Martin Bregman, who had a newborn child, spent much of the year fending off threats from Cuban exiles, and not just in Miami. A group of New Jersey Cubans called a meeting across the Hudson River to tell him "that it would be very unsafe for me, my family and everybody involved in this enterprise to make this film." His costume designer in Miami witnessed set spectators with guns holstered on their ankles. "The exiles," he recounted, "said they were aware—and they used the word *aware*—

that Castro was financing this film to embarrass the good Cuban community."

Equally absurd, said Bregman, was their contention that Cuban-American drug dealers were a rarity. "I had just gotten back from Miami with Oliver Stone and we spoke with nothing but Cubans and they were all in the drug business. Not all Cubans, but the people we talked to, the big guys in the drug trade."

In August, Commissioner Perez wrote a column in the *Herald* proposing that Tony Montana instead be a Communist agent that Fidel Castro had planted in the US through the Mariel boatlift. Half a century earlier, Washington censors demanded that producer Howard Hughes rewrite the original *Scarface* script with less violence. A furious Hughes had ordered his crew to proceed. "Screw them!" he said. "Make it as realistic and grisly as possible."

For his part, Channel 4's Ralph Renick, Miami's foremost TV news personality—a fixture at the bar at the Mutiny every afternoon, where he crossed paths with *Scarface* scouts and cast—offered this on-air commentary:

Miami wants to be a lot of things . . . even a place where Hollywood movie producers make their films. This is all to the good. But you can't have your cake and eat it, too. Just as we can't insist that all visitors using our beaches must have slim waists and trim shapes, we can't insist that all movies shot here have plots that reflect positively on Miami. . . . Now: lights, cameras, acción. Good night, and may the good news be yours.

In the end, opposition from Miami exiles was just too much for Universal Studios to stomach. *Scarface* was filmed chiefly in Los Angeles. "That's no way to get up in the morning," remarked Martin Bregman about the extraordinary security that filming in Miami would have entailed, "with a policeman sitting by your bed with an Uzi."

Not that this meant the real Miami and Mutiny were again PG-rated. In August, Mutiny security chief Fernando Puig and his wife headed to a banquet at the University of Miami. Things were on cruise control for a predictably huge night at the club. Driving in his dark blue Cadillac Eldorado, Puig pulled up to a curb near the campus police station and asked his wife to get out before he parked in a puddle beneath a streetlamp.

As she got out, a man ambushed her from behind, stuck a gun to her neck and demanded her jewelry. Puig, whose Cadillac slowly lurched forward as he tried to phone deputy Willy Gomez, apparently did not hear her scream in Spanish: "Fernando, help me! They're going to kill me!"

The assailant, a young black man, then ran to the driver's-side door and stuck his gun in Puig's rib cage. As his wife rushed back to the car, she slid and fractured her ankle. In the ensuing confusion, the gunman shot Fernando Puig through his left shoulder. The bullet sheared through his massive chest and exited his right shoulder.

"Oh my God, you've killed him!" Puig's wife yelled at the robber, who frantically dug through Puig's bleeding shirt and pants in search of money. He found no cash in his billfold, but he did snatch Puig's .45-caliber pistol. Mrs. Puig handed the gunman her Rolex watch, her gold bracelet, her six gold bangles and her purse. She had managed to toss her diamond wedding ring beneath the idling Cadillac.

Fernando Puig, forty-three, was pronounced dead at a nearby hospital just before midnight. His murder was Dade County's 346th homicide of the year.

Shortly after, recalled his deputy Gomez, a Venezuelan air force general showed up at the Mutiny just as Puig's widow asked Gomez to meet her at an enormous warehouse by Miami International Airport. He figured she needed help with another client from their family security business.

Upon arriving, Gomez observed the extraordinary security details of the warehouse, which had a rolling iron gate activated by special IDs and even wrought iron grilles over the vents and HVAC units on the roof. Inside, the building was packed with giant pallets containing parts for F-14 and F-15 fighter jets. Venezuelan military officials were all over the place.

Gomez said it was only then that he realized his boss, Fernando Puig, apparently had had a hand in a clandestine operation to smuggle fighter jets and parts to South and Central America in giant Venezuelan C-130 aircraft. The beneficiaries: the Contra rebels fighting the Nicaraguan Communists, who had deposed and assassinated his best friend, former strongman Somoza. The big planes would then fly back to Miami filled with cocaine and cash.

Much of that would come to light nationally several years later during the Iran-Contra hearings. And much of that set the stage for the next kings of the Mutiny.

"Look," said Gomez, "Fernando didn't tell me everything. I respect him for it."

Chapter Thirty-three

A MARKED MONKEY

EXACTLY ONE YEAR after he pursued Amilcar from outside the Hotel Mutiny, Raul Diaz was felled by a headline in the *Miami Herald*: "FBI Probes Homicide Supervisor: Metro Officer Denies Corruption Allegations."

It took just hours after the article was published for police brass to banish their star homicide lieutenant to a security job at Miami International Airport. Though two official boards of inquiry later cleared Diaz of wrongdoing—and he was even offered a promotion to major in mid-1983—Diaz resigned in disgust in September. "I used to feel good putting on my uniform," he said. "Now I couldn't stand it anymore."

What happened to Raul Diaz? "They didn't want waves," he said. "You had to fucking break eggs to make an omelet. I broke eggs. I didn't break any laws, though. But I did bend them."

Fellow homicide detective June Hawkins thought that Diaz was done in by political enemies across Miami law enforcement.

"Because he was unorthodox," she said, "he'd get out there with us, interrogate people, chase people down, be there in shoot-outs with us. That was just not what a lieutenant did. He had great loyalty from his troops—he was the best supervisor I ever worked for; he taught me so much—but it was threatening to the rank-and-file establishment."

Shortly after Diaz was demoted and reassigned, Hawkins downshifted out of homicide and into a Monday-to-Friday patrol job in South Miami. "I have no real understanding of why they did him like that," she said. "You shoot and kill the leader of a group and you deflate them. It just wasn't the same. How could they take the wind out of our sails?"

Diaz said his next CENTAC target would have been Griselda Blanco, the Colombian cocaine "godmother" who had had dozens killed since having Dadeland Mall shot up in 1979. (Blanco was assassinated thirty years later, in 2012, after having been linked to as many as two hundred murders.)

As for Ricardo "Monkey" Morales, Diaz's longtime informant: the two men had been irreconcilably separated after the Tick-Talks disaster. "He was a drunk by then," said Diaz. "It was all lost. I no longer knew Ricardo."

But Morales was not quite done. In early December, he taped a tell-all interview for a local Spanish television: *"Historia de una Intriga."* As Morales sat there in his jeans, fidgety and seeming fifty pounds heavier than he looked on the Tick-Talks stand, he told the show's host that exile drug dealers in Miami and Communists aligned with Fidel Castro were in cahoots. While this wasn't *Harper's* or *Esquire* or *Newsday*, it was more than enough to raise hell in Little Havana.

The watering holes of Miami—and all floors of his erstwhile headquarters, the Mutiny Club—were now abuzz with talk of competing bounties for the Monkey's head. How *dared* he libel Bay of Pigs hero and exile charity czar Rafael Villaverde—now presumed dead—and his grieving brother Jorge, who had suffered for eighteen years in Fidel Castro's prisons? The rumor now was that Morales was plotting to do in pot smuggler and militant anti-Castro activist Juan Cid. Maybe, sniffed the old men at the domino tables in Little Havana, the Monkey had been working for Castro all along. See, I told you!

Ricardo Morales could now barely show his face in Miami. "*Ratón*" was what he was being called across town, having shown the temerity to get so many Brigade freedom fighters ensnared. And for what?

Still, he kept refusing witness protection.

On Monday, December 14, Morales went to visit Jerry Sanford, now in private practice, at his office. Sanford said he had important news. "Grayer, heavier and looking tired," observed Sanford, "he smiled enthusiastically when I greeted him at the door."

Morales had assumed Sanford would be leaving private practice to return to government life, and they could pick up where they had left off three years earlier. Instead, the former federal prosecutor asked the exile what he thought about working with him in the pursuit of Nazi war criminals in South America. This foray was personally important to Sanford: his wife was the daughter of Holocaust survivors. Morales was a known quantity to Israeli intelligence, which he had helped during his stint in Venezuela; Prime Minister Golda Meir had given him a medal of appreciation.

Morales agreed to help Sanford. Meanwhile, he added, the book he was shopping would offer irrefutable proof that a high-ranking CIA-trained Miami exile was actually in the employ of Fidel Castro. In fact, he told the ex-prosecutor, he had hatched Tick-Talks precisely to out this operative.

Morales looked happier and reconstituted. The men shook hands and he promised Sanford he'd call.

Less than a week later, on the evening of December 20, Morales picked up Nancy Cid in his red Cadillac for a preholiday night out. They drank and tooted blow at a Little Havana restaurant before crossing over the causeway to Key Biscayne, where Nancy's estranged husband, pot smuggler Juan Cid, owned a club called Roger's on the Green.

In Roger's dimly lit, heavily mirrored discotheque, as a TV set showed the Cincinnati Bengals at the San Diego Chargers, Morales, more than a little inebriated, got into a loud argument with a guy named Orlando. He kept storming in and out of the lounge. A bystander heard the word *maricón* ("faggot") uttered. As Morales reportedly reached for the gun in his ankle holster, he took a bullet to the head.

The place quickly emptied out. Police and an ambulance arrived to find Morales facedown in a pool of blood. He was rushed across the bay to the nearest emergency room.

Which raises the question, why did Ricardo "Monkey" Morales, multiple bounties on his head, even go to Juan Cid's club in the first place?

"I have no fucking idea," said Douglas Williams, his Tick-Talks interrogator and Juan Cid's attorney. "Ricky was an over-the-top, really insufferable self-promoter. He had an ego as big as Donald Trump and thought he was bulletproof. He thought if he hung out with Nancy—who was psychotic—it would gall Juan. All the behind-the-scenes intersections of these terribly fucked-up relationships. It was like a circular firing squad."

Juan Cid, for his part, claimed his estranged wife, Nancy, wanted him dead. He said he'd been convinced of as much after he'd recently tested her during a romantic, supposedly conciliatory evening. He left four of his unloaded guns out near his nightstand and shut his eyes. "I played stoned and dizzy," he said. "She picked up each gun and pulled the trigger." After he perked up and threw her out of the house, he said, the next thing he heard from her was her vow to have Monkey Morales kill him (and how many times did Morales shoot to kill and escape sentencing in his twenty years in Miami?). "Then," he said, "they both showed up at my restaurant."

"Bullshit," said D. C. Diaz, the Miami police detective who was deposed during Tick-Talks. "It was a fucking hit."

Morales was intubated at Mercy Hospital, just north of the Mutiny, where a gunman had infamously broken in a year and change earlier to finish off a drug dealer.

At her mother's behest, Morales's niece, Annette, kept an eye on Nancy Cid, who commandeered a hallway pay phone to make two dozen calls, mostly with updates such as "still alive," "not yet" and "I will tell you."

A private-attorney friend of Morales's was blitzed with calls from reporters, to whom he described his on-and-off client as a "real-life James Bond." "I find it hard to believe he would get shot in a bar," he told the *Miami News*. "He's too careful. He's too smart."

On the day before Christmas Eve, doctors disconnected Ricardo Morales's respirator and declared him dead. He was forty-three.

John Rothchild, the journalist who had once profiled him in *Esquire* and gotten him on the cover of *Harper's* to start the year—only to watch him self-immolate in Tick-Talks—read the headline in the morning paper. He called Mercy Hospital for the name and number of the funeral home to send flowers to.

But when he called the funeral home, he was told there wasn't a body.

Chapter Thirty-four

YO SOY SCARFACE

SCARFACE CAME OUT in December 1983 to mostly solid reviews. But the 25-million-dollar production did not exactly blow away the box office or compel Miami exiles to take to the streets. Liza Minnelli saw it at a red-carpet premiere with Steven Bauer, the Mutiny member who played Manny, and almost felt sorry for him. Other actors and luminaries at big debuts across the country fell asleep or walked out.

If it wasn't the film's 226 f-words that alienated audiences, the savage chain saw murder and shoot-out scene filmed in the middle of South Beach (a final "fuck you" to Miami for stymieing the production) did it.

Some of the actors admitted feeling a bit ashamed about the film, which one critic wrote "plays like a crude *Godfather* parody, the sort that might amuse as a ten-minute sketch on *Saturday Night Live*, but curdles and collapses as a 143-minute film."

Funny thing is, Miami's Cuban drug lords were kind of enamored of this Tony Montana character. "I thought it was exaggerated, but pretty accurate," said Juan Cid. At *Scarface*'s Babylon Club, for example, Tony Montana had a phone plugged in at his table—straight out of Burton Goldberg's Mutiny. Wayne Doba, who played the dancing mime that got shot up by Latin gunmen at the film's club, was discovered by the producers working at the Mutiny, where he would go from table to table, entertaining guests.

This is how Oliver Stone's screenplay set the scene:

EXTERIOR OF THE BABYLON CLUB—NIGHT

We know this is no workingman's dive when Lopez piles them out of his Rolls, and the carhops are moving Bugattis, Lamborghinis and Corniches in a long, snaking line down the driveway. Single girls in high-collared silver lamé jumpsuits with cinched waists prowl like big, glistening tents back and forth across the entry doors, rich, young, coiffed playboys in their Porsches honking their horns in appreciation . . .

INTERIOR BABYLON CLUB

The interior is built like three or four plush apartments that run together on three separate levels with imaginative angles, mirrors, swimming pool, bars, twenty-piece band, hundreds of tropical plants, dance floor, video games, computers and a restaurant. It's a lavish fun spot that will play a central role in the film,

*a drug dealer haven and nighttime capital of South
America.*

*The crowd, a combination of Caucasian and Latin, is
mostly young, rich and happy and a lot of them coked;
the girls, upper-class in sleek dresses, trim figures,
heels, hats, sensuous bodies, yell as they dance to a
black American music beat, "Celebrating" or "Partying
Down Tonight." . . . The waitresses, mostly blondes,
hats pinned to their heads and the barest pants with
hose and high heels. Rich young guys with a lot of
gold and diamonds on their necks and hands huddle
briefly in groups or chat.*

"Every doper in Miami thought *Scarface* was based on them," said Juan Cid. "It was well researched and familiar: the big Mutiny-like club, banks opening up just for them to count their cash. It was our life."

An associate of Mario Tabraue, the wildlife-loving kingpin with the pet chimp, insisted that Tony Montana was chiefly based on his boss. Montana, after all, had the big cats on his grounds, not unlike Mario's Coconut Grove zoo-manse. The fictional villain-hero's throne, with letters *TM*, was pretty much a replica of Tabraue's throne, which had the letters *MT* in the same style.

When convicted coke lord Jorge Valdes got out of jail in 1984, *Scarface* was still playing in some ninety-nine-cent theaters. He said he walked out of the movie convinced it was at least partially based on his life. "Tony Montana had the big cat," he said. "I had a cougar. Also, I battled a guy in Bolivia."

Ray Corona, for his part, told the *Miami Herald* that he detested *Scarface*. He thought it typecast all Cubans as thuggish, overly flashy hotshots. (Never mind that the banker so fond of fur coats and Rolls-Royces was given to beating people up and threatening Mutiny staff with a loaded gun.)

However much or little you thought art truly imitated life in *Scarface*, the real events of 1984 Miami were worthy of their own Hollywood treatment. That year, Corona and his father were indicted for running a drug bank. On the night of the announcement, Willie Falcon and Sal Magluta showed up at Corona's bank with suitcases that they had stuffed with fifty- and hundred-dollar bills. If anything, maybe *Scarface* wasn't exaggerated enough: for all his flash, Tony Montana's cocaine empire never saw anything like the fortunes thrown off by Muchachos Corp.

Parallel to the indictment of the "bad-boy banker" from Table 3, Burton Goldberg had never been so absentee from the Mutiny. Rumors wafted around Miami that cops would shut down the now-infamous hotel and club.

The prior year alone saw two of the Mutiny's cornerstones, Monkey Morales and Fernando Puig, shot dead, Rafael Villaverde presumably lost at sea and Carlene Quesada's Poop Deck gang Tick-Talked and scattered. Dressed-down Marielitos were showing up with relatives and cursing at the membership director to let them all in, or else. "The quality of the clientele fell enormously," said Baruch Vega.

Meanwhile, exclusive clubs were opening up across Coconut Grove, including in the penthouse of a new five-star hotel, Regine's—the tuxedos-only Miami debut of international hot spot doyenne Régine Zylberberg.

A few buildings down, Suzanne Johnson, the Mutiny's former general manager, opened her offshoot, Suzanne's in the Grove. She was aggressively poaching Mutiny girls and cribbing from the membership list.

Both tried to emphasize an exclusivity that the increasingly déclassé (read: Marielito) Mutiny did not have.

"The Mutiny by now was full of Tony Montanas wanting their fifteen minutes," said Sam Burstyn, the cocaine attorney who had kept a table there since the place made it big in the mid-1970s. "It was a pirate town for them, where they could do whatever the fuck they wanted—prostitutes, gambling, drugs. There was no class anymore."

In 1983, Mario Ortiz, a speedboating and smuggling pal of Upper Deck habitué George Morales, was running security at the Mutiny. His deputies were ex-enforcers of Jean-Claude "Baby Doc" Duvalier, Haiti's murderous dictator.

At the Mutiny one night, Morales, a Colombian, invited Ortiz to dinner with a guest who said he wanted to meet him. In walked Pablo Escobar, the head of the Medellín cocaine cartel, alongside his cousin. They apologized that Griselda Blanco—"*La Madrina*"—could not make it.

Escobar's being at the Mutiny in 1983 and owning a mansion in nearby Miami Beach took balls. Vice President George Bush, the White House's drug czar, was often in town to trumpet his South Florida Drug Task Force. Bush and his procession stayed at the Mayfair, a posh hotel mere yards from the Mutiny, where the international king of cocaine was now dining.

Not that Pablo Escobar was exactly public enemy number one at the White House. Indeed, he had just posed for a photo with his son along the fence of 1600 Pennsylvania Avenue. Back home, moreover, Escobar bought a modicum of legitimacy by winning a seat in Colombia's congress. He had designs on its presidency.

At the Mutiny, Escobar and the men sat in a secluded booth in the Upper Deck. The VIP from Medellín asked if Chef Manny could possibly whip together *bandeja paisa*, the official dish of his home-town: a deep, hearty bowlful of corn, pork rinds, beans and rice.

Escobar, soft-spoken and betraying little emotion, told Ortiz he had heard good things about him through the Muchachos grapevine—that, like them, he was that rare Cuban who could be trusted in the highest layers of his organization. To cut to the chase: Would he be willing to come to Colombia to work for him?

Ortiz said he was flattered and took pains to praise Escobar, but begged off. He had just agreed to do stunts for NBC's upcoming *Miami Vice*. He was making famous friends with the show's number two actor, Philip Michael Thomas, who was interested in moving his family and entourage into the hotel.

So desperately did the Mutiny need Ortiz and his Haitian heav-ies running security that management agreed to pay him in ad-vance. But a sense of safety alone was not enough to bring back the old big spenders. By the end of 1983 and into 1984, membership sales slowed down to a trickle, and there were constant rumors that the club was having trouble making payroll. "You were just letting people in," recalled a saleswoman.

A pair who did like the place, however briefly, were Don John-son and Philip Michael Thomas, the actors who played Crockett and Tubbs on *Miami Vice*.

First-season *Miami Vice* writer Gustave Reininger dined with FBI agents and drug dealers at the Mutiny. "Every gangster wants to be in showbiz," said the late Reininger in a 2005 newspaper in-terview. "Sometimes they wanted to tell me too much. I'd just ask them for patterns, what a typical day was like. 'Well, last night at midnight we brought in a load from New Orleans.' No, no, no! I don't want to know specifics—I don't want to be called in to testify!"

Cocaine smuggler Jon Roberts was introduced to the two lead actors at the Mutiny. The late Roberts, subject of the hit indie doc *Cocaine Cowboys*, recalled the scene in his memoir, *American Desperado*. "'Jon,'" he said, quoting a friend at the club, "'meet the guys who pretend to be hunting you every week on TV.'"

"The Mutiny was blowhead heaven," wrote Roberts in his book, "and I'm there with people who got to be stars playing cops and smugglers on TV.... Nose powder [made] us all instant friends...."

Chapter Thirty-five

BY THE NUMBERS

THE POOP DECK and Table 14, rocked by Operation Tick-Talks, were now the stomping grounds of flamboyant kingpin Juan "Johnny" Hernandez. This heavily protected cocaine dealer's weekly tab at the Mutiny often broke twenty-five thousand dollars, which didn't even include the 3,500-dollars-a-week rent he was paying for use of the panoramic Sailboat Bay penthouse suite.

Hernandez was married to a Playboy Bunny, but kept a mistress at the Mutiny. The same Upper Deck waitress who not long before kept Monkey Morales's gun for him in a bread basket now prepared Hernandez's steak tartare tableside.

Hernandez came to the US from Cuba in 1960. In Spanish Harlem, he and his parents were so poor, they had to cover themselves in newspapers on cold nights; the couch they lugged upstairs off the curb had fleas.

The family left New York for South Florida after a Puerto Rican gang jumped and robbed them. They came to Hialeah, the densely packed center of Latin life in West Miami. Here, Hernandez came under the influence of Alberto San Pedro, a property developer who had a hand in every racket, from narcotics to official bribery to assassination plots. Nicknamed the "Great Corrupter of Hialeah," San Pedro taught Hernandez how to steal cars. "In fact," admitted Hernandez, "I lost my virginity in a stolen station wagon."

But what really clicked for this juvenile delinquent was the *bolita*, the illegal Mafia-linked street lottery that was a way of life with Miami's many immigrants, especially before Florida had a state lottery. By his twenties, Hernandez was one of Miami's biggest *bolita* runners, overseeing 700 thousand dollars in play per drawing, with eight drawings a week. So flush was Hernandez's racket that he had five Miami cops on his payroll and literally could not spend money fast enough at the Mutiny. "My guys were like 'Johnny, bro, there's too much cash coming in. Buy more bottles. Get tables. Food. Spend it.'

"I loved that place," he said. "It was the place to be."

Hernandez said he now felt so at home at the Mutiny that he sometimes arrived with grocery bags of produce and seafood to give Chef Manny to cook up, not just for himself but also for the rest of his Poop Deck delegation, including bodyguards and their girlfriends—and the girlfriends' girlfriends.

At the end of the evening, they would all follow him out the front door and wave him off at the Mutiny's valet. "I paid five-hundred-dollar tips to my waitresses," he said. "I put them through school." He said Burton Goldberg bought him a cast-iron Johnny Hernandez likeness.

Hernandez tried to diversify his numbers racket into money counterfeiting. When a Colombian printing-supplies vendor was short on cash, he asked him to instead accept a kilo of uncut cocaine as payment. "Dude," said Hernandez, "I never even did coke. And I never, never, never wanted to get into the drug business."

How quickly could he convert it to the cash he was owed? Hernandez had many black employees in his *bolita* racket, a couple of whom were connected to Harlem's top dope dealer. As fate would have it, the kilo of coke that Hernandez was sitting on was a buttery variety that was especially in demand in the inner city. Said Hernandez: "It was exactly the kind the blacks wanted; it was better for crack."

Hernandez netted 300 thousand dollars in three days, and with minimal effort. And as with Rudy Redbeard and Jorge Valdes and Willie and Sal before him, all he could think about now was selling his next load. "What the fuck?" he said. "I was in the wrong business."

Hernandez flew down to Medellín, Colombia, where he was picked up in four Toyota SUVs packed with bodyguards. A helicopter transfer later, he found himself at a huge ranch, where he was greeted by deputies to Pablo Escobar.

Hernandez negotiated wholesale access to their buttery product, via an alternate route. His supply conduit would be the Venezuelan Air Force, with a Colombian senator as their official go-between. The Venezuelans would fly one thousand kilos per trip on camouflaged C-130s, landing at Miami International Airport.

Hernandez asked if they could tack on an extra three kilos apiece of their special "Juicy Fruit" variety that he had sampled—a blow so aromatic and smooth that women at the Mutiny were begging for it.

Deal, they said: 1,003 kilos a pop, into a special hangar at Miami International.

At the Mutiny, Hernandez said he was approached by one of the top producers of *Miami Vice*, who confided to him that many of his cast and crew were users of cocaine. He didn't want them out in the mean streets of Miami, dealing with tabloid-bound dealers and middlemen to score blow of questionable quality. Would Hernandez agree to discreetly supply them? The producer would be sure to pay him what he needed. Sure, said Hernandez, who in turn put the producer on the spot: Would he get Hernandez on his show? The producer stuck him on two episodes. Hernandez depicted a stolen-merchandise runner in 1985's "Made for Each Other," and Marco, a goon, in "The Fix" (1986).

"Don Johnson was a pain in the ass," said Hernandez, who recalled him as a whiny, petulant ego who always had to get his way. The show's leading man moved in to the floor below Hernandez's massive penthouse condo in downtown Miami. Johnson was mad that Hernandez refused to let him land his chopper on the roof.

Chapter Thirty-six

BOYS IN THE GROVE

WHEN KINGPIN NELSON Aguilar got out of jail in 1983, he immediately returned to dealing cocaine. "I came out itching to kick ass and take numbers," he said. Knowing his hometown of Miami was already well supplied by pals Willie and Sal— prices were now falling; coke was everywhere; he had lost market-share while he was behind bars—he went prospecting in Alaska.

At the Great Alaskan Bush Company, an Anchorage strip club, Aguilar met a dancer who went by the name "Good-Booty" Judy. The Cuban convinced the pasty blonde to ditch the cold and fly back with him to Miami.

Upstairs in the first-class bathroom of their cross-country 747, they smoked freebase cocaine, an indulgence Aguilar had picked up in prison from Rudy Redbeard. ("Can you believe that?" Aguilar said. "When I first walked into the Mutiny [circa 1977] and saw him [Redbeard] up there with all the women and bottles, I never imagined he would even acknowledge me. But when you're two Cubans in jail together . . .")

Upon landing in Miami, Aguilar and Good-Booty Judy went straight to the Mutiny, where Aguilar had stashed ten kilos of cocaine in the closet of the Egyptian Suite. He cooked up a special batch with acetone. "You're going to love this shit," he told his guest. After taking one hit of the stuff, however, she felt wobbly and started to tremble. Within minutes, she fell to the floor and hugged her knees as she rocked back and forth.

The next evening, Aguilar put the terrified stripper back on a plane to Alaska. He might have accompanied her on the five-thousand-mile ride had he not had more pressing plans: he had committed "to party" with Rick James, whom he spotted on the way out of the Mutiny. The multiplatinum-selling funkster would be mobbed by women whenever his stretch limo pulled up on South Bayshore Drive.

James and Aguilar booked neighboring rooms and got tied to their bedposts, and vice versa, by various women, in between obligatory hits of *yeyo*. James, a heavy crack smoker, would often get especially paranoid after a binge. Aguilar recalls being midcoitus with two women who'd tied him to a fixture when James, presumably freed from his silk cuffs, started banging frantically on his room door.

"What's that sound?" yelled James. "You hear it, Nelson? What is that sound?! Nelson!"

Outside of Rick James, the gregarious Aguilar built a lucrative book of business plying NFL players, including and especially the Miami Dolphins, with cocaine. He recalled a big Dallas Cowboys–Dolphins *Monday Night Football* game marked by a bad showing by All-Pro Dallas running back Tony Dorsett, who had partied hard with Aguilar the night before. The Dolphins won the game by a touchdown.

After the game in the parking lot of Miami's Orange Bowl, a dismayed Dorsett spotted Aguilar giving high fives to his best pal and client: Dolphins wide receiver Mark Duper. "You motherfucker!" he yelled. "You know each other?" (The Duper-Aguilar cocaine scandal was later outed by *Sports Illustrated*.)

Sometime in 1983, Aguilar bumped into Sal Magluta after an all-nighter in Coconut Grove, either at the Mutiny or at its offshoot, Suzanne's. No one remembers for sure (too much coke).

By now, Coconut Grove was one big pub crawl for high rollers: you might see Don Johnson at Cat's—and all the girls would head there—or maybe a Miami Dolphin or Rick James at the Mutiny. And a bunch of tuxedo-clad celebs at Regine's in the penthouse of the Grand Bay Hotel.

Aguilar says he and the chief Muchacho, Sal Magluta, had been discussing a run to the Bahamas. A preoccupied Magluta cut him off. Glancing at Venao, the Deer, he snapped: "Just talk to him, man."

It was no secret that Bernie *"el Venao"* Gonzalez was now handling the boys' Bahamian weight. Word on the street was, Willie and Sal wanted to focus more on the West Coast, what with things in Miami getting dicier (their outside moneyman, Ray Corona, was facing an indictment; Vice President Bush had his South Florida Drug Task Force; they were still appealing their 1980 state cocaine conviction).

Magluta gestured to Venao to cover Aguilar's several-thousand-dollar tab: claws, steaks, lobsters, open bar, endless magnums of Dom, fine wines. The next day, said Aguilar, he attempted to call

Magluta to arrange to pay him back—"I didn't want to be sponging on these guys; they were generous; I didn't want to be seen like that." But a Muchachos deputy told him to forget about it.

Such liquidity was all still new to Aguilar, who had been in jail for four years, where he could barely believe the stories fellow inmate Rudy Redbeard (for long the master of Table 14) would tell him. "Those guys would spend one hundred thousand dollars at the Mutiny like you and I would order a spaghetti dinner at the Olive Garden."

In hindsight, Aguilar said he realized why there was a chill in the air of the perennially hot and humid Grove. For one, Jack Devoe, a pilot who worked for the Muchachos, was caught and in November gave testimony to the President's Commission on Organized Crime. His humblebrag was written up in a *New York Times* piece, "Drug Smugglers Say Hard Part Is What to Do with Money." Why would a busted drug pilot appear before the Feds, and probably the nightly news, if he wasn't amenable to a deal?

Meanwhile, Ray Corona, the Muchachos' banker—the J. Pierpont Morgan of cocaine who lorded over Mutiny Table 3—was apparently going down. On December 12, the Feds swooped in and cuffed Corona, thirty-five, and his sixty-five-year-old father, on charges of running Sunshine State as a drug bank since the late 1970s. A volatile man was now in the hands of the law, which would no doubt try to mine him for intel.

In Washington, no less than the attorney general crowed that Corona's bust "demonstrates one of the important aspects of the scope of drug trafficking activities: the penetration of the financial and business communities." Ray Corona was charged with creating more than thirty business enterprises and shell companies in

Miami and Panama to launder and reinvest drug proceeds. He faced as much as sixty years in jail.

By the summer of 1985, a month before his trial, Corona tried to wax contrite in a long profile in the *Miami Herald*: "Bad Boy of Miami Banking on the Ropes." "Ray Corona blames his troubles on the movie *Scarface*," began the piece. "'It became fashionable,' he complained, 'to think that anyone who is young and Latin and out with a girl at night and is rich and has a Rolls-Royce has got to be a hood.'"

While donning a gold fob attached to a Rolex and sitting at a mahogany table whose brass legs were shaped like curvaceous strippers, Corona argued that he was humble and misunderstood. He was also severely under the influence of cocaine.

The reporter went on to detail how Corona owned Rolls-Royces, limos, Jaguars and Cadillacs and how he would have wine flown in from Chile. "Several times a week, he could be found at Table 3 at the Mutiny, sipping Château Lafite Rothschild and munching special-order fish teriyaki. He wanted a phone at his table, always. He was a big cash tipper. Everyone called him 'Dr. Corona,'" in recognition of a PhD he actually didn't yet have. Corona explained that he was working on a dissertation, "The Influence of God on the Latin-American Businessman."

"He watches movies on his VCR," closed the piece. "But not *Scarface*. It depresses him."

Chapter Thirty-seven

BURTON BOLTS

BEHIND THE SCENES, cops were telling Burton Goldberg that they had seen enough of his den of iniquity. There was, for starters, a brazen burglary commissioned by a group of Mariel refugees. They had drilled through a concrete wall and lifted about 100 thousand dollars' worth of jewels in display cases—a warm-up heist ahead of robbing nine banks across Dade County. Apparently, someone on the inside had tipped off the Marielitos to the Mutiny opportunity: the hotel fired its hairstylist, whose salon the robbers bored through.

A speedboating pal of Willie and Sal's shot up the upstairs wine room over a girl. Another member, a Colombian, pulled a gun on a Cuban. The last straw, for many members, was Luis "Weetchie" Escobedo, the Marielito who looked like Magnum, P.I., firing his gun in the Upper Deck sometime in mid-1983. "Stop shooting up the fucking hotel," a manager screamed, before running for cover. "The fucking Cubans are shooting!"

"Weetchie looked like a spider crawling out of a dark hole," recalled a Mutiny girl who saw him fleeing from hotel security. "We ducked and ran out of the building," said member Laura Costanzo. "That place was over. No one was going to go back."

The cops stuck Burton Goldberg with an ultimatum: sell or get shut down.

In January 1984, a month after *Scarface* debuted at the box office, and with the blessing of his psychic, Goldberg struck a deal to sell the Mutiny at Sailboat Bay to an investor group for 17.5 million dollars. "I knew that place would be dead without me," he said.

It took almost no time for the hotel and club to fall into a cash-flow crunch. Magaly Migoya, the Mutiny's comptroller, said the new owners made a concerted effort to whiten the place's image (and its clientele).

Pammy Scoop, a blond darling who worked on the Upper Deck and was close with Willie and Sal, quit when she was warned the place was now too hot with both dangerous criminals and law enforcement.

When she dropped in one Sunday afternoon to see old coworkers and customers, she saw the club clear out when there was yet another shooting. "You could feel things going down the tubes," said Migoya, who doubted she'd receive her next paycheck.

The Mutiny now had to offer free trial memberships in a desperate all-caps mailer:

DEAR PAST MUTINY MEMBER:
HAVEN'T YOU HEARD ALL THAT'S GOING ON AT THE
MUTINY THESE DAYS? WOULDN'T YOU LIKE TO COME
BACK AGAIN AND JOIN IN THE FUN? UNDER NEW
MANAGEMENT, THE MUTINY CLUB IS ON THE RISE . . .

On many nights, José "Coca-Cola" Yero, the flashy Mariel refugee coke dealer, largely had the place to himself. The new owners tried in vain to urge sales staff to market instead to businesses and more well-heeled white couples who frequented the country clubs of North Miami. They increased the lighting and dispensed with expensive flower shipments and menu items. When the hotel's countless one-of-a-kind room fixtures were broken or stolen, they'd be replaced with mismatched pieces—say, a contemporary glass vase in the Gypsie Caravan Room or Chinese replacement plates in the (Japanese) Shibui Suite. And that begot a vicious cycle: fewer full-paying guests and members led to more cost cutting and fewer full-paying guests. Until the cost cutting hit the mortgage payments.

When its loan to the new Mutiny went into default in April of 1985, Sunrise Savings and Loan brought foreclosure proceedings in state court. In July, however, Sunrise itself went broke and was seized by Washington. "The insolvency was caused by poor underwriting practices, high-risk direct investment and acquisition, development and construction loans which went sour," said the Federal Home Loan Bank Board. The upshot was that the Mutiny at Sailboat Bay—for a while the favorite den of iniquity in the murder capital of America—was now owned by taxpayers.

"They ran the business into the ground," said Burton Goldberg. "Never once did they talk to me. Fuck it. I should have turned it into a condo building. The Latins would have bought it up and I'd have made twice as much."

From the minute Goldberg handed over the keys, the Mutiny spiraled to insolvency. Oscar Paz, the off-duty cop who used to administer staff lie-detector tests for Goldberg, visited while the new owners were painting some walls pink. The menu was streamlined, with quirky favorites like the "Goldburger" and Ma Flo's

[Goldberg's mother's name] chicken soup jettisoned. "I wanted to cry," said Paz.

In December and January, when the hotel was supposed to be at peak occupancy with flocks of snowbirds, the Mutiny was half-full and discounting even its biggest suites. In the spring of 1985, the hotel's new management had to let go of thirty-two staffers—20 percent of its head count. Those who did remain were unsure about when they'd get paid. The elevators worked half the time and were especially expensive to maintain. To say nothing about all the theme suites.

Even seemingly big VIPs who still came to the Mutiny assumed it was in no position to turn them away for boorishness. Singer El DeBarge—"to the beat of the rhythm of the night"—came to the place to sexually proposition his favorite waitress, Jane Podowski. "He thought he could just pay me and I'd go up to a room with him," she said, laughing.

Philip Michael Thomas, the wingman on TV's top show, *Miami Vice*, was still living at the Mutiny with his mother and girlfriend. He had annexed pretty much the entire fifth floor facing the water and turned the panoramic corner suite into his "office." Glenn Frey, his *Miami Vice* costar and former Eagle, liked to visit him there in the "Smuggler's Blues" days.

Gone, however, were the Ferraris, Rollses and Lamborghinis that once jockeyed for "pride of place" at the valet stand.

Thomas liked to park his tricked-out purple Machiavelli out front along South Bayshore Drive. It was a Pontiac Trans Am dolled up to look exclusive, elusive and foreign.

"It was a shitbox," said former Mutiny manager Chuck Volpe. Thomas was making thirty thousand dollars an episode, half-kilo chump change to the dopers of Mutiny's yesteryear.

A longtime general manager acknowledged that—on second thought—the new management's efforts to clean up the hotel's druggie image had been a big mistake. "It was the downfall of the Mutiny in financial terms," he told the *Miami Herald*. "[Drug dealers] supported the club, and the club accounted for 65 percent of the revenues of the hotel."

He should know: turns out, Ricardo "Monkey" Morales of Table 14 had informed on him, too, in the late 1970s—telling police and prosecutors that the manager was storing machine guns and silencers at the Mutiny for Rudy Redbeard and Carlene Quesada.

Chapter Thirty-eight

NEW COKE

On May 28, 1985, Metro-Dade Police responded to reports of shots fired in a residential Miami area. While the arriving cop questioned several homeowners and scribbled on his pad, a young Latin male walked up to volunteer that whoever called 911 had probably heard firecrackers going off in his house. He invited the officer to come in and see for himself.

The policeman came in to indeed observe spent fireworks. But he also noticed white powder on a dish. He handcuffed the man and his housemate and called in backup from narcotics detectives, who showed up to test the substance.

In the ensuing sweep of the house, police found numerous kilogram wrappings—the kind smugglers most often used to pack compacted cocaine. One search warrant later, they managed to seize 1.6 million dollars in cash, ten ounces of cocaine, guns, jewelry and various documents that identified the home's owner as José "Coca-Cola" Yero.

Police opted to let the dopers bond out, the better to keep them under surveillance and hopefully lead them to more people and product. Sure enough, Coca-Cola and his crew continued smuggling between the Bahamas and various South Florida marinas, as if the firecracker bust had simply never happened.

Two weeks after the incident at his house, undercover detectives pulled Coca-Cola over near another address they had been monitoring. In the trunk of the Mercedes 500 SEL he was driving—it belonged to his partner Rene "Raspao"—they found 350 thousand dollars in cash.

They seized and impounded the money and the sedan and let Coca-Cola go free—again, to keep chumming the waters for a more comprehensive takedown of what smelled like a huge cocaine enterprise.

That night, Raspao and Coca-Cola got into a heated argument about the latter's carelessness. If it wasn't bad enough that Coca-Cola hired the kinds of guys who shot off fireworks in a cocaine stash house—and then invited the police to come in! *While cocaine was on display!*—Coca-Cola himself also managed to lose a Benz and all that cash in one swoop. What the hell?

Coca-Cola, recalled Raspao, shot back, "You think I give a shit about three hundred fifty thousand dollars?" yelled the Mariel refugee. He grabbed his crotch. "*Pff!* Fuck," he sniffed. "I have more than that in my left nut!"

Raspao and his girfriend, Nancy "the Big Blonde" Mira, thought back to when Yero was tied up and begging for his life. Was that really just four years ago? Was he still so clueless? "Coca-Cola," she said, "was useless. He was flash."

Still, even after Raspao read him the riot act, Coca-Cola Yero went right back to business as usual, toggling between various cocaine stash houses and marinas and big nights at the Mutiny—all under the careful watch of cops and the DEA.

Finally, in late June, Coca-Cola and his nine-man crew were arrested when agents seized thirty duffel bags packed with fifty to seventy-five pounds of cocaine—the product of flying a ton of the stuff from Colombia to the Bahamas every ten days. From there, the cocaine was put on speedboats and delivered to waterfront homes along the South Florida coast, before getting processed and packed for national distribution in Miami.

Confiscated in the bust was a ton of cocaine, worth as much as 200 million dollars. The DEA reported the Yero haul as the largest seizure of cocaine in the history of Palm Beach. United Press International blasted out the stranger-than-fiction specifics to newspapers around the world:

> *The federal agent who asked not to be identified said Yero, who also goes by the nickname Coca-Cola, compared himself to Al Pacino's character in the movie* Scarface. *The agent said he has a picture of Yero facedown in a pile of cocaine and a picture of him with a gun in one hand and a fistful of money in the other. He said agents found gold Rolex watches in the pockets of eight or nine different suits at Yero's home. He said Yero wore a gold necklace and a gold wristband with the words* Coca-Cola *on them.*

Agents seized two Lamborghinis, three Benzes and a dozen Rolex watches color-coordinated to his suits. On the doper's neck was a gold medallion in the shape of a speedboat stamped with the words *Coca-Cola*. He told police he was just a boat mechanic.

In September, the DEA stormed his partner Raspao Rodriguez's condo in Coconut Grove. As they cuffed Raspao and other smugglers, agents seized a mobile phone, thousands of dollars of leather luggage, ostrich- and eel-skin cowboy boots and fine furniture. They also arrested Bert "Super Papi" Becerra, the guy who first hooked up Coca-Cola at the Mutiny back in the day.

"They blatantly flaunted their wealth," remarked a narcotics detective to the *Miami Herald*. DEA agents said they observed the Coca-Cola gang "sipping Dom Pérignon in reserved champagne booths" in Coconut Grove. "It was, 'Here it is, folks. I'm a doper—come and catch me.'"

As this news flooded the local papers and word got out that the Mutiny Marielito had run out of time, Coca-Cola's attorney attempted to float an insanity defense: he told a judge he had found the former bicycling champion in his jail cell, shivering in a fetal position, having swallowed twenty-five cold pills. The defendant, he argued, was psychotic and unable to stand trial.

"Coca-Cola was the ultimate rags-to-riches story, especially the amount of money he spent at the Mutiny," said then-prosecutor Greg Kehoe. "His supposed mental health issues were just that: supposed."

Chapter Thirty-nine

MIA TO LA

1985 ALSO SAW the Feds finally nail Carlene Quesada for smuggling cocaine, albeit in Los Angeles, where he had moved after 1982's Tick-Talks fiasco. A judge there slapped the fast-talking Cuban with a twenty-five-year sentence. "From the moment of his arrival in this country, he has been involved in one criminal enterprise after another," she said. "I'm obliged to send a signal to Miami. . . . Don't do it; it's not worth it. This community does not need the exporting of *Miami Vice*."

Across the map in Miami, the *Herald* kept running a headline that wouldn't die: the mysterious circumstances surrounding the death three years earlier of Quesada's Mutiny tablemate and betrayer, Monkey Morales.

On a Saturday morning in January, Rogelio Novo, the front-man owner of the disco where Morales was shot late in 1982, was found dead on a deserted road near Fort Lauderdale. A motorist called the cops when he saw the man facedown on the road.

The police arrived, assuming they were dealing with a traffic fatality—until they flipped Novo over to find a bullet hole in his forehead. The sixty-one-year-old exile mobster was still wearing a gold chain and had more than one hundred dollars in cash on him. The police ruled out robbery and the case remained open. Word in Little Havana and Hialeah was that Pucho Morales, the Monkey's otherwise upstanding and law-abiding big brother, had finally exacted his revenge for what was widely viewed as a setup and hit at Novo's disco.

1985 was also when Willie Falcon's mother was kidnapped by a gang of Mariel refugees. Falcon, now a father of twin boys, paid 500 thousand dollars to have her returned, never involving the police.

That same year, he and Magluta were nabbed for trying to sell cocaine in Los Angeles, but under the phony names Wilfredo Fernandez and Angelo Maretto. Their fake IDs were so convincing to the local court that they were able to bond out of custody.

The Muchachos skipped town as the "Angelo Maretto–Wilfredo Fernandez" case lingered in an LA court—not unlike their 1980 state drug case, which stagnated 2,700 miles away in downtown Miami. In early 1987, the LA detective who arrested the men in 1985 almost spit out his beer when he spotted that "Maretto" in a nationally televised ESPN powerboat race. Only, the broadcast's chyron identified him as champ Sal Magluta.

When Magluta was arrested on perjury charges and taken back to LA jail, a bunch of Muchachos associates accompanied his wife, Isabel, cross-country to bond him out yet again. Neither Magluta nor Falcon had any intention of showing up for their August court date.

WHILE THE FEDS were either too preoccupied or too clueless to nab or interrogate Falcon and Magluta—who remained so big in the powerboat race circuit that they both appeared on ESPN at least three times in the mid-1980s—they did manage to seize their old headquarters: the Mutiny.

In September 1986, the Federal Savings and Loan Insurance Corporation took the keys to the twelve-story property, which by now had 109 hotel rooms and thirty-nine offices and condos. The country's savings-and-loan crisis, the decade's defining financial scandal, was just getting started. "Don't look at me," said Burton Goldberg, who had by then decamped to Colorado.

It turns out, the cops who chased Goldberg out of Miami at the end of 1983 did him the favor of a lifetime: he sold at the market's top.

Chapter Forty

THE MUTINY'S LAST STAND

COME 1987, THE Mutiny Club barely registered on Miami's party radar: management complained that many members, past and prospective, incorrectly assumed that the joint, so connected with 1970s Miami, had closed. With paid membership having tanked as much as 30 percent, the latest iteration of club management loosened restrictions on who could dine at the club (now: anyone).

The new-look Mutiny also flooded Miami with trial membership cards. "If you don't like one club," said Jennifer Caramatti, long one of the highest-grossing Mutiny girls, "you can go to another." She was now membership director at nearby Ensign Bitters, where Willie and Sal made occasional cameos. Her head of security was former CENTAC-26 chief, Raul Diaz, now a private investigator.

Another exclusive Mutiny offshoot was Cats in the Grove, which was designed by Carolyn Robbins, the visionary Burton Goldberg hired in the late 1970s to help him convert his hotel into a free-spender's fantasyland. "We are strictly private," the manager of Cats remarked to the *Herald*, before getting in this dig at the struggling Mutiny: "Other clubs are part of hotels and they are forced to allow hotel guests in."

In March of 1987, undercover narcotics detectives busted a hundred-strong bash in the Mutiny's fading Cappuccino and Santa Fe suites. But this was no fifty-thousand-dollar Rudy Redbeard boondoggle.

Amid the cries of hysterical teenage girls, cops arrested an adolescent who went by "Manky" for carrying a Ziploc with a few pinches of cocaine. A sixteen-year-old DJ who had been spinning the Beastie Boys and Run-DMC sobbed as he told officers that his father had driven him to the bash.

The saddest part: the shindig wasn't even supposed to happen at the Mutiny. The teens had had no luck checking in to the newer hotel down the road. Either way, quipped a writer for the *Miami Herald*, "Police did not exactly find *Scarface*-size mounds of cocaine."

That August, Mutiny hotel engineer Jose Rotger, a deputy to the late Fernando Puig, was shot dead, execution-style, at his hunting cabin in the Florida Everglades. The father and husband, who had borrowed Baruch Vega's yacht to retrieve his loved ones during the Mariel boatlift, was forty-seven.

A month later, 250 former Mutiny staffers and Burton Goldberg descended on Coconut Grove for a reunion. Only, not at their old stomping ground, which was so rapidly deteriorating and understaffed that Goldberg & Crew could not bear to see the joint.

Goldberg, now sixty and relatively mellowed, had since reinvented himself as an alternative-health guru. His former workers had a surprise: they hired a near-naked woman to jump out of a pasta-filled bathtub—a nod to Goldberg's rumored Ronzoni fetish.

These days, the old nightlife mogul was far more keen to talk about all the impurities in everyday foods and nontraditional treatments for cancer and depression. He urged former staffers with ailing family members to call him for a consultation.

An undercover DEA agent who used to case the Mutiny reminisced about his job description in his heyday to the *Miami News*, which wrote about the staff reunion: "The company pays for my [membership] card and all I do is sit here and eat, drink and watch the big dealers watching me."

In October, the Mutiny's central banker, Ray Corona, was sentenced to twenty years in prison. As fate would have it, the onetime free-spending patron known for making loans he never collected on owed more than five million dollars to Sunrise Savings and Loan, the insolvent bank that financed the sale of the insolvent hotel he frequented.

Corona's beloved Table 3—and everything else at 2951 South Bayshore Drive—was now property of the federal government, which just a week after his sentencing put out a press release announcing that the property was up for sale. Though the hotel remained open (barely), the Feds quietly shuttered the Mutiny Club, which was hemorrhaging cash. At its peak, the place was pulling in sixty thousand dollars on Friday nights alone.

Much of the magical thinking that made the Mutiny at Sailboat Bay so hot just a few years earlier now made it radioactive to Washington, which was being assailed in the press for the collapse of the financial system and the commercial real estate market. So many banks were failing that the Federal Savings and Loan Insurance Corporation was already insolvent and needed tens of billions in taxpayer-footed bailouts.

"The rooms will have to be toned down a bit," admitted an official from the quasi-governmental agency handling the Mutiny's sale. "I don't think the French bordello look is in anymore."

Offers came and went, and came and went, until the property became such a money pit for the Feds that they finally shuttered the Hotel Mutiny as well in 1989.

By this point, the government was also pursuing a criminal case against Robert Jacoby, the hotshot former chairman of Sunrise Savings and Loan. Nicknamed "banking's boy wonder," the then-thirty-three-year-old Jacoby told *Forbes* magazine: "I'm an ego-status person. I have a pretty wife, a Jaguar, a Mercedes, a beautiful home, a yacht. I want a Ferrari, a bigger house, a bigger boat. I want an airplane, an apartment in New York."

Such tales of conspicuous consumption and risk-taking by bankers rotted across Miami's skyline, as building after shiny building fell into receivership. Government officials were coming to terms with the fact that it would probably be cheaper to burn down certain properties than to operate them and hope for a sale. The savings-and-loan crisis dragged on the economy well into the 1990s, ultimately costing taxpayers an estimated 124 billion dollars.

Chapter Forty-one

COCAINE, CANNONS, COMMIES

THE *POLITICAL* SCANDAL that would come to define the 1980s was, of course, the Iran-Contra affair, Washington's covert scheme to sell arms to the embargoed regime of Iran to secure the release of American hostages and fund antileftist Contra rebels in Central America.

Miami's peculiar role in that imbroglio was now a priority for a newly elected Democratic senator from Massachusetts, John Kerry.

Opposition to aiding the often-ruthless Contras had been a liberal cause célèbre for a while now, with publications like *The Nation* running ads for charities that helped victims of the rebels' atrocities in Central America. For the most part, however, with Ronald Reagan still glowing from his landslide 1984 win, Democrats were fearful of taking on leftist-seeming issues.

In Miami, home to the country's biggest Nicaraguan population, the Contras were, to Cuban exiles and Cold War hawks, all but synonymous with the Bay of Pigs Brigade. The prevailing belief in South

Florida's exile community was that a proxy rematch against Fidel Castro and Latin American leftism could be waged in and around Nicaragua: wrest back Central America from the Commies, and the US could exert new leverage in the region to pressure Fidel Castro.

In December of 1985, the Associated Press reported that certain Contra units were "engaged in cocaine smuggling, using some of the profits to finance their war against Nicaragua's leftist government." Senator Kerry, a former prosecutor, was intrigued. One of his senior staffers was the sister of attorney John Mattes, who himself was following this trail down in Miami. She tipped off the senator.

You might recall Mattes from his first day in Miami in 1981, when, while sitting in a café just yards from the Mutiny, the law school rookie encountered a man who'd had his throat slit.

Mattes had since graduated and was now a public defender with a client in jail on machine-gun possession charges. The inmate protested that he believed he was working for the US government all along, having also loaded military-grade cannons onto camouflaged military planes at Miami International Airport. How, he asked, was no one asking or doing anything about that?

Mattes repeatedly met with the client at Miami's Metropolitan Correctional Center (MCC). "The place was like one big fraternity reunion for anyone involved in running cocaine or arms in 1980s Miami," he said. Juan Cid, the prolific pot smuggler, was there. Carlos Quesada and Rudy Redbeard, the old pals from Mutiny Table 14, passed through the forty-two-acre penitentiary. Upper Deck speedboating phenom, George Morales, was at MCC after getting busted attempting to smuggle upward of a ton of cocaine into Miami.

Had the Feds much cared about the Muchachos' growing cocaine empire, George Morales might have been in a good position to trade information for leniency. In his 1985 record-breaking boat race from Miami to New York, the Colombian was assisted from the air by Ralph "Cabeza" Linero, the Muchachos' pilot—who himself had set a record in 1978, albeit in a lighter class of craft. George Morales's throttle man was Gustavo "Taby" Falcon, Willie's brother and cosmuggler. "We were friends," said Linero.

But Willie and Sal were at this point still tiny footnotes in the War on Drugs: a pair of young exiles who were still appealing a 1980 cocaine charge in between appearances at speedboat races.

Inside MCC, Morales and Mattes's client commiserated about how they believed they'd been screwed by intelligence agents. At the client's suggestion, Morales buttonholed John Mattes: "Son," said the flamboyant doper, "I hear so much about you. We have so much to share. You're going to represent me."

"Why?" replied Mattes. Morales, after all, was a drug lord and Mattes was looking into illegal arms exports. He didn't get it.

Morales laughed and put his hand on the lawyer's shoulder. "You will," he said. "And you won't believe what you've walked into."

The Colombian then gleefully recounted his story. Rewind back to the Mutiny: After Operation Tick-Talks blew up in late 1982, anticommunist exiles joined a new scheme. With the help of a CIA-linked rancher, they would work Miami's drug smugglers into the effort to arm the Contras in Nicaragua. While Congress forbade the Reagan administration to fund the rebels, the White House's body language suggested it would look the other way if friends of the Contra cause came up with innovative off-the-books methods of fund-raising.

In 1983, George Morales accordingly directed his planes to start flying arms down to Central America and narcotics on the trip back to South Florida. A year later, he was arrested and indicted for trafficking in pot and Quaaludes. While he was free on bail, he told Mattes, CIA-connected agents reassured him they would have his back. So Morales continued smuggling, and up-shifted to cocaine (much more money per plane trip); he duly hiked his arms loads and cash payments to the CIA-backed Contras.

In 1986, however, Morales, the defending three-time world powerboat racing champion, landed in jail when the DEA arrested him for smuggling as much as 1,500 kilos of cocaine—on top of his 1984 pot and Quaalude charges.

Long story short: Morales explained to Mattes that cocaine smuggling was the return leg of the gunrunning to Nicaragua that he was looking into. They were one and the same, inextricably related to what he and Senator John Kerry were investigating.

"He was so comfortable laying out the landscape for me," said Mattes. "It was, 'Look, I'm going to plead guilty to cocaine, OK? But top Contra and CIA leaders are guilty, too. Why are they outside while we are in here?'"

That summer, after George Morales refused to appear before a grand jury, he was held in contempt of court and placed in solitary confinement. The Colombian returned to court after his time in the hole with even more resolve: "Judge," he announced, "I appreciate and respect this court, but I do not trust the men standing in this room. I will only talk to the US Senate."

That stunt, said Mattes, won Morales the attention of Washington, as well as the ardor of various drug and arms smugglers back in the MCC. An admiring inmate offered to custom-tailor his prison-issue khakis. "He had a large personality that brought people in," said Mattes. "He developed a reputation of confidence."

George Morales parlayed this momentum by introducing Mattes to fellow speedboat smugglers. "They all came and shared their stories," he said.

At MCC, Mattes received José "Coca-Cola" Yero, who had just been slapped with a four-decade prison sentence for running cocaine. "I remember the day I met him," said Mattes. "He was so flashy, reminiscing about how much he missed his custom-painted pink Lamborghini."

"Wait," said Mattes. "You mean that thing out in front of the used-car lot on US-1 right across the street from my law school?" Coca-Cola told him the lot was merely a front for the speedboat warehouse behind it—an operation that belonged to Falcon and Magluta. That, said Mattes, was the first he had ever heard of Willie and Sal. "Coca-Cola was not as refined as George Morales," he recalled. "But he definitely wanted a way out."

The Marielito illustrated the sheer interchangeability of South Florida cocaine smuggling. "Everyone worked for everyone else," said Mattes, whether George Morales or Sal and Willie. "I was learning all of the infrastructure of the South Florida cocaine scene, the interconnectedness. Between Miami and Bimini, it got crowded at night. You could hire an off-load crew that worked for several cocaine kingpins. It was like going to a staffing firm."

Coca-Cola explained that the Mutiny "was like a central clearinghouse for these gigs. I mean, it's not like you could look up those kinds of jobs on Google."

Mattes met Fabio Ernesto Carrasco, aka "Hemingway"—as in the patron saint of the Florida Keys—one of George Morales's most trusted cosmugglers. At night, in his leading speedboat, Hemingway would wear an Armani suit and carry a rocket launcher, threatening to "vaporize anyone in a boat who left his sight."

The inmate told Mattes about the time he encountered General Manuel Noriega at a party thrown by Pablo Escobar in Medellín. Wasn't Noriega supposed to be Washington's foremost ally in the region? he asked. Why, then, would he be drinking and whoring with the world's biggest cocaine kingpin?

Juan Cid and George Morales shared war stories at MCC. Though Cid had been a go-go Contra booster in the early 1980s, he said he had no illusions about the real Reagan-Bush agenda. "The War on Drugs," he said, "was a big farce, for political brownie points—a marketing theme for the administration. It was a big facade. People would get arrested. But others would not, and would be getting bigger all the time."

In December of 1986, George Morales's attorney outright declared to a district judge that his client "was working at the behest of the government of the United States"—in the interest of national security.

Morales also introduced John Mattes—now working double duty in conjunction with Senator Kerry—to Sarkis "Merchant of Death" Soghanalian, the Middle Eastern arms dealer who used to hold court at the Mutiny. He was at MCC for selling the Iraqi army choppers with machine-gun mounts. The men talked about the arms-for-cocaine Contras connection. "Sarkis exuded an unusual confidence for a federal inmate," said Mattes, "as if he had cards to play. He wouldn't be in there for long."

The prisoners all reiterated the same thing to Mattes: the roads he was looking down in his investigation all led to cocaine.

Mattes related much of what he learned to Senator John Kerry, who flew down to Miami to debrief George Morales. The publisher of the *New York Times* called Mattes to verify what his editors were hearing via leaks from Congress.

At MCC, George Morales also met with former federal prosecutor Jerry Sanford. They had a two-hour conversation about Panama, the CIA, Nicaragua and everything that went into running a quasi-protected global cocaine conglomerate in the 1980s.

Sanford says he got a lump in his throat when thinking back to how he nearly indicted Manuel Noriega for arms smuggling in 1980, only to be thwarted by Washington.

John Mattes upped the ante by introducing George Morales and other dopers at MCC to producers at CBS News who were covering the CIA's campaign in Central America. In April of 1987, Morales and other inmates appeared on CBS's evening newsmagazine *West 57th* to charge that the Contras and the CIA were intimately involved in drug smuggling.

Morales flew up to Washington to testify before the Senate Foreign Relations Committee.

"George went up to Capitol Hill, wearing his finest London Savile Row suit," recalled Mattes. "He was so proud of how he and John Kerry both wore Ferragamo ties."

Under oath, he told lawmakers that in 1984, after he had been busted for running pot and Quaaludes, he was approached by three Contras, two of whom identified themselves as CIA agents. Morales said the men vowed to "take care of my legal problems."

Over the next eighteen months, he testified, he loaded his planes with their weapons. The quid pro quo: hardware down to Costa Rica and El Salvador and cocaine back to South Florida, with millions of dollars funneled to the Contras as tribute.

"He was one of the first big guys on the dark side who came over to the other side to point the finger at the CIA," said T. R. Cimino, a fellow speedboat racer who was marine coordinator on *Miami Vice*.

Back down in South Florida, however, no one looked askance when, in late 1986, Fort Lauderdale's top newspaper, the *Sun-Sentinel*, cast George Morales as the bad guy and Sal Magluta as the good one:

While unresolved smuggling charges against world champion George Morales remain the last prominent blemish from that period, the core of honest sportsmen has made significant strides in restoring credibility and respectability to the offshore circuit.

Another example of the racing fraternity's emerging good-guy image is evident in Miami driver Sal Magluta's offer to lend his best boat and a crew member to the rival Apache Racing Team for Saturday's race. The Apache boat, second in the open-class standings, was damaged in a crash this month at Rochester, NY. Magluta, in sixth place and out of contention for the national title, made his 36-foot Seahawk and throttleman Gus ["Taby"] Falcon available to Apache driver Ben Kramer, even though Magluta's other boat, Team Seahawk—driven by Gus's brother, Willie Falcon— still has a mathematical chance at the championship.

"It's a tremendous thing, a very sportsmanlike thing [Magluta] is doing," remarked fellow racer Ben Kramer's father to the newspaper. "You have to understand the camaraderie among these racers. They all understand the risks they face, and it brings them close together. Sal is just a good person."

Maybe. But Sal, Willie, Taby and Ben Kramer were also prolific drug smugglers.

"Good to see white hats outnumbering the black these days in powerboat racing," closed the piece, however cluelessly.

Unbeknownst to speedboat beat reporters, the DEA and federal prosecutors were now homing in on Willie Falcon and Sal Magluta.

Chapter Forty-two

SHIPWRECKED

IN THE SPRING of 1987, shortly after he raced his Team Seahawk Aston Martin at the Miami Grand Prix, Ralph "Cabeza" Linero, the Muchachos' trusty pilot, ran aground with the law.

As Linero's cocaine-laden Cessna approached the Bahamas, the pilot contacted flight control officials in Nassau, saying the plane was on its way to Freeport from Iowa. Linero also gave officials a false identification number for the craft.

As soon as the Cessna readied for its descent to Chub Cay in the Bahamas, DEA agents sent a helicopter holding US and Bahamian officials. On the ground, Bahamian police arrested Linero and two other men. Officials seized 761 pounds of cocaine and threw Linero in the Bahamas's Fox Hill Prison, notorious for its overcrowding, high inmate mortality rate and overall barbaric living conditions. "It was," said Linero, "the hellhole of the world. Six guys in a six-by-ten cell. One bucket to shit and one to pee."

But he said he was at peace with his commitment to remain

quiet about Muchachos Corp.; he wasn't going to just hand in the guys who had rescued him from that Colombian prison and made him a millionaire. He'd take whatever the law threw at him. "Look," he said, "I was together with my friends, had a great time for a few years, and I knew what I was doing. They needed me to tie Willie and Sal to the Colombian connection. I told them to go and fuck themselves."

For his intransigence, Linero was slapped with an eighteen-month civil contempt charge. At the end of that stint, he still refused to talk, and a prosecutor in Miami further charged him with criminal contempt. "The civil one," said Linero, "was to coerce me into talking. And the criminal one was to punish me. What a crock of shit!" The Muchachos' pilot ultimately received a twelve-year prison sentence.

Though Linero's boss and pal, Sal Magluta, was now shorn of his beloved Team Seahawk racing partner—and though Sal himself was due to appear in an LA court for dealing cocaine and skipping town—he could not resist the rush of the raceboat circuit. Public eye be damned: in June of 1987, Magluta piloted *Seahawk* at a tourney in the rough waters of Lake Pontchartrain. It was an all-out disaster for the repeat champ: his multimillion-dollar craft sank. Sal Magluta never again appeared in a speedboat race.

Just weeks later, Willie and Sal's appeals from their original 1980 state cocaine bust were finally exhausted. When the men failed to surrender, warrants promptly went out for their arrest. Seven years removed from pleading guilty in that Miami court, Falcon and Magluta were only now declared fugitives from the law.

To make matters worse, their attorney, Mel Kessler, was now facing his own indictment. In November, a federal grand jury in Miami charged him with racketeering and participating in an international syndicate that laundered drug money. He was looking at up to 165 years in prison.

With Cabeza Linero keeping silent, authorities zeroed in on nabbing and pressuring Justo Enrique "Dr. J" Jay, one of Willie and Sal's top lieutenants and favorite fellow speedboaters. By all outward appearances, Jay was a law-abiding sportsman. Witness this bit from a November 1987 *Sports Illustrated* story:

> *The waters off Key West, with their dark history of piracy, make an apt setting for major powerboat racing. Some modern-day pirates are drawn to the sport . . . absent—though not exactly missed— from last week's World Offshore Championships: George Morales, a Colombian who was the 1983, '84 and '85 Superboat champion, is serving 16 years in Miami for cocaine smuggling . . .*

Justo Jay, the story wrote, had Willie Falcon's *Cougar*, a black forty-one-foot catamaran, "howling as she soared over the one- to three-foot swells sprinkled with whitecaps."

Just a few months later, in February of 1988, Jay found himself charged with cocaine trafficking—up in North Carolina, a hot market for the Muchachos in their domination of the East Coast. Though Miami was still the nation's undisputed cocaine entrepôt, the price of the drug there had been in free fall; a kilo smuggled to South Florida now only fetched between 8,500 dollars and 14,000 dollars, compared with 50,000 dollars in 1982.

Even so, now-warring families from Medellín and Cali, Colombia's top cocaine cartels, kept on deluging the US with their kilos. Building and defending market share was the name of the game. It was said that Pablo Escobar, the Godfather of Medellín, was spending one thousand dollars a week just on rubber bands for all his cash. And so prices kept falling. (As did bodies—it was a bull market for contract killers in South America and the US.)

Muchachos Corp. was only indispensable to Colombia as long as it kept expanding its market into more states. If you hustled into other markets up the seaboard and out in Southern California, you could score upward of eighteen thousand dollars for your kilo. Atlanta, Baltimore, Washington, Los Angeles and New York were in the throes of an epidemic of crack cocaine, the dealers and users of which weren't as discriminating when it came to the quality or consistency of product.

Crackheads. Crack whores. Crack fiends. Crack mothers. Crack babies. *Playboy*'s 1975 declaration of cocaine as the champagne of drugs was officially over. It was now the scourge of America's most destitute zip codes.

Justo Jay's 1988 indictment was rife with language indicating that the long arm of the law would be reaching out to grab more Muchachos:

> *That from in or about the fall of 1978 and continuing thereafter up to and including the fall of 1984 . . . the defendant, JUSTO ENRIQUE JAY, knowingly, willfully, and intentionally did engage in a continuing criminal enterprise . . . doing, causing, facilitating, and aiding and abetting the importation, possession with intent to distribute, and distribution of cocaine . . . and which violations were a part of a continuing series of violations undertaken by defendant, JUSTO ENRIQUE JAY, in concert with at least five other persons with respect to whom defendant, JUSTO ENRIQUE JAY, occupied a position of organizer, a supervisory position, and*

*position of management, and from which defendant, JUSTO EN-
RIQUE JAY, obtained substantial income and resources . . .*

But Jay, thirty, who had grown up with Sal Magluta since arriving in America from Cuba in 1961, also let it be known that he was
keeping his mouth shut. He even invoked Christian duty. This
time, though, the Feds hit back mercilessly: in September of 1988,
the father of two, including a three-year-old boy, was slapped with
a 115-year prison sentence.

This would have been a most opportune time for his bosses, Willie Falcon and Sal Magluta, to go into deep hiding, ideally overseas
and with the help of plastic surgery, Swiss bank accounts and a network of safe houses. But the pals apparently felt immortal enough
that—DEA dragnet be damned—they stayed in South Florida.

Sal Magluta, moreover, just survived the closest of calls with
authorities. On March 30, 1988, he was at a Miami office supplies
store when he bumped into someone who immediately recognized
the fugitive. The guy knew him from Miami Senior High. But this
wasn't any old classmate. Jorge Plasencia was a Metro-Dade police
detective and alum of Raul Diaz's CENTAC-26 force, and he was
with his squad partner, Alex Alvarez.

When the cops accosted Magluta as he left the store, he claimed
his name was Maretto, and provided fake IDs to that effect. "But,"
said Officer Alvarez, "we knew him."

In the backseat of the police car, the cuffed Magluta fessed up
to his real identity. He offered to take the officers to one hundred
kilos of cocaine—akin to a multimillion-dollar payoff for two guys
making forty thousand dollars a year—if they let just let him out
somewhere. No one would know a thing. But Plasencia and Alvarez tuned him out.

At the police station, agent David Borah, the DEA's emerging Muchachos point man, hurried over and tried to talk to the trophy catch. But Sal said nothing.

Less than a week after his arrest, Magluta was sprung loose. Papers transmitted to his holding facility somehow specified that he had been in jail for north of seven years, which would have more than satisfied the original fourteen-month sentence he and Willie Falcon received back in 1980.

As in the case with Rudy Redbeard's hit man, Mon, a decade earlier, someone on the inside had manipulated the documents. To this day, no one knows exactly what happened. It stands to reason that the Boys had more than enough money to bribe the dirty cops and prison officials that teemed all over 1980s Miami.

When Officers Plasencia and Alvarez learned that Magluta had *again* gotten away, they went ballistic.

All of which only swelled the Boys' Robin Hood–like legend across Miami. It was all but official: Willie and Sal could not be caught. This was 1988 and they had consistently Houdini'd out of 1980 Miami and 1985 Los Angeles drug raps, and kept dealing more and more and more and more coke throughout.

Word wafted around town that Muchachos Corp., now a billion-dollar-plus multinational, had just pulled off a stunt for the ages. When one of its tractor trailers full of Mexican cocaine got stuck in a ditch on a Texas highway, the driver was able to CB in special choppers to winch it out. Discreet roadside service took care of axles and tires. "Bro," recalled an affiliate, "it's like they had Mac-Gyver working for them."

The Boys' product was everywhere. Nelson Aguilar, the Muchachos-connected cocaine dealer, rocked headlines in December 1988 when *Sports Illustrated* linked him with Pro Bowl Dolphins wide receiver Mark Duper, who had just been suspended by the NFL for drug use. Aguilar was serving a thirteen-and-a-half-year prison sentence in Wisconsin, where he was interviewed for the *SI* article. "Mark's a very good friend," remarked the inmate.

In 1988, a Miami grand jury indicted Willie Falcon for providing false information to purchase a gun. Now, to actually find Willie Falcon . . .

"Good luck with that," whispered followers in exile and night-life circles. Miami law enforcement was crammed with all sorts of bullshit leads about the Boys: that the duo was supposedly spotted at a Julio Iglesias concert, where they reminisced about the late, great Mutiny; no, they were at a huge street fair in Little Havana; on houseboats in Sailboat Bay; at some new nightclub in Coconut Grove.

There was even a legend that Willie and Sal had paid obscene amounts to have rare lasers recast their faces and fingerprints. The domino tables of Little Havana were again abuzz.

Chapter Forty-three

THE HUNT FOR WILLIE AND SAL

IN 1988, GEORGE H. W. Bush resoundingly won the presidency. By this point in his history, with the Iran-Contra scandal in full stink, and with people openly talking about the Nicaraguan Contras' ties to the cocaine trade, the former CIA chief had little need for bad headlines emanating from Panama. There were photos of him meeting with General Manuel Noriega in the 1970s.

Now that it was all but an open secret that the strongman was running a "narco-kleptocracy," his usefulness to Washington had diminished to nil. In February of 1988, after a fourteen-month investigation by the US attorney in Miami, the Justice Department indicted the general for essentially running a cocaine republic. (Just ten years earlier, the DEA publicly praised him for his cooperation.)

Senator John Kerry's massive subcommittee report "Drugs, Terrorism and Foreign Policy" weighed in at four hundred pages, with an additional six-hundred-page appendix. It concluded:

Noriega attempted to manipulate the DEA in Panama by feeding officials cases and providing information leading to arrests and seizures, but which did not affect his drug operations. As a result, the DEA ... ignored Noriega's obvious and ultimately quite public involvement with the Medellín cartel ... In the mid-'80s [our] government did nothing regarding Noriega's drug business and substantial criminal involvement because the first priority was the Contra war.

As prosecutors learned more about Noriega's outsize role in international cocaine finance, the parallel pursuit of the Muchachos shifted to the battlefront of asset forfeiture—where law enforcement seizes property potentially bought with ill-gotten gains, and in effect dares defendants to step forward and prove they were obtained lawfully. If they don't show, they lose. The more they lose, the more they hurt. Willie & Sal Corp., they calculated, had hundreds of millions of dollars to lose.

In 1988, the Feds moved to annex a Miami ranch that they claimed was used by the Boys to coordinate communications via air and sea with their network of smugglers. The US attorney for the Northern District of Florida seized KS&W Offshore Engineering, the Boys' beloved speedboat front upstate in Saint Augustine. Owned by one of their dummy companies in Panama, KS&W was a perfect vehicle to take in and wash enormous amounts of cash: it built custom high-performance engines for the speedboat circuit's most expensive craft. In the process, alleged prosecutors, it had laundered millions in 1980s drug money.

Across the country, the US attorney in Colorado successfully seized a 340-thousand-dollar condominium owned by Falcon and Magluta in the resort town of Vail.

One Muchachos-related property that the Feds wished they didn't have to seize was the the now-defunct Mutiny. For more than three years, Uncle Sam had tried to find a buyer for 2951 South Bayshore Drive. But deal after deal kept falling through. A Coconut Grove ghost walking tour pointed out the twenty-year-old edifice as haunted. There was a massive tab to abate asbestos. Banks were skittish with their financing commitments. The property, now a poster child for the savings-and-loan scandal, was eulogized in *Newsweek*:

> When spectacular cocaine profits first flooded Florida in the early 1980s, the swank bar at the Mutiny Hotel in Coconut Grove seemed like a Chicago speakeasy during Prohibition, a mixture of respectability and underworld. Drug lawyers in cowboy boots mingled with traffickers like businessmen courting new accounts.

"How's this for irony?" added *Fortune*. "The federal government owned a notorious drug den in Miami."

At the turn of the decade, the moldering hotel held an auction of its fixtures from the Carolyn Robbins era. Every last piece of furniture, from the spaceship dashboard in the bed of the Lunar Dreams Suite to the ceiling mirror in the Bordello Room, had to go. Even door numbers were fair game. "One last chance to reflect on the Mutiny's past" was how the *Miami Herald* put it.

Jane Podowski showed up with another former Mutiny girl and promptly snapped up a watercolor of the hotel from Burton Goldberg's old office. There was a brawl over something in one of the rooms—perhaps an ersatz antique lamp. "When we heard the unmistakable sounds of fighting," she said, "we split down the fire stairs, then came out the front lobby." The women saw police cars and ambulances pulling up to the valet circle. Passersby were wagging tongues about a shoot-out at the Mutiny. "We almost died laughing," said Podowski. "What a fitting end to an era."

Actually, it was far from over.

Chapter Forty-four

EMPIRE STRIKES BACK

ONE OF THE Mutiny's last big spenders was José "Coca-Cola" Yero, the Mariel refugee who stuck around the club well into 1985, when his cocaine gang was busted. By 1989, serving a forty-year prison term, Coca-Cola was cooperating to get his sentence reduced. Doing this as an inmate was far safer than doing so in the open.

As Thomas "Hap" Arnold, a boat captain for the Coca-Cola smuggling gang, testified against his fellow smugglers in April of 1986, the girlfriend of one of the defendants ran a finger across her neck. In February of 1989, Arnold was shot and killed outside a North Miami bar. He was supposed to testify in the second leg of the trial, scheduled for that June and called "Son of Yero."

This time around, however, ringleader Coca-Cola Yero and smuggling partner Rene "Raspao" Rodriguez were themselves testifying on behalf of the government. Both were hoping for reduced sentences and keeping a close eye on the pursuit of Willie and Sal.

Meanwhile, though Sal Magluta was still on the lam, his wife pleaded the Fifth nearly five dozen times when a federal prosecutor subpoenaed her for a deposition.

One of the many key figures in the setup of Muchachos Corp. was Juan Acosta, a Miami international attorney who had been recommended to Sal and Willie by Mel Kessler back in 1980. Acosta helped the Boys launder money through their now-seized speedboat front, KS&W Offshore Engineering. Critically, he was their Miami-based fixer in the narco-financial laundering haven that was Panama.

You would think Acosta would have been relieved that his old law partner there, Guillermo "Porky" Endara, was now rumored to be the White House's handpicked man to replace Manuel Noriega. Washington must have done enough due diligence on Endara to be satisfied that his ascendance would not sully President Bush.

But Acosta's fate wasn't purely in the hands of Washington or Panama: in South Florida, Mel Kessler was headed to jail (where he was more likely to talk and implicate Acosta) and the DEA was hot on the trail of Willie and Sal.

In 1988, while Bush was running for president, a federal prosecutor subpoenaed Juan Acosta to testify before and furnish records to a grand jury into the Boys' decade-old cocaine syndicate and its links to Colombia and Panama.

Acosta's lawyer managed to drag out negotiations with the US Attorneys Office well into 1989. In September of that year, just weeks before he was set to finally appear before the grand jury, Acosta got a call from a woman who said she needed help structuring a divorce. The lawyer received her and another man in his office and walked back to his chair. The woman excused herself to use the bathroom.

Acosta looked up to see the man pointing a gun with a silencer at him. Clueless as to what was going on, he frantically offered his wristwatch. To no avail: Acosta took several bullets to the face. His secretary shrieked as the man and woman bolted in two separate getaway cars.

Investigators arrived at the scene of Acosta's murder to find a treasure trove of papers linking the attorney to Guillermo Endara. The new leader of Panama and his law partner had been treasurer and president, respectively, of at least six Muchachos front companies.

Though US authorities didn't realize it at the time, the Colombians had had Juan Acosta killed. Medellín's cocaine cartel was in a full-fledged war with the government of Colombia, killing and bombing police, civilians and public servants until Bogotá took back its vow to extradite the country's drug lords to the US. Acosta's cooperation with the Justice Department could well have given it the damning testimony it needed to connect enough dots to haul South America's biggest cocaine lords to the US.

In October of 1989, Colombian troops arrested Mono Abello, the number four guy in the Medellín cartel, who initiated Muchachos pilot Ralph Linero into cocaine smuggling and brought him to the Mutiny, where he had pioneered the champagne hot tub with fellow Colombian Baruch Vega. Abello was nabbed by cops at a Bogotá restaurant, where authorities noticed his surgically changed appearance. The US had him extradited by month's end.

Medellín hit back hard. That November, Pablo Escobar and a top deputy ordered the downing of a national airliner, Avianca Flight 203. It exploded midair, killing all 107 people on board. Medellín also coordinated a car-bomb attack on the federal intelligence agency in Bogotá that killed more than sixty people and wounded 1,000 others. A Colombian presidential candidate who was supposed to have been aboard the jetliner changed his plans at the last minute.

The Colombian street pushed for unpopular president Virgilio Barco to strike a truce with the drug cartels. He narrowly averted a congressional no-confidence decision on his war against the drug lords.

But President Barco doubled down, siccing his intelligence service on the murderous G. R. Gacha, "the Mexican," Medellín's number three guy. A decade earlier, when Baruch Vega shuttled to Medellín to negotiate on behalf of Colombian smugglers, Gacha presented the fashion photographer and Mutiny emissary with a bucketful of severed human hands. "He was trying to intimidate me," said Vega. "It was his way of doing business."

By 1989, Gacha had a noose dangling over the front lawn of one of his ranches and an estimated net worth of four billion dollars, appearing annually in *Forbes* alongside Pablo Escobar. On December 15, hundreds of Colombian soldiers and policemen surrounded Gacha and his seventeen-year-old son. In the ensuing shoot-out, the father and son were killed, in addition to fifteen bodyguards—on top of the Medellín cartel's number eight guy.

Less than a week later, US troops invaded Panama in Operation Just Cause. As Manuel Noriega went into hiding, Guillermo Endara was sworn in as the new president. While they were being debriefed on a military base, Endara and his old law partner agreed to discuss their involvement in the Muchachos' front companies in exchange for a promise of confidentiality from Washington. Remarked a State Department official: "We took the position that if it turned out Endara did something naughty, he will have to live with it."

It took just weeks for the US to arrest Manuel Noriega and extradite him to Miami. For the first time in history, the American justice system was trying a foreign leader. As *Time* magazine put it, the government would charge him with "turning Panama into the ultimate full-service center for Colombian drug lords, offering everything from secure landing strips and labs to money laundering and passports for dealers on the run."

The DEA only started bringing up successor Endara's past with him months after he took office. *U.S. News & World Report* subsequently observed: "Documents seized after the murder of Endara's American legal colleague, Juan Acosta, alerted federal investigators to the role of Endara's law firm just about the time that the Bush administration made the decision to invade Panama."

Up in Miami, Manuel Noriega was kept segregated in an enormous cell at MCC, which was by then a who's who/*This Is Your Life* for 1980s drug and arms smugglers. Officially considered a prisoner of war under international conventions, Panama's former "Maximum Leader" was warehoused in the MCC's "Dictator Suite," two-room quarters where he took in telenovelas on a small TV and blew his fifty-dollar-a-month commissary stipend on Oreo cookies. Late at night, after lights-out, the little general would be accompanied by several armed guards for his lone daily taste of freedom: a walk around the lake at the middle of the penitentiary.

The US government would allege that Noriega, its longtime ally in Central America, took nearly five million dollars in drug payoffs into the mid-1980s, precisely as Washington was ramping up its War on Drugs.

Dopers in Miami who had been ripped off by the general quipped that the real figure must have been multiples as much.

Chapter Forty-five

A BUSTED FRATERNITY

JORGE VALDES, THE Muchachos' original connection to both the Mutiny and Medellín, had spent much of the eighties in and out of marriages and prisons, as his cocaine-dealing prowess faded. By the turn of the decade, on parole, having found Jesus Christ and on the verge of marrying his third wife, he was touring the country to check out prize horses.

Still, Valdes said, he had a heavy heart for his original Colombian mentor, cocaine kingpin Manuel Garces, who had been nabbed in February and flown to the US. Bogotá had so far extradited fourteen drug lords.

But it also gave him more than a chuckle to see Manuel Noriega, his betrayer and torturer, seized and smeared by the US military. As the *New York Times* wrote shortly after Christmas: "The United States military headquarters here, which has portrayed Gen. Manuel Antonio Noriega as an erratic, cocaine-snorting dictator who prays to voodoo gods, announced today that the deposed leader wore red underwear and availed himself of prostitutes."

Traveling to a horse show in Illinois, Valdes and his fiancée were mysteriously pulled over by state troopers who checked his license and did nothing. He assumed he was being ethnically profiled by a rural cop.

The next day at the show, Valdes felt paranoid. Though he had been out of the cocaine business for a few years, he could not help but notice a bunch of serious-looking white men in the crowd constantly staring at him. Most weren't wearing hats or boots.

Valdes's filly won the show. As he was celebrating the victory, a large man tapped him on the shoulder and brandished his badge. "United States Marshal!" he yelled. "You're under arrest."

While Valdes was led to a holding cell at the county jail, the DEA ransacked his hotel room.

Though he'd had no dealings with Willie and Sal for a decade, Valdes, it turns out, was still hugely valuable to the many authorities now pursuing his old pals. He could help the Feds map the beginnings of their "continuing criminal enterprise"—and, in a best-case scenario, testify against the ringleaders when (if?) they were hauled into court.

Valdes was transported to a courthouse and interrogated by a panoply of Florida-based law enforcement officials, spanning the FBI, Customs, the DEA and the IRS. They asked about his ranch in central Florida, and the corrupt father-son sheriffs in Clewiston he and other cocaine smugglers had kept on their payroll for a decade, allegedly to look the other way as they moved tons of cocaine.

Back down in Miami, sometime after midnight on June 1, 1990, a Colombian hit squad placed a bomb in a van belonging to Tony

Posada, a cocaine-dealing chum who had worked with Willie and Sal. Shortly after Posada's wife turned the key and pulled out of their driveway to head to work, the bomb blew a door off the van. Though the blast shattered windows across their block, Mrs. Posada survived largely unhurt.

Elsewhere in town, a Corvette that belonged to the sister of Hector Valdez, another Muchachos friend and associate, was stolen and set ablaze; Valdez received telephone threats.

In July, a federal grand jury in northern Florida indicted Sal Magluta and Willie Falcon as fugitives, charging them in absentia with conspiring to launder cocaine profits between 1979 and 1985.

That November, Juan "Recotado" Barroso, the Boys' trusty speedboat navigator, was arrested and charged with dumping 249 kilos of cocaine from a disabled boat near Fort Lauderdale. He told police he was a car mechanic. But they already knew Recotado was for years responsible for smuggling boatloads of cocaine from the Bahamas to South Florida after Ralph Linero and other Muchachos pilots flew the stuff up from Colombia. The Feds now had another potential cooperating witness behind bars.

Quitting cocaine and not having dealings with the Boys since the disco days offered no legal cover to Jorge Valdes. The government was targeting Muchachos Corp. as a "continuing criminal enterprise": since the Boys were smuggling into the present, founding Muchacho Valdes was still criminally on the hook, even if he had last sold drugs years earlier.

It seemed unfair and harsh. But Valdes had little recourse. He accepted a prosecutor's offer to trade all his money and property for reduced time in prison. He pleaded guilty to the government's charges, and received a sentence of ten years.

Inside MCC, Valdes bumped into "Mutiny Mel" Kessler, his onetime defense attorney and the lawyer who represented Willie and Sal during their fateful 1980 no-contest plea. Kessler had just been sentenced to thirty years for laundering drug money. A decade earlier, when Valdes was sentenced for the bust in Panama, he had learned that Kessler had betrayed him to the DEA in order to get the Feds off his scent. Though Kessler looked horrified to reunite with Valdes behind bars, the former client said he hugged his old attorney, praised Christ and told him he forgave him.

DEA agent David Borah, the Muchachos' chief pursuer, paid Valdes a jailhouse visit. Channeling a nonthreatening "good cop," he introduced himself and calmly explained that he knew about Valdes's long-since-lapsed ties to his childhood pals Sal and Willie. What Borah now needed was information that could lead to the capture of the ringleaders.

Naturally, Valdes's cooperation could get his time behind bars slashed. Old prison sentences meant nothing. (Ask cocaine kingpin extraordinaire Carlene Quesada, who in 1985 was sentenced to forty years in jail by an LA judge, but was out by 1990 for cooperating.)

Valdes said that he felt a Christian affinity toward both Borah and David Odom, another DEA agent who had visited him earlier and welled up at news that this nefarious kingpin had turned to Jesus. He even wrote a Christian poem in their honor. So, as Valdes described it in his autobiography, *Coming Clean*: "Keeping my promise to God meant breaking my word to my good friend Sal, something I had never done before."

When an attorney representing Willie and Sal showed up two days later to see what Valdes had dished to the DEA, the inmate waxed noncommittal, insisting he was good with God now—and that was all that mattered. (Serving a life sentence, and then some,

Muchachos lieutenant Justo Jay was also invoking God—but instead to justify his unwillingness to testify against his friends.)

The Feds then upped the stakes by trapping "the Deer." In January of 1991, Bernardo "Venao" Gonzalez Jr., the Muchachos' head of Caribbean operations, pleaded guilty to drug and tax fraud charges. Facing life in prison, he got a fourteen-year sentence and, in exchange for the prospect of more leniency, agreed to cooperate in the government's unfolding case against the rest of the Muchachos.

At the MCC, Venao agonized over this decision with Carlos Ruiz, the fellow smuggler who used to help him in the rough waters between Miami and the Bahamas and send him drinks upstairs at the Mutiny. "I think I'm going to do this," he said, looking out at the lake at the center of the prison.

"You do what you have to do," said Ruiz. "Just don't bear false witness, you know?"

Chapter Forty-six

UNDERCOVER SAL

YOU WILL RECALL Owen Band, the Boston University salutatorian who went rogue in Miami and became a small-time doper after he didn't get into Harvard Law. Back when cocaine practically poured down from the vents at the Mutiny, he was in clover. When the Muchachos lorded it over the club's Upper Deck, the nice Jewish kid got kilos on consignment—"Whatever, man, name your terms"— which he then larded up with various store-bought powders, en route to banking on all the rich kids up in Manhattan and Long Island. He would count his blessings while ogling Morgan Fairchild's backside at Studio 54.

At his peak, Band was bringing in a couple of million dollars a year in cash. "I never looked at the prices on a menu," he said. "I had the best cars. The best women. I can't believe I lucked into that."

But failing health, chronic depression and a 1988 car crash that nearly flatlined him in the ER pretty much derailed his budding cocaine career. It didn't help matters that cocaine had since blanketed New York while Willie and Sal, his ultimate benefactors, were now far more cautious about whom they were supplying.

Glass half-full, though, he was lucky to have been a runt dealer who had been out of the business at a time when the Feds could have snagged him in their sprawling hunt for the Muchachos. Jorge Valdes, the other honor student at the Mutiny, was not as fortunate.

Sometime in 1991, Band, still limping from his car accident, finally mustered the strength to go clubbing again. By then, Miami's nightlife scene had shifted across the bay from the abandoned Mutiny, Ensign Bitters and their Coconut Grove like to South Beach. Long a warren of efficiencies for dying snowbirds, south Miami Beach was now enjoying its Art Deco revival, with new restaurants, dance clubs and boutique hotels drawing national attention. There was serious talk that Studio 54 cofounder Ian Shrager was going to restore a 1940s hotel there.

Band went to Club Nu, a consistently packed South Beach joint that was throwing a costume party. He figured he might bump into an ex–Mutiny girl who helped manage the club. That night, shortly after getting past the bouncer and surveying the scene, he thought he was hallucinating when he witnessed Sal Magluta, flanked by three bodyguards, walking in dressed as Zorro. "What the fuck is he thinking?" he thought to himself.

Dismayed looks across the club echoed that emotion. "Everyone knew it was Sal," he said. "It was common knowledge the Feds were after him. The room was astonished to see him. You heard the whispers: 'Sal is crazy to be here, bro.'" Women in masks were mouthing, "Oh. My. God."

While strobe lights flashed and booming bass shook the big venue, Band watched as Magluta and his heavies ascended to the club's elevated glassed-in VIP section. It all seemed to transpire in slow motion. Or it felt like a hallucination.

He felt revved enough to do a bump of coke in the VIP bathroom. Using the white stuff, he said, still gave him desperately needed confidence and a sense of escapism, reminding him of the old days with Bernie at the Mutiny.

Tonight, the mere thought of blow gave him enough audacity to head upstairs and follow Magluta, the fugitive, into the men's room. As soon as Band opened the door, one of Magluta's bodyguards blocked him and kicked his steel-tipped shoe in between Band's legs, splitting them apart to check for a gun or knife in an ankle holster. It was a move you were taught in police academy.

"No!" exclaimed Magluta, looking up from the sink mirror. "No! He's cool."

Had Owen Band already been in jail and needed to talk, or had some other small-time dealer ratted him out to the DEA, he could have been called to testify against the Muchachos. After all, it was their Caribbean operations chief, Bernie "Venao" Gonzalez, who had brought Band upstairs at the Mutiny that night to recuit him as a distributor.

In June 1990, Venao's West Miami home was firebombed. Rusty unexploded grenades were later found in the front yard. The following January, Venao pleaded guilty to drug running and tax evasion and agreed to assist prosecutors in their pursuit of his bosses.

Gonzalez cooperating with the Feds, said fellow powerboat aficionado T. R. Cimino, "was when you knew that the Boys' fraternity was fractured, irrevocably. The government broke them up."

"You started hearing that the prosecutors were looking pretty much for anyone who had hung out with them at the Mutiny," said Nelson Aguilar. "There's no honor among thieves," he said. "When they told everyone they were going to get forty years, it became snitch time." He said he was miffed that in spite of this tightening noose, Sal Magluta was still making cameos in South Beach. "When you're the most wanted man in Miami? Please."

On the inside, inmate Venao lobbied to flip other jailed affiliates over to the government's side. "He went state's witness and broke in a lot of other cooperators," said Cimino.

Another enthusiastic inmate was José "Coca-Cola" Yero. Hustling overtime to shave down his forty-year sentence, the Mariel refugee made a prison call to his coconspirator, Nancy "Big Blonde" Mira, who had been behind bars since 1989. He exhorted her to "jump on the bus"—prisoner speak for cooperating with the government to buy a reduced sentence. He told Mira that her ex-boyfriend, Rene "Raspao" Rodriguez, serving twenty years, was already talking.

"Back me up," he urged her, via prison phone, explaining that the DEA was willing to go to bat for their old smuggling crew for cooperating in the pursuit of Los Muchachos.

"No way I was jumping on the bus," she told him. "My feet are staying on the ground." She ultimately served four years.

"We never did nothing with Willie and Sal," said Super Papi Becerra, Coca-Cola's coconspirator, who was serving a twenty-year sentence. Coca-Cola pressed him, too, and FBI and DEA agents visited him to seek his cooperation in the case against the Muchachos. "Everybody should jump on the bus!" blared Coca-Cola into the prison phone headset to Super Papi.

Super Papi told the agents he could lie if they offered him leniency. They packed their pads and pens and left.

"They're traitors, all of them," said Becerra. "They wanted to get their time off. Even if I wanted to cooperate, I knew nothing about Willie and Sal."

"It was like open recruitment for informants," said Juan Cid. "People who had nothing to do with cases would just get debriefed and would rehearse. The Feds encouraged it."

High-priced attorneys for the Muchachos visited Super Papi Becerra. Would he testify for Willie and Sal against untruthful government witnesses? "I would," he said, "but I got my own problems, you know? Why don't you give me money to help me out?"

They, too, passed.

"I could have been their savior," he said. "I could go in front of the judge and say none of these fuckers worked with them."

The Feds opted to go full bore with what they already had, including the cooperation of Coca-Cola, Raspao and Venao. It all culminated in a sweeping twenty-four-count indictment handed down in April of 1991. The list of the accused read like a Mutiny reunion:

United States vs.
Augusto Guillermo Falcon
    aka Willie Falcon
    aka Wilfred Fernandez
Salvador Magluta
    aka Sal
    aka Santiago Mendez
    aka Angelo Maretto
Orlando Begnino Lorenzo
    aka Bennie B
Juan Adriano Barroso
    aka Recotado
Luis Escobedo
    aka Witchie . . .

 ... Louis Mendez
 aka Pegy
Gustavo Falcon
 aka Taby

The government alleged that the Muchachos Corp. conspiracy had made north of two billion dollars since 1978—and indeed went out of its way to spell out the ill-gotten gains with three commas: $2,130,871,500. For perspective: that was 68 thousand kilos of cocaine brought into the country since 1978, when Sal Magluta first hesitated to take Jorge Valdes's thirty-kilo consignment.

Cabeza Linero and Justo Jay were already in jail, having pleaded guilty years earlier and refusing to cooperate. Notably absent from this list was associate Bernardo "Venao" Gonzalez, who was already helping the Feds behind the scenes. When the indictment was unsealed a month later, Recotado Barroso and another defendant, Tony Garrudo, were arrested without incident.

Of course, one gaping hole remained in the Feds' case: they still had to find Willie and Sal.

Chapter Forty-seven

SUNRISE, SUNSET

AUTHORITIES CALLED IT Operation Sunrise. On October 15, 1991, a special assault team of two dozen men with heavy machinery and access to boats and air surveillance surrounded a *Miami Vice* set–like mansion on La Gorce Island, an ultraexclusive enclave in Miami Beach. A few hours earlier, US Marshals had watched as a guy who looked like Orlando "Benny B" Lorenzo—number three on the Muchachos indictment—drove up to the house.

Behind the scenes and behind bars, Venao prevailed upon indicted coconspirator Louis "Pegy" Mendez to draw a map of Magluta and crew's approximate whereabouts. When Venao handed the sheet to marshals, they looked blindsided: Sal and the other fugitives were pretty much right across the causeway from downtown Miami, where federal prosecutors had handed down their forty-four-page indictment.

Authorities quietly idled a speedboat in the waterway behind the mansion and readied tear gas canisters and a police helicopter.

It had been raining most of the day. At sundown, several cops and special agents finally approached the house and yelled for hands up. Though various occupants scattered and tried to bolt out the sides of the mansion, they were all apprehended within minutes. La Gorce Island teemed with police dogs and armed agents, with choppers and speedboats at the ready to nab any escapees.

One of the marshals showed the men Sal Magluta's photo and asked if anyone had seen him. When everyone kept a poker face, cops called for Magluta to come out of the house with his arms above his head.

Silence.

They lobbed in tear gas. Magluta jumped out of a window on the second floor. The agents thought they heard something and unleashed their baying German shepherds. Almost instantly, a man started howling. They ran to the north end of the mansion, where Magluta, wearing just underwear, was frantically trying to get a canine's jaws off his bloodied wrist. He was cuffed after paramedics treated his wounds.

While checking out Magluta's mansion, the sting team found papers that contained Willie Falcon's address—twenty-five miles up the road in Fort Lauderdale. They showed up a few hours later and he surrendered without incident. The Feds noted finding a bar of solid gold that he was using as a paperweight.

Sal Magluta's seized notes alluded to the Muchachos selling more cocaine in just three years—120 thousand pounds—than in the entire preceding decade. Theirs was by far the East Coast's biggest cocaine ring to date, and one of the largest in the world.

IN PRISON, VENAO—the slick deer who could not be caught on the seas or in sport—became an advocate for plea bargains. He wrote

Magluta and Falcon, his fellow Miami High dropouts, and urged them to plead guilty and negotiate fines and sentences.

At the same time, Venao hedged his bets by urging other drug runners who had crossed paths with him and the Boys to cut their own deals and testify against the ringleaders.

Chapter Forty-eight

BLOODY 'NINETY-TWO

IN FEBRUARY 1992, Alina Falcon, Willie's wife, wrote a letter to the *Miami New Times*, which was covering the government's case against the Muchachos:

> Willie and Sal's case is based on government information received from convicted informants who are bargaining for a reduction in their prison sentences. Specifically, Mr. Ray Corona, a very unreliable source who is presently serving time, is cooperating and supplying the government with false information to reduce the length of his prison term.
>
> Your article also states that Willie and Sal were drug dealers in high school. This is a false statement.
>
> Prosecutor Ken Bell states that Augusto Jay has a perverted sense of honor. On the contrary, Justo Jay, in his refusal to assist the government, has displayed courage and a strong sense of character. Justo fully understands the high price he has had to pay

*for his decision not to cooperate with the government in exchange
for a lighter sentence. It is my opinion that this commitment
toward friendship is rare and, indeed, should be admired.*

*It is a shame that the government has had to revert to cheap
bargaining in order to make their cases stronger. If this is the
way the US government operates, this is not justice. Whatever
happened to the democratic principle that one is innocent until
proven guilty?*

*Finally, it is my opinion that the media, including your
publication, have distorted the facts regarding this case to
achieve your own sensationalistic purpose.*

*Alina Falcon (Mrs. Willie Falcon)
Miami*

August 6, 1992. While her husband was in jail awaiting trial,
Alina Falcon drove her tan Jaguar to a posh beauty salon in Coral
Gables, a stone's throw from Coconut Grove. She got out of the car
to run inside for some bottles of shampoo.

On the way out of the parlor, she was jumped by two men who
lunged for her handbag. Falcon snatched it back and made a run
for her car. One of the assailants then shot her in the face through
the window. After the other wrested back her purse, both men fled
in a getaway car.

Willie Falcon was taken to his wife's burial in shackles and flanked
by prison marshals. He sobbed. Tatico Martinez, the Mutiny's resident armed robber, crossed paths with Falcon in a penitentiary in
Atlanta. He tried to cheer up the ashen-looking inmate with old
tales about the Mutiny and how he had ripped off Ray Corona and
even Johnny Hernandez.

"Willie," he said, "was devastated about Alina. He loved her very much." Tatico says the widower used coke heavily on the inside; he had guards at his beck and call.

During his twenty-four years in jail, Tatico Martinez also roomed with Coca-Cola Yero. They hit it off, with the Marielito always reminiscing about his meteoric rise and fall in Miami. "He compared himself to *Scarface*," said Martinez. "'One minute, I'm on the streets, you know? The next thing I know, I'm getting fifteen hundred dollars a kilo to move a boat two hours to Bimini. The next day I'm driving a fucking Benz up to the Mutiny and ordering Dom for everyone!'"

Martinez said that unlike Justo Jay and Ralph Linero, Coca-Cola did not subscribe to any sort of exile code of honor; he hadn't fled Castro's prisons and risked the treacherous Mariel boatlift—then, in Miami, shark-infested smuggling waters and the barrel of a gun from jilted dealers—to spend forty years in the pen. No—he would testify against Willie and Sal and take his chances. "I can either die in here or out there," he would say.

As the US Justice Department zeroed in on Colombia's cocaine cartels and their American syndicates, a posse of hit men snuck up across the Mexican border and into Florida to take out suspected government witnesses. In Miami, they cased targets.

In January 1992, Lazaro "Tattoo" Cruz, a doper with some 1980s Muchachos ties, was shot outside his home in Hialeah as he opened his front door. He took a bullet but ran back inside and survived six more shots through the door.

In late August, Juan "Recotado" Barroso, out on bond, was with his seven-year-old son at a gas station in west Dade County. Reco was machine-gunned by a group of men. Seven bullets pierced his abdomen and back. "Don't shoot!" pleaded the boy, while his father bled atop him.

Though Reco had succeeded in shielding his son from bullets as they made a run for the convenience store, they couldn't get inside after the terrified attendant locked the door. Both survived.

The gunmen then drove to the hospital where Louis "Pegy" Mendez, the youngest gun in the indictment, and the guy who drew that map for US Marshals, was with his wife in the delivery ward while out on bond. The hit men waited in the parking lot. But when the new father never emerged, they lost their nerve and sped off.

When Venao was sprung loose in November of 1992—having served less than four years—he confessed to his attorney and parents: "I'm a marked man." Still, he refused witness protection, despite unsuccessful appeals to his probation officer to let him carry a gun. The government's trial against Willie and Sal was slated to start in a year and Venao, their head of Caribbean operations, would be a pivotal witness.

He still tried to prevail on the ringleaders to cut a deal. "Hey, guys, the prosecutors have a lot against you," Venao urged them, in calls and letters. "They have me, and I know a lot. You have to make a deal. It's your only way out."

But Falcon and Magluta blanched at the government's demands. Though prosecutors were alleging a more-than-two-billion-dollar conspiracy over a decade, the men were only willing to pay twenty to forty million dollars and serve about a decade in prison.

So they dug in their heels and resolved to go to trial. "Sal and Willie were cash cows for private investigators and the criminal defense bar," said attorney John Mattes. "They were never going to come to Jesus. You didn't need an exit strategy, they must have thought. You could buy anything."

Mattes says he was blown away by the freedom of movement and visitation Magluta and Falcon enjoyed at the fairly low-key MCC facility, where Mattes was now the government's cooperation point man for figures like Pegy, Coca-Cola and George Morales.

He said he witnessed a constant procession of supposed attorneys and paralegals visiting with rolls of quarters for the vending machines. They would come in shifts, including gorgeous women in spiked heels and black miniskirts going into rooms with them that guards never looked into. "It was absurd," he said. "You realized there were so many levels of the game they could play."

One of the paralegals was Magluta's longtime mistress Marilyn Bonachea, who was in charge of his financial affairs and kept a ledger of payoffs from concealed stacks of cash and offshore accounts. When it handed down its indictment, the government had frozen the Muchachos' known assets, from property to boats to bank accounts. In the six months leading to their capture, they scrambled to hide their money and line up rainy-day reserves.

In 1992, when Magluta was being held in MCC, Bonachea was arranging payoffs to fellow inmates who took special care of the kingpin. One example: during an unannounced shakedown search, a cellmate was busted hiding a small mobile phone in his shoe. He ate thirty days of solitary confinement, refusing to admit that the phone was Magluta's.

When the young inmate emerged from the hole, he learned that his mother had been given the keys to a Nissan Maxima. Moreover, someone had put money in his prison commissary account, as well as those of friends he had made behind bars. Magluta, through his mistress paralegal, had also arranged to front money to a Miami criminal defense attorney who would appeal the man's cocaine conviction. For good measure, he paid for the funeral of the inmate's father and got cash to his kids' mother to buy them Christmas gifts. For his help, the inmate and his family collected 82 thousand dollars in all.

On the outside, it was still open season on Muchachos affiliates who had agreed to help the government.

Bernie "Venao" Gonzalez's bodyguard was Mario Ortiz, who'd headed security at the Mutiny a decade earlier after Fernando Puig was killed and Burton Goldberg sold to new owners. He pleaded with Venao to hang low now that he was out on bond, what with what had happened to Juan Acosta and what had very nearly happened to Recotado and his little boy. At Venao's family ranch in west Dade County horse country, Ortiz installed an elaborate closed-circuit camera system, including a panoply of monitors in the kitchen.

The bodyguard was annoyed that Venao's mother would often watch soaps at full blast in another room, when she should have been cognizant of what was going on over the surveillance screens.

Venao, for his part, was annoyed that Ortiz was always so worried. "Relax, bro," he would tell him, grinning. "You're always seeing ghosts everywhere."

Chapter Forty-nine

THE HIT LIST

In April of 1993, a rather unprecedented ad appeared in *The Champion*, a popular trade publication for the criminal-defense-attorney set that also made its way into prisons.

Placed by the six power attorneys representing Falcon and Magluta—one of whom had represented mob boss John Gotti—the ad read: "Information Wanted." It listed the names of thirty-one potential witnesses in the mega drug case, including Coca-Cola Yero, Bernardo "Venao" Gonzalez, Rene "Raspao" Rodriguez, Pegy Mendez, Recotado Barroso, the Boys' former pilot Jack Devoe (owner of their front company Devoe Airlines at Miami–Opa Locka Executive Airport) and even Johnny Hernandez, the Mutiny doper who appeared in two episodes of *Miami Vice*.

Hernandez, who had been in jail since 1989, said federal prosecutors visited him after they handed down their Muchachos indictment. "I only partied with Willie and Sal at the Mutiny," he said. "I didn't do business with them." He thought that he might have been included on the list because he had been involved with some of the Muchachos's ex-girlfriends and ex-mistresses. In prison, Hernandez was cuffed and placed in isolation—"for my protection"—when the list came out.

Two months after the ad was first published, Venao and his brother Humberto were contacted by a group of men who claimed to be interested in buying their fishing boat. They arranged to meet at the Gonzalez family ranch in West Miami.

Though bodyguard Mario Ortiz warned Venao that it looked like a trap, he ignored him. "*Mahito*," he said, over and over, "I'm telling you: you are seeing ghosts everywhere. Chill. Just chill."

On June 23, the prospective buyers arrived to find Venao's brother Humberto outside the house. They rushed him, tackled him and pushed him into the garage, where they tied him up and taped his mouth shut in anticipation of his brother's arrival. Their mother was busy watching soaps, oblivious to all this going down on the screens of the surveillance monitors in the kitchen.

After half an hour, Venao himself drove up to the house in his blue Jeep Cherokee. As he lowered the driver's window and opened the door, he took several bullets and died immediately. The hit team then returned to the garage to shoot his brother before speeding off. He later died at the hospital.

Venao, his beard perfectly sculpted, was wearing shades when his bullet-riddled corpse was photographed for the papers.

"They're animals!" yelled their sobbing father, his body shaking with anger on the evening news. "They're cold-blooded assassins!"

Days later, one of the gunmen was watching television when footage of Willie and Sal in orange prison suits appeared. Pointing at the screen, he told his girlfriend that the Boys "now had to pay the office" for the death of Venao. "Snitches," he said, "end up dying by squashing. Flies don't come into a closed mouth." The hit man fled back to Colombia the next day.

Carlos Ruiz, the Muchachos' old pal, couldn't believe Venao was hit. "He was a jet-setter. Slick. Hard to catch," he said. "Six foot tall. Beautiful girls, always. They never should have killed him. You do not kill a cop, an agent or a witness. You just don't. Plus, what does it mean to kill six out of dozens of witnesses in that ad?"

"Sal got crazy," he said. "He got obsessed with beating the US government. But no illicit organization ultimately beats the government."

Tatico Martinez, then serving hard time, said he was surprised at all the news of the Muchachos murders. "Willie and Sal were nonviolent," he said. "*I* was violent. Very violent. 'Damn,' I thought, 'these guys have gone hard.' You corner a dog and it will bite you."

"They believe the way to fix these affairs is to get the witnesses out of the way," target Coca-Cola Yero told the *Miami Herald*. He said Willie Falcon confronted him in June 1993 in a courthouse hallway. "He was out of control. He said to me this is something personal between me and him. He said, 'I'm going to get you, wherever you go.'"

When the *New York Times* featured the hit list later in October, it was revealed that shortly after Venao's murder, a lead defense attorney received a call from a man who told him that one of the thirty-one listed people was then in the federal witness protection program. For a price, the caller offered to tell him the guy's new identity and location.

INMATES WERE JOKING that the Boys had hunted a deer—now they were going to pop open a Coca-Cola.

Two years had now passed since Sal and Willie had been captured.

Key witnesses were dead. Despite the government's seemingly prohibitive freeze on their assets, the Boys were retaining the country's most expensive criminal defense attorneys and paying off all manner of accomplices inside and outside the prison system. CBS News was calling the prosecutor's office about the hit list in *The Champion*.

The "Drug Trial of the Century," as it was being called in Miami, was nowhere close to starting.

Back down in Colombia, Pablo Escobar's Medellín cartel was in tatters, having seen eighty members killed by government security forces. The competing Cali cartel was taking market share. In November 1991, Carlos Lehder, one of Escobar's top deputies, a guy who loved the Mutiny, was on the stand in Miami, testifying in the government's trial against Manuel Noriega.

Escobar himself was on the lam, having escaped a year earlier from a luxury prison that he had built and staffed after turning himself in in June of 1991. Escobar had been listed by *Forbes* as the planet's seventh richest man, and made the list of international billionaires for seven years straight.

He was somehow worth thirty billion dollars, very little of which he could enjoy while he ran from the several thousand troops and agents the government had dedicated to his capture.

On Thursday, December 2, 1993, hundreds of police and soldiers surrounded his suspected Medellín hideout, which they homed in on through a phone call they traced with US technology. The "Godfather of Cocaine" had just turned forty-four a day earlier.

They spotted their target, who tried to escape on the roof. After a twenty-minute shoot-out, troops proudly posed for photos with Escobar's bloodied corpse.

Chapter Fifty

MIAMI'S TRIAL OF
THE CENTURY

"*Los Estados vs. Los Muchachos*," as the government's case was nicknamed, finally got under way in October 1995, fully four years after Willie and Sal were captured. Three potential prosecution witnesses were dead. Another two had been injured in shootings. By comparison, O. J. Simpson's murder case, the concurrent legal spectacle, took just sixteen months from arrest to verdict. The Boys and the NFL Hall of Famer used to bump into each other at the Mutiny.

The Muchachos' legal saga was so big that *60 Minutes* sent Steve Kroft to Miami to cover its spate of witness assassinations and that supposed hit list. The piece aired with the headline "It Pays to Advertise."

"Swans don't swim in sewers," a prosecutor told Kroft about the government's cultivation of witnesses. "If you're going to go down in the sewer to catch a drug dealer, you're going to have to use the kind of bird that swims around down there."

The security measures at the Boys' downtown Miami trial were extraordinary and unprecedented. More than a dozen armed marshals were posted inside the tenth-floor courtroom and the hallway leading to it. All visitors had to clear a metal detector in the lobby and then another one as they got out of the elevator upstairs.

Prosecutors were up against what was being billed as a dream team of the defense bar, led by Roy Black, who had successfully defended William Kennedy Smith against rape charges, and Albert Krieger, the masterful cross-examiner who repped Gambino mob boss John Gotti. Another lawyer had argued before the Supreme Court.

The *Miami New Times'* Jim DeFede billed it as "the last great drug trial of the Cocaine Cowboys eighties . . . a drama that has taken nearly two decades to produce."

Despite all the government witnesses and the supposedly damning evidence collected from Willie and Sal's compounds, conviction was no foregone conclusion. "One element missing from this trial," wrote DeFede, "is a victim. Prosecutors are unable to show a cause-and-effect relationship between the thousands of pounds of cocaine they claim Falcon and Magluta smuggled into the US and the havoc that cocaine wrought in people's lives . . . [They] can't hold up a snapshot of a newborn baby, for instance, and assert that it was born an addict . . . because the mother abused cocaine imported by Falcon and Magluta."

In his opening statement, prosecutor Chris Clark declared: "May I present to you the case of the United States of America versus Augusto Guillermo Falcon and Salvador Magluta. Willie and Sal. *Los Muchachos*. The Boys." He stepped aside and gestured to give the jury an unobstructed view of the ringleaders.

"So well-known in the drug community were these two individuals," he remarked, "that among fellow drug dealers the mere mention of the name 'the Boys' or 'los Muchachos' indicated to those in the drug trade the biggest drug dealers in Miami during the nineteen eighties."

The defense team countered that the Boys had long ago (April 1980) ditched the cocaine business. In its zeal to nail Willie and Sal, they argued, the government overinvested in the testimony of career criminals serving long terms whose only hope for leniency was a manufactured snitch. Star witness Jorge Valdes himself would say he'd had no contact with them since he was double-crossed by General Manuel Noriega and shipped to prison in 1980.

The government was using his testimony to contend that his late-seventies initiation of his childhood friends into cocaine trafficking launched a continuing criminal enterprise—the likes of which Willie and Sal used to haul in nearly half a billion dollars in the three years leading up to their 1991 capture. "They stood at the top of the drug trade and lived like kings," said Clark, "spending untold amounts on prostitutes, speedboats and Rolls-Royces."

The lead defense attorney opened by excoriating the government's dependence on the testimony of the Muchachos' friends and associates. He singled out the example of Jorge Valdes, whose cooperation with prosecutors chopped more than a decade off his fifteen-year sentence. "He got the benefits he bargained for," argued attorney Martin Weinberg. "Every other prisoner saw him as their ideal." He further alleged that Valdes had leaned on fellow prisoners to jump on the bus.

By now, Willie and Sal looked like hulls of their former hard-partying selves. Magluta was now bald and had an ulcer. Falcon, mourning his slain wife throughout three years of prison transfers, looked uncharacteristically menacing. A defense psychiatrist testified to the mental toll exacted by spending endless hours in prison isolation, awaiting trial: "I've become a barbarian," court documents quoted Falcon as saying. "I don't use the exercise equipment in the day room. I want to be lonely again. I can't stand all these people. . . . I feel a sense of insecurity, like my mind's not strong anymore. I feel like I'm inside a shell."

Willie's brother and codefendant, Gustavo "Taby" Falcon, was on the lam; the producers of TV's *America's Most Wanted* were calling around about the fugitive. Which only added to his and his parents' anguish.

In an echo of the Tick-Talks hearings of 1982, when Monkey Morales greeted all the tablemates he was betraying, Willie and Sal now had to face their old Mutiny pals turned informants, including Coca-Cola Yero and Rene "Raspao" Rodriguez. And, of course, Jorge Valdes, the childhood pal who had started them in the biz.

On his way out of prison recently, Valdes had felt the huge satisfaction of passing by inmate Manuel Noriega, his original betrayer. They made eye contact; Noriega's trademark acne scars looked even worse now that he had lost skin color behind bars. "He looked like an animal in a cage," said Valdes, who thought back to the broomstick episode, torture and double cross that ultimately broke him apart from Willie and Sal.

He admitted that part of him wanted to bark a "How you like me now, motherfucker?!" to Noriega (not that Noriega would necessarily remember him; more than fifteen years had passed since their lurid rendezvous in Panama). But Valdes said he remembered his pact with Christ.

Plus, he was grateful that he was not in Willie's and Sal's shoes. They were both facing life in prison.

A free man since April, Valdes took in the Muchachos developments in the morning papers and the evening news. He thought it more than a bit surreal how everything that started off so innocently—"so high-society Mutiny"—back in the late 1970s devolved into this mass funeral for this brotherhood of exile boys.

"It was just bootlegging," he said. "We were kids in a bubble making more than we could ever imagine. We were poor immigrants suddenly among the rich and famous in Coconut Grove."

Valdes's conversion was pilloried by defense attorneys.

"The core of the case, what it all boils down to, is whether you trust their witnesses," Martin Weinberg said to begin his opening statement, ". . . [who] have learned—as cunning criminals, as experienced criminals, as very intelligent people—how to avoid the consequences of their career of crime . . . [pointing] false fingers of accusation at Sal Magluta and Willie Falcon."

Jorge Valdes, he argued, "is out of jail today, in four and a half years, because DEA agent David Borah and Chris Clark went to bat for him. They rewarded him for his cooperation. And every other prisoner, every other drug trafficker who will take the stand, knows what happened to Jorge Valdes. He is their ideal. His sentence, his cut, his breaks, his ability to avoid the consequences of what he did, is what motivates ten and twenty and thirty of the government witnesses. And again, they are the foundation of this prosecution."

Mel Kessler, the Muchachos' longtime attorney now serving a thirty-year sentence for laundering drug money, was rumored to be cooperating with the prosecution behind the scenes. Mutiny banker Ray Corona, sentenced to twenty years in jail in 1987, told the DEA's David Borah that he had laundered for the Muchachos syndicate. He was released from prison in June of 1993.

After Valdes, the prosecution called Earl "the Preacher" Dyess Jr., the former sheriff of Hendry County, Florida, who was serving eighteen years for drug smuggling. In 1979, before he went to jail, Jorge Valdes introduced Dyess's late father to Willie and Sal. They agreed to pay the officials to leave them alone when they flew their planes in and out of their ranch near Lake Okeechobee in central Florida.

"It didn't take me but a minute to figure out that [Valdes] had to be in the drug business," the former sheriff testified. "He had a lot of gold on him and he drove a somewhat flashy car. He was somewhat of a flashy fellow himself."

Valdes was in jail when the cocaine sorties started in 1980. Dyess Jr. testified that Falcon and Magluta picked up where their old pal left off. By looking the other way while dozens of flights full of cocaine and cash landed at the Clewiston ranch, Dyess Jr. said he pocketed 354 thousand dollars for a little more than a year's work. (By late 1981, Willie, Sal and crew had shifted primarily to speedboating cocaine to South Florida from the Bahamas.)

During his cross-examination, defense attorney Martin Weinberg pounced on the slow-speaking sheriff.

"You were a corrupt sheriff, were you not?" he asked.

"I was a crooked sheriff," Dyess responded.

"What is your definition of a bad sheriff?" Weinberg asked.

"I can say a good one is one that doesn't break the law," Dyess answered. "And a bad one is sitting right here."

In January of 1996, another Mutiny Muchacho, confessed smuggler Manny "Veneno" Hernandez, took the stand to dish on his harrowing 1987 drug runs to the Bahamas, where he had to protect his cash and contraband from marauding pirates.

The prosecution also got quality insider testimony from Pedro "Pegy" Rosello (aka Louis Mendez), who first tipped off the Feds to Sal Magluta's whereabouts and was pursued by assassins outside the hospital where his son was born less than a year later. His sister was married to Taby Falcon, Willie's fugitive brother and code-fendant. Pegy was serving twenty-four years. But thanks to his cooperation, he would ultimately do less than five.

Prosecutor Clark called up Jorge Plasencia, the Metro-Dade Police detective who arrested Magluta in 1988 outside the office supplies store. The veteran cop testified that Magluta offered to take him and his squad partner to one thousand kilos of cocaine if they let him go and forgot about the incident. The prosecution was trying to make the point that this would have been uncharacteristic access, to say the least, for someone who swore to having quit the cocaine business back in 1980. Should the jury be expected to believe that Sal the honest businessman just knew someone who knew someone who was warehousing a ton and change of cocaine?

In all, the government called more than two dozen witnesses. Their testimony filled at least eleven thousand pages of transcripts piled from the floor to the ceiling of the courthouse.

Chapter Fifty-one

THE BEST JUSTICE THAT MONEY CAN BUY

WHILE THEIR TOP-SHELF defense attorneys hammered away at the credibility of the government's witnesses, friends of Willie and Sal worked another front: jury tampering.

Juror Miguel Moya was employed as an airport mechanic making a little under forty thousand dollars a year. On January 31, a guy identifying himself as Eddie called Moya at home. His then-wife picked up and handed the phone to her husband, Miguel, who went to another room to converse with the caller.

When he'd put the phone down, Moya bolted out of the apartment. He returned shortly after with a bag of cash—a down payment, he told her, on his "not guilty" vote for Willie and Sal.

"Eddie," it turned out, was a guy who played for the Falcon-Magluta semipro Seahawks softball team. It took him all of six minutes by phone to buy a vote in the biggest cocaine trial in Miami history—an alleged two-billion-dollar conspiracy—for somewhere around 500 thousand dollars.

Another juror, Gloria Alba, was also on the take. The Boys discovered her identity and whereabouts when she told a family friend that she'd been summoned to serve on their jury. That friend worked in the real estate business alongside a childhood pal of Falcon and Magluta. That old friend then procured a private investigator's license in order to visit Magluta in jail as a "member of his legal team." There would be a broker's fee to collect by negotiating the sale of Alba's vote. The upshot: Alba would pocket 500 thousand dollars just for her "not guilty" and another 500 thousand dollars if Falcon and Magluta were ultimately acquitted.

Closing arguments from the Muchachos' legal dream team clocked in at almost five hours. Roy Black invoked Martin Luther King Jr. and Bobby Kennedy. Pointing to the humbled-looking Falcon and Magluta, he argued: "It is not just them, but it is our country, our Constitution that is at stake."

The gist of their argument: the government was scapegoating their clients and depriving them of their civil rights, cutting deals with convicts in order to win two giant trophies in the War on Drugs. The judge cut Black off when he was about to brandish a poster of the unknown tank man from Tiananmen Square.

During the jurors' sequestered deliberations, they selected Miguel Moya, the most avid among them, as their foreman. The airline mechanic insisted on acquitting and refused to deliberate, telling the other jurors that he could remain sequestered indefinitely.

A black juror voiced displeasure at the special treatment wealthy nonblack drug defendants like Magluta and Falcon were given over African-American crack and heroin dealers. The oldest member of the panel, he experienced a diabetic seizure during the deliberations and was attended to by paramedics.

He was replaced by a young Hispanic woman who leaned toward voting not guilty. After a bit of pushback, the rest of the jurors relented. They had agreed to exonerate Sal Magluta and Willie Falcon.

On Friday, February 16, 1996, at 6:30 p.m., the Boys were acquitted in *United States v. Augusto Falcon, et al.*, case number 91-6060-CR-MORENO. Magluta and Falcon cried and thanked their attorneys and the heavens.

Prosecutor Chris Clark gave the jury a disgusted glare. "We had enough evidence to convict one hundred times over," he said.

An exuberant, breathless Magluta told TV cameras: "I just hope that our justice system respects the system, and respects that a jury found us not guilty. We went to trial. We did it the way this country and this constitution was meant to."

As news of the evening verdict got out, prisoners started stomping, clapping and pounding up and down the floors of downtown Miami's huge federal prison tower. Fans walking into nearby Miami Arena for a hockey game reported feeling the ground shake; Miami doesn't have earthquakes.

In a past life, the Muchachos would no doubt have celebrated by cordoning off the Upper Deck and several suites at the Mutiny—and tipping a room service kid more cash than he'd ever handled to hoard all the Dom and Perrier-Jouët in Miami. And maybe even letting up some Hare Krishnas—you know, for shits and giggles.

But their old haunt had been abandoned for seven years now. As the *Miami New Times* put it, "Across South Bayshore Drive . . . sits the rotting hulk of the infamous Mutiny Hotel, the vortex of Miami's cocaine-fueled party era of the late seventies and early eighties. It was a favored hangout for drug dealers, renowned for its anything-goes-and-everything's-served bashes. . . . Among its most ardent customers: Willie Falcon and Sal Magluta, who were recently acquitted of charges that they imported more than seventy-five tons of cocaine, valued at more than two billion dollars, over a thirteen-year period. No doubt the pair frequented the place because they just loved the food."

Chapter Fifty-two

EMPIRE STRIKES BACK II

THE SYSTEM WASN'T buying it.

"We knew we lost via corruption," said Pat Sullivan, a veteran prosecutor. "Our strategy was to tie them up while we investigated jury tampering, bribery and witness murders."

Just weeks after the bombshell acquittal, the IRS accordingly slammed Sal Magluta, still in jail on unresolved money laundering charges, for nearly 2.5 million dollars in federal income tax liabilities for the 1982 calendar year. The Southern District of Florida immediately followed up with an indictment on several offenses relating to the use of false identities.

Uncle Sam also stuck Willie Falcon with a 1982 tax assessment of 4.88 million dollars; the Southern District of Florida slapped him with firearms violations for the gun found in Operation Sunrise's 1991 raid.

The IRS's justification for this action: Magluta and Falcon had not filed their respective income tax returns for the 1982 calendar year. In August, a revenue agent who had been investigating their criminal careers testified that he was acting now to get money the IRS was owed fourteen years earlier.

"The federal government," said Christopher Clark, "is thorough, if nothing else."

Using the full bureaucratic reach of Washington to tie up Willie and Sal was a good way to buy time for a new case. But that could only keep them behind bars for so long. And if they got out, they'd be flight risks.

What prosecutors really needed now was not to prove that the Boys were prolific coke lords as much as a smoking gun to show that they'd rigged the jury that acquitted them.

The government got its big break when one juror who felt bullied out of convicting by foreman Miguel Moya approached authorities. He recounted how Moya reacted to the not-guilty verdict with a victory dance and offers of high fives to other jurors.

Turns out, this was the least of Moya's indiscretions. It was a cinch for authorities to discover Moya had had extensive telephone contact with a Muchachos associate during the trial. The jury foreman and his parents had recently bought a 198-thousand-dollar house in the Florida Keys, taking just a few months to pay off its mortgage. The family also shelled out 31 thousand dollars in cash for a speedboat and thousands more on cars, jewelry and furniture—none of which jibed with the airport mechanic's small salary and normal ATM records.

The Feds also went back to scrutinize the accounts of Willie and Sal's legal dream team, which was estimated to have cost the men upward of twenty million dollars. After their acquittal, prosecutors subpoenaed the financial records of defense attorneys and private investigators, bent on demonstrating that they had accepted payments from drug proceeds that the 1991 indictment put a freeze on.

It took only until August for a grand jury to issue a ten-count indictment against Sal Magluta. Put aside for now the government's contention that this man was the ringleader of one of the biggest cocaine conspiracies in history; he was a passport and social security fraudster. That rap, they calculated, would at least keep Sal tied up until the government readied *US vs. Los Muchachos: The Rematch*.

Chapter Fifty-three

MIAMI VICE COMES TO LIFE

IN MID-OCTOBER, a federal prosecutor got an anonymous phone tip that Marilyn Bonachea, Magluta's on-and-off mistress, had kept revealing documents about the jury-fixing conspiracy. The tipster said that she would have the papers in her car later that afternoon, en route to an attorney's office.

The DEA and Miami cops arranged to arrest her for speeding and possession of marijuana. In the orchestrated search of her rental car, a police sergeant opened the trunk and found a cardboard box with what he recognized were drug ledgers.

In February 1997, while on trial for passport fraud, and under less-than-maximum security conditions, Magluta walked out of a downtown Miami courthouse. He never returned. Jurors convicted his empty chair the following day.

Rumors raged across Miami that Sal had finally fled the country and had his fingerprints lasered down, alongside elaborate plastic surgery to alter his appearance.

Instead, he was captured two months later during a traffic stop near Palm Beach. Just not with any kind of James Bond–caliber disguise: donning a shoulder-length salt-and-pepper wig, he was carrying twenty thousand dollars in cash and the key to a thousand-dollar-a-night oceanfront suite at a nearby Ritz-Carlton. In his car were handwritten notes regarding the whereabouts of his cash, new cars, places to store new fake IDs and land where he might build a compound.

FAST-FORWARD TO AUGUST of 1998: ex–jury foreman Miguel Moya was indicted on charges that he took a 500-thousand-dollar bribe to vote to acquit Willie and Sal. Prosecutors alleged that Moya, with the help of his parents, spent his payoff on a Cadillac, a Rolex, a house and a boat. They taped Moya fessing up to the bribe to a 350-pound government informant posing as a Muchachos enforcer.

Though *Miami Vice* had been off the air for nine years, headlines like this one seemed like they were ripped right from the show:

MOYA'S "DATE" WILD AND WIRED
September 19, 1998 | By LARRY LEBOWITZ
Staff Writer, *Sun Sentinel*

MIAMI—Miguel Moya was bragging about all his new toys to the provocatively dressed woman "dirty dancing" with him in South Beach nightclubs.

Little did the former jury foreman know that the woman in the low-cut dress was an undercover FBI agent wearing a wire.

And little did he know that the Feds would one day take those taped boasts of new cars, houses, watches, vacations and gambling trips to build a case that he accepted up to $1 million in bribes to fix the trial of reputed cocaine cowboys Augusto "Willie" Falcon and Salvador Magluta.

Prosecutors kept recruiting and leaning on more informants within the Muchachos' sprawling conglomerate. They succeeded in flipping Marilyn Bonachea to their side. In September, she met with an associate of Magluta's while wearing a hidden recorder. In their second meeting, she expressed concern about the outing of a bribed female juror from the 1996 trial. The associate assured Bonachea that the bribed juror was "under control" and, unlike foreman Moya, not spending her payoff ostentatiously. The Feds got it all on tape.

In September of 1998, Richard "Blondie" Passapera, a Magluta worker, personally delivered 1.2 million dollars in cash to another Magluta associate—who himself had recently become an FBI informant.

The informant handed the money over to the FBI, and flew to New York to retrieve the cash. Under surveillance, he transferred it to a pair of Magluta associates who then flew it to Israel and deposited it in an Israeli bank under a fictitious Jewish-sounding name. The FBI informant was then given eight blank checks from that Israeli account. The Feds watched him hand them to Blondie Passapera, who then got them to Sal Magluta, who then used them to pay his lawyers.

In November, just over seven years after he was captured at his Miami Beach mansion, Magluta pleaded guilty in a Miami courtroom to conspiring to use false identification and falsely presenting himself to arresting officers.

On the same day, Gilberto Barrios, the Muchachos' head of road transport, was found guilty of trucking cocaine across the country for the conglomerate. A truck-loading deputy was also convicted, while a man in nearby Broward County who maintained a stash house for Muchachos cocaine pleaded guilty and agreed to testify.

The government mined ever deeper into Muchachos Corp.'s huge org chart to nail coconspirators with long jail sentences. That then gave it a powerful capital with prisoners: "The more you talk, the more you could walk."

Chapter Fifty-four

REMATCH

On August 20, 1999—a little over twenty years since the Boys inherited Jorge Valdes's Medellín supply line—the Feds handed down their second Magluta-Falcon conspiracy indictment. But this wasn't so much about cocaine. The government's forty-four-page, forty-seven-count case was decidedly focused on the organization's regimen of witness and jury tampering and obstruction of justice. In addition to assassinations (successful and attempted), the Justice Department was alleging twenty-three payoffs totaling 711,500 dollars to inmates in federal prisons for either their silence or false testimony at trial.

The *Miami Herald* called the sweeping indictment the "latest episode in the government's continuing chase of what they have so far been unable to prove was the longest-running cocaine business in South Florida history."

The defense, for its part, called the Feds' redoubled pursuit a "never-ending vendetta."

"I'm all for zealous prosecution," said new attorney Richard Diaz, "but when you take your shot and it doesn't result in a conviction, that's enough. You have some prosecutors who are just sore losers. They make these cases career projects, and that's not what it's supposed to be about."

By April of 2000, twenty years had passed since Willie Falcon and Sal Magluta pleaded no contest in court after they were hauled in by a state cocaine sting. They would have served a maximum of fourteen months—probably much less, in light of all the violent criminals shooting up South Florida in the wake of the Mariel boatlift. The system and prisons were hopelessly overwhelmed.

Their ultimate pursuer in the 1980 case was state attorney Janet Reno.

Their ultimate pursuer at the turn of the century was US attorney general Janet Reno.

Chapter Fifty-five

SEQUESTRATION

SHIFT AHEAD TO 2002. Eleven years after they were taken by marshals in successive raids, Willie and Sal had been spirited in and out of various penitentiaries across the country, in and out of solitary confinement; given and deprived of email rights; taken in shackles to the funerals of loved ones.

Gary James, the valet at the Mutiny who used to collect two hundred dollars a pop for parking their fancy cars, crossed paths with Falcon at the federal penitentiary in downtown Miami. James was doing time for dealing ecstasy, the it drug of the South Beach party scene that had taken over Miami while the Boys were in jail. The men immediately recognized each other, then hugged and reminisced before a guard moved Falcon back to his cell.

Nelson Aguilar recalled a spat between Falcon and Magluta over fellow inmate Gilberto Barrios, the Muchachos logistics specialist who in March of 2002 had agreed to cooperate with the government's case. Just a few days earlier, Magluta had confided to Barrios that he had been scrutinizing jury questionnaires in his jail cell and was convinced he had dated one of the women.

In a holding pen adjacent to the courthouse, when Magluta got up in Barrios's face, Falcon cut in and got up in Magluta's face. "What, are you stupid, bro?" he yelled. "This guy knows everything."

Aguilar said Falcon then turned to Barrios and said, half fatalistically, "Do what you gotta do, man, OK?"

Gilberto Barrios proceeded to testify that Sal Magluta was now plotting to fix this new jury, with one juror having already received a threatening phone call. He added that Sal had an emissary send him a menacing message before his 1999 grand jury appearance.

Now, he revealed, "[Sal] had people already investigating the members of the jury, that is investigating the whole pool, to try to get to know who was involved. The story was that he had to give the right instructions to the jurors this time. . . . This next time, it's not going to happen like it happened before."

Sequestration was an overarching priority for prosecutors this second time around. They would be trying Magluta and Falcon independently.

In April of 2002, the government won a key motion to isolate jurors from the outside world for what was expected to be a four-month trial. To call this measure extraordinary was an understatement: no jury had ever been sequestered *during* a trial in Florida's Southern District; at most, and in extreme cases, juries were sequestered only during deliberations.

In June, Marilyn Bonachea took the stand as the government's star witness. Twelve sequestered jurors and six alternates listened as the ex-mistress admitted that she and other associates smuggled a cell phone into the federal detention center in Miami and made plans for a never-attempted escape. Bonachea said Magluta was going to act as if he was sick so he could be transported off the prison grounds. "He had a group of Colombian mercenaries," she testified. "They were going to stop the bus and fly them out."

In June, the jurors (now anonymous and sequestered) heard the testimony of several convicted Colombian hit men involved in taking out lawyer Juan Acosta and associates Luis "Weetchie" Escobedo and Bernardo "Venao" Gonzalez. Their ringleader, now dead, was a Colombian cartel chief known as Tocayo who'd recruited assassins from New York and Texas to kill up to a dozen witnesses cooperating with the government's case against the Muchachos. Successful hits earned 50 thousand to 125 thousand dollars apiece.

ALL OF THIS was going down exactly twenty years after Miami's last big cocaine courtroom spectacle: the Tick-Talks hearings. As government witnesses were testifying against Magluta in a highly secure downtown Miami courthouse, Jorge Villaverde—Tick-Talks' defendant, Mutiny Table 14 habitué and anti-Castro crusader—was gunned down in front of his West Miami horse ranch. The sixty-seven-year-old had a pair of nine-millimeter guns tucked in the back of his pants.

Villaverde had spent eighteen years as a political prisoner in Castro's jails. In the 1990s, he served two years behind bars in the US for stockpiling machine guns and silencers, adamant that there would be a forthcoming battle to retake Cuba.

Who would want him dead in 2002? "It looks like Castro ordered this," the head of Miami's oldest anti-Castro group told the *Miami Herald*.

TWO MONTHS LATER, on August 16, 2002, the federal jury came to its decision on Sal Magluta: it convicted him—not for murder or his 1980s rise to the top of the cocaine trade, but instead for his 1990s obstruction of justice, juror bribery, witness tampering and money laundering. All told, three dozen Muchachos associates had been convicted since 1996.

Magluta, especially pale, kept his head down and eyes closed while the verdicts were read; it seemed like he was deep in prayer. But he smiled and looked up to the heavens when the jury acquitted him on the most serious charge, of hiring Colombian hit men to kill government witnesses.

The thinking was Magluta would ultimately face twenty years of prison at his sentencing later in the year. His attorneys were optimistic that he'd see freedom again. "He knows that he has his life back," said one.

But prosecutors had very different plans. They were going to lobby the judge to dispense with sentencing guidelines and come down much harder on Magluta.

This second go-around, not a single person in the courtroom knew a thing about the individual jurors' identities. Since the trial commenced, they'd been under strict twenty-four-hour guard by US Marshals at an undisclosed hotel.

Behind the scenes, jurors twice voted to suspend the proceedings so that one of them could fly out of state, guarded closely by marshals, to be with sick relatives; they all agreed to come in on Saturdays to make up for her sick leave. Even after the verdict was read, they asked the judge to maintain their anonymity.

On January 23, the judge, siding with the prosecutors' recommendation, sentenced Sal Magluta to 205 years. "I would like to begin by apologizing to this country," said a clearly devastated Magluta, who looked unrecognizable after having been in solitary confinement for nearly four straight years. "I know I failed it and all it stands for—and for that I'm truly sorry."

Choking on his tears, Magluta turned to his parents, his children and his friends and thanked them for their prayers throughout the process. "You deserved much better for the way you raised me," he said.

Magluta then addressed his children, including his oldest son, Christian, who with Magluta's father (Christian's grandfather) was facing drug-money-laundering charges. "I'm sorry for not being there for you, and, more important, for not being an example of what a father should be."

But he tempered his contrition by implying that the court was ignoring the will of the jury by sentencing him for the worst charges. "I have come to the sad conclusion that . . . this court has tried and convicted me of every allegation," Magluta said. "My fears have now become reality."

Sitting in the courtroom was *Miami Herald* reporter Jay Weaver, who had been following the Muchachos saga since he first got to South Florida a decade earlier. "I'll never forget the look on Sal's face," he said. "No more cocky, arrogant nineteen eighties cocaine cowboy. He was so diminished. Stooped. Ashen. Completely broken. It wasn't that he had fallen from grace. He looked like he was being buried alive and had to look down into his grave on that day."

"One down, one to go," remarked lead prosecutor Pat Sullivan.

London's *Telegraph* could not resist running with the headline "205 Years for '*Scarface*.'"

Later that year Magluta's son, Christian, and father, Manuel, were sentenced to prison for helping Magluta conceal and launder drug cash. Christian Magluta, then twenty-nine and having completed a year and a half at the University of Miami's law school, said he agreed to a five-year sentence in his plea bargain in the hopes of keeping his grandfather, who raised him, out of prison. The government also agreed to let the younger Magluta delay the start of his prison sentence until after his wife gave birth to their second child in a few months.

"I have suffered deeply for years," Manuel Magluta, the eighty-one-year-old baker, said after he was sentenced to three months in jail. "Sadly, I don't know whether there is an end to this in the near future. I don't know whether I will be able to see my son."

"I think Sal became a victim of his own jailhouse legend," said a fellow inmate and drug dealer. "He was never a thug, physically; he had never done any serious time. Then, all of a sudden, he's in Miami prison surrounded by all these Marielitos and other small fish treating him like he is the Almighty. Maybe he believed that legend too much."

In June of 2003, Willie Falcon pleaded guilty to using laundered drug money to fix his trial. He looked forlorn and exhausted, having spent nearly twelve years in a variety of penitentiaries, often in solitary confinement. His plea agreement with the government entailed a twenty-year prison sentence and not having to testify against past associates.

Not that there was really anyone left to testify against. "In my mind's eye, I see a runaway train, with Magluta as the conductor and Willie in the back," said Falcon's defense attorney, Jeff Weiner. "These two men factually, legally and in every other way are different."

"Willie just fell on his sword and copped the plea," said Jay Weaver. The example of Sal's double life sentence, he said, was just too sobering: "Screw around with the judicial system the way they did," he said, "and you are going to get slammed."

Still, the judge overseeing Falcon's trial made attorneys on both sides convince her to accept their extraordinary deal, which she argued did not exact enough prison time. The contentious hearing lasted more than three hours.

On his way back to jail, Willie Falcon blew kisses to his infirm parents, Arsenio and Mirta, and three children in attendance: Aileen, twenty-eight, Jessica, twenty-three, and William, eighteen. The parents and sister of his wife, Alina, murdered eleven years earlier, were there as well.

A month later, the judge agreed to sentence him to twenty years. She commended his "gentlemanly demeanor" and recommended that the Bureau of Prisons assign him to an appropriate facility in southern or central Florida. "I will probably not live to see my son a free man," wrote Falcon's seventy-four-year-old mother. "Please, at least allow me in my late years to continue to see him. Given my health, this will only be possible if you keep him nearby."

In her final face-to-face with Willie Falcon, the judge wished him "all the best," and told him, "Each day is the beginning of the rest of your life."

In January of 2004, two more jurors from the Muchachos' original corrupted 1996 trial got their own prison sentences. Fort Lauderdale's *Sun-Sentinel* was ready to eulogize the cocaine cowboys: "It is a tale that inspired the opening credits of the 1980s TV hit *Miami Vice. . . .*" Think gorgeous women in bikinis, enormous speedboats, Rolls-Royces, the Miami high life. "In the end, about 40 people, including a fourth of the duo's 1996 jury, were sent to federal prison."

With the heads of the Muchachos syndicate now in jail, their loyal deputy and holdout, Justo Jay, was clear to get his life sentence slashed by cooperating with the government. He had a lot of incentive: Jay's son, who was all of three years old when his dad went to prison, was now a star pro baseball player, drafted high up by the Saint Louis Cardinals after covering himself in glory at the University of Miami.

In July of 2006, eighteen years after going to jail, Justo Jay testified for the government in a case against a Cali, Colombia, drug lord who had supplied the Muchachos. "It's very hard to have a friend go over and testify against you," he said, holding back tears.

Under oath, Jay explained that Manuel Garces, one of the founders of the Medellín Cartel and Jorge Valdes's mentor, was the middleman between Falcon and Magluta and Colombia. By 1981, he said, the Muchachos had been moving so much cocaine that they were working directly with Pablo Escobar, the notorious overlord of the Medellín cartel. He testified that he had been present several times when Sal Magluta communicated in code words with Escobar over a short-wave radio.

Justo Jay appealed to President George W. Bush to commute his life sentence. Was it not risky business to testify against the biggest drug lords of Colombia? The thinking, says reporter Jay Weaver, was that "here in Miami, all of the violence had subsided long ago and the Feds already had Willie and Sal."

So with the blessing of prosecutors, Justo Jay was released in March 2007.

Which was shortly after the movie version of *Miami Vice* hit theaters.

Director Michael Mann finally took his landmark show to the big screen, plugging in Colin Farrell and Jamie Foxx for Don Johnson and Philip Michael Thomas. In the movie's breathless opening sequence, you can see stuntman Ralph "Cabeza" Linero, a free man since 1999, racing a speedboat while Tubbs mentions the pursuit of "Sal Magluta." Another drug lord in the film was named José Yero—Coca-Cola's real name.

Linero brought Magluta's daughter to the set to meet heart-throb Colin Farrell. She and Ralph were now distantly related: while Linero was in prison, his middle daughter married Sal Magluta's nephew. Linero felt especially close to Magluta's daughter, having lost one of his daughters to a car accident while he was in jail. He went to her funeral in shackles.

In November of 2006, three years after he was sentenced to 205 years in prison, Sal Magluta, bald, pale, hunched and shackled at the feet, appeared before the same judge to plead for leniency after an appellate court threw out one of his obstruction charges. As his parents, relatives and old pals watched, Magluta cried.

His voice cracked as he spoke about espousing the Bible. "I can't change the past, Judge," he said. "If I could . . . I would. I wake up every morning—it's a constant reminder of the errors I have made. You pray, you confess, you put it all out but you can't get rid of it."

Magluta said he didn't come with "any hidden agenda. Other than that," he said, "all I can say is, I'm sorry."

Though the judge claimed to be touched by the "Saint Paul's conversion," her decision suggested otherwise: she only trimmed ten years from Magluta's 205-year sentence. He was fifty-two.

His lead attorney slammed this as "unreasonable" and "unconstitutional" under federal guidelines—particularly compared to Willie Falcon's twenty-year sentence: "Even Einstein would not be able to calculate the net disparity of two centuries. How can Magluta, with this record, be ten times worse?"

At this point, Falcon's camp was happy to stick to its line that Magluta was the brains of the operation—the Muchacho who went rogue enough to hire Colombian assassins, don wigs and romance the idea of an elaborate prison escape. The story line now echoed across old Miami Muchachos circles: "Sal lost his mind, bro."

Still, other friends think Magluta was the victim of a government vendetta.

"Do you really think Sal deserves to be in jail the rest of his life, underground with no visits?" said former associate Nelson Aguilar, who spent a total of twenty-five years in prison for cocaine dealing. He now owns a Miami Beach restaurant with surveillance cameras installed throughout. "Look, Sal's not a saint. But really. Really? Is he really, really, really like the Hannibal Lecters he's surrounded by?"

Aguilar suggests that the thinking back in the early 1990s was, the Muchachos needed to buy jurors to counter the government's buying of witnesses (with freedom) to testify against Willie and Sal.

Had Willie and Sal opted to snitch, he said, "there'd be a lot of institutions dead, rotting and stinking in Miami right now." Everyone from the pro football franchise to cruise ship conglomerates to properties on the skyline to legitimate politicians and businessmen, he said, have the Muchachos' cocaine or coke money on their hands. "You have no idea how much stink there would be in Miami if these guys snitched."

INCREDIBLY, THE MUCHACHOS saga continues into the present. Yuby Ramirez, a single mother in Miami, was dating one of the assassins who took out Muchachos witnesses in the early 1990s—the very guys who had since testified for the government and entered federal witness protection.

In 2001, after taking her attorney's advice and refusing government plea deals, Ramirez was sentenced to life in prison for aiding and abetting her ex-boyfriend and the other hit man (she housed and fed the men). In May of 2012, no less than the *Wall Street Journal* was reporting that she was the first beneficiary of the US Supreme Court's recent decision that a defendant's conviction could be voided if they reject a plea agreement thanks to legal incompetence.

The *Miami Herald*'s Jay Weaver was once again pulled into the Willie and Sal saga, a decade after the men were convicted and twenty years after deputy Bernie "Venao" Gonzalez Jr. was assassinated: "A couple of days after [Venao] was executed by a Colombian hit team," wrote Weaver, "Yuby Ramirez was making a meal in her Kendall town house for the crew's boss . . . [who was] smiling as the TV flashed images of Magluta and Falcon in orange jumpsuits . . ."

Ramirez was released from immigration custody in late February 2013, fortunate to be spared deportation to her native Colombia after thirteen years behind bars. She would most likely have been assassinated there. As for Magluta and Falcon, "I had never heard of them," she said. "I never knew them at all."

TO THIS DAY, precious few people in Miami will say anything about prodigal Muchachos Marielito Luis "Weetchie" Escobedo—aka *Ton* Selleck, aka the Marlboro Man.

Which is noteworthy. After all, Weetchie got off a boat from Cuba, finagled his way into the Mutiny, stole tips, bedded a wealthy attorney who gave him her Corvette—and within a decade became an indicted conspirator in a two-billion-dollar cocaine bust, the biggest in Miami history. He was the fifth name down on the government's first case against the Muchachos.

On August 22, 1992, ignoring a judge's warning to hang low now that he was cooperating with the government, Weetchie drove his Porsche to Suzanne's in the Grove, the Mutiny offshoot on South Bayshore Drive.

Laura Costanzo, a girl who used to party with him and other Marielitos at the Mutiny, was now behind the bar at Suzanne's.

The tall, mustached Cuban walked in dressed in a white suit, white shoes and a white shirt. "Weetchie!" she blurted out, looking around. "What the fuck are you doing out here?"

Willy Gomez, now the head of security at Suzanne's, warned the staff about the heat Weetchie could bring. Just two days earlier, the cooperating codefendant had survived a shooting attempt while driving back from a club up in North Miami Beach. The judge overseeing the Muchachos' trial admonished him for being so out and about.

"Weetchie looked tired," said Costanzo. "Burned-out. Nothing like how I remembered him." She asked him why he was dressed all in white.

"Hey," he replied, shrugging, "because you never know when it will be your time to go, right?" His eyes welled up as he took a long drag on his cigarette.

Weetchie then struck up a conversation with a very eager brunette sitting at the bar. They took a table and ordered a bottle of champagne. Laura went downstairs. She later heard machine-gun fire—that MAC-10 sound redolent of 1979's Dadeland Massacre. She fell to the floor and covered her head.

An off-duty cop told everyone to stay inside, as there had just been a shooting in the parking deck. Costanzo looked through a window to find Escobedo on the ground in a pool of blood, vermilion streaked across his all-white outfit. Witnesses reported that a guy had called out to him, "Weetchie!" and shot him in the head as he was walking to his parked Porsche.

Escobedo was thirty-nine. The brunette who had hit on him was a spotter for the gunmen.

"I heard you were out partying," a federal agent had warned

him a week earlier. "They are going to track you down, and you are going to get yourself killed!"

"He wouldn't listen to me," the agent later remarked. "Not only did I warn him, but another person did, too. He didn't listen."

If you were ever going to put a hit on someone in Miami, that day in 1992 would have been it. Because already barreling toward South Florida at 175 miles per hour was category-five Hurricane Andrew, the strongest storm to hit Florida in sixty-six years and, to that point, the most destructive in US history.

Having already clobbered the Bahamas, Hurricane Andrew proceeded to shred up much of Miami, leaving 175 thousand people homeless and more than a million without power.

With especially low-lying Coconut Grove evacuated, Andrew's winds were powerful enough to send metal street signs through palm trees. Suzanne's was finished—Weetchie Escobedo's residual bloodstain scoured by the howling winds and surging salt water.

A block south stood the hulking shell of the once-great Mutiny. Abandoned now for three years—the subject of as many as nine failed investor bids—the hotel was an off-the-grid hangout for goth kids, crack addicts and graffiti artists.

Andrew's winds and 150-mile-per-hour projectiles did a number on the twenty-four-year-old tower, ripping apart the awning of the club's bay windows, collapsing its parking garage and forcing water and debris through balconies and broken windows. The rooms, all shorn of their fixtures and furniture, were coated in mold, bird droppings and asbestos from warped popcorn ceilings.

By the time the news trucks and choppers made it out to the Grove the following morning, dozens of boats had been propelled up from the marina and onto Peacock Park and South Bayshore Drive.

Vessels plunked themselves right in front of the Mutiny, a quarter century after developer Burton Goldberg parked a houseboat as a sales office for a place he was calling Sailboat Bay.

TWO YEARS LATER, a high school senior had a weekend job slinging cups of frozen lemonade at street fairs. In his last months in Miami before heading up north for college, senioritis was in full bloom and the honor student needed spending money.

The campy Coconut Grove Bed Race was this weekend's assignment. A big Frozade truck deposited him on an overshaded corner of South Bayshore Drive, in the semicircular driveway of an abandoned building.

He looked behind him and through a hole in a tarped-off fence with some government insignia that said NO TRESPASSING. The pool area was intensely overgrown with weeds and miscellaneous foliage.

Across the street on a stage in Peacock Park—behind a grownover softball field—was rocker Eddie Money, the day's musical entertainment. He was belting out a classic:

"I wanna go back, and do it all over, but I can't go back, I know."

The crowd from the race and concert was treating the fence to the building's pool like a huge trash bin, just launching gyro wrappers, ice-cream cones, cans and Zima bottles into the patio area. A Dumpster in the driveway overflowed with food waste, broken windows and arguing crows. Above it was a shattered sign: it kind of looked like a winking pirate. But your author wasn't sure.

Raccoons, rats and turkey vultures were feasting on the detritus by the pool, whose contents were an antifreeze green. Broken chairs and tables bobbed in the sludge.

He stepped back and checked out the side of the tower overlooking South Bayshore Drive and the softball field full of Eddie Money fans. Leaning out of a broken window was a gaunt-looking black man, smiling at a guy and a women leaning out of another window. A couple of silhouettes could be spied behind one of the big tinted bay windows that hadn't been boarded up with plywood.

The lemonade boy looked back around in the pool/patio area, next to a huge tear in the tarped-over chain-link fence. Sitting on a keg was a burly, bearded guy in a Miami Dolphins jersey and heavy gold bracelets and necklaces. He was smoking a joint.

"Hey!" he hollered from inside. "Yo!"

The man walked through the hole and toward the lemonade cart.

Your author saw police to his right, along the marina. If the man tried anything, he thought, he would just dart toward them.

You could smell him from yards away: Drakkar Noir and b.o. and pot marinated in nicotine. He was breathing heavily.

"What you got here, bro?" he asked.

"Frozade," said your author. "It's frozen lemonade. We also have piña colada, but I'm waiting for a refill from my manager."

"Gimme a cup," he said. "Whatever."

(Awkward pause. Silence.)

"You know this place?" he asked. He pulled out a card from his wallet. It was gold. It looked like some sort of platinum credit card. "How old are you?"

"Sorry," he responded. "I'm finishing high school. Two dollars."

He felt a pang of guilt for catching the man smoking pot. He needed to show him he was cool. "Wait," he said to the stoner. "You know what? This is on me. Here."

"Free?!" The man laughed and took a huge lick off the side of the cup and the back of his hand. "No way!" he exclaimed. "Naw! You're in school, bro."

He put the cup down, took a money clip out of his shirt pocket, peeled off a bill and slammed it on the top of the lemonade cart. It was a fifty-dollar note.

"Sir," I said. "I can't. No, here . . . Wait. No, really."

He put away his clip.

"Study hard and say no to drugs!" yelled the man. He laughed and coughed thunderously as he waddled away and was absorbed back into Miami.

Afterword

RUDY REDBEARD GOT out of jail in 1998. Waiting for him was Carlene Quesada, the childhood friend who had testified against him—and presumably others—to get his twenty-five-year sentence slashed down to less than five years. You're very likely to bump into these old Poop Deck pals at one of the many Cuban diners of Coral Gables.

Two years later, in 2000, their pursuer Raul Martinez became the first Latino to be named Miami police chief. Ironically, the Cuban immigrant ascended to the top job after his predecessor was fired in the furor over his handling of another Cuban immigrant: six-year-old boatlifter Elián González.

In 2001, O. J. Simpson, his girlfriend and a *Penthouse* model filmed a sex tape in room 310 of the new, gutted and completely sanitized Mutiny Hotel—in an area where a swath of the Upper Deck once stood.

SAL MAGLUTA, SIXTY-TWO, is now in Florence, Colorado's super-maximum-security ADX prison. Nicknamed the Alcatraz of the Rockies, the thirty-seven-acre penitentiary houses the Unabomber, the Shoe Bomber, and various busted double agents, white supremacists and cartel and Mafia bosses. His email was cut off.

THE FILM *SCARFACE* has traversed the past thirty-four years as nothing short of a pop cultural totem. You see Tony Montana's lines referenced everywhere: in *The Simpsons* and on ESPN's *SportsCenter*; in the hit show *Breaking Bad* (pitched to AMC as "Mr. Chips meets *Scarface*") and in video games, rap lyrics and even porn scripts. The 1983 movie has been rereleased multiple times.

In Ken Tucker's 2008 book *Scarface Nation: The Ultimate Gangster Movie and How It Changed America*, screenwriter Oliver Stone recalled:

> *The first time Brian [De Palma] came to Miami, I took him to the Mutiny . . . It was a great drug hangout and in those days it was chic to be a druggie, and all the girls were beautiful, the clubs were rich and modern—this was new to America . . . The Mutiny Club was one of those places that had forty or fifty hotel rooms, each of which had a different color. I stayed in a red- or white-colored room, but fuckin' Brian chose the black room! Completely black.*

Early in 2017, Universal Studios announced a remake of *Scarface* that will involve the Oscar-winning Coen Brothers and a screenplay pivot: this time the protagonist will be a Mexican immigrant conquering Los Angeles.

BACK IN FLORIDA, two related headlines hit the news tape in April: the South Beach location of *Scarface*'s infamous chain saw scene is being turned into a CVS; Gustavo "Taby" Falcon, on the lam since he was named in the original 1991 Muchachos indictment, was arrested without incident while bicycling with his wife near Disney World. His brother, Willie Falcon, gets out of jail in June.

MUTINY MOLLIE NOW owns a limo company that chauffeurs Matt Lauer. In 2015, she reunited with J. D. Barker, the Miami cop—"my guardian angel," she calls him—who in 1982 intervened to help get her sober and into the taxi-dispatch business. It took her years to get off cocaine and alcohol and then learn how to sleep at night without medication. She now trumpets for her church choir.

Burton Goldberg lived in Tiburon, California, where he devoted his life to alternative health. You can look him up on YouTube, where in 2011 he exhorted the late Steve Jobs, founder of Apple, to seek him out for cancer treatment. Goldberg died peacefully in late 2016.

Owen Band and Alberto Bover were in the hospital on the same day I finally met Alberto—after at least seven years of putting out feelers for the Marielito who spoke so many languages. He passed away just weeks later.

CINDY PROIETTI IS a flight attendant. She recently ambushed Julio Iglesias in first class, and they reminisced about the Upper Deck.

IN 2009, THANKS to Mario Tabraue, I finally made it through to Bernardo de Torres, who wanders the grounds of Miami. We met four times. The first time, he was surrounded by black cats and a wake of vultures. The second time, he checked out my license plates.

The final time, he pleaded for ten thousand dollars—showing me two checks that JFK investigator Jim Garrison had written him during the Kennedy investigation. "Buddy," he said, "this is my life we're talking about."

He admitted to me that he received radio waves from a balcony at the Mutiny, and that he never paid a penny of his own money there. He also hinted at something about the KGB. Bernie made me drive him home, where the license plate of my rental car was photographed at his guard gate. He refused to connect the dots any further for me.

"Forces had intersected at the Mutiny in ways no one could imagine," said T. R. Cimino, the author who advised the production of *Miami Vice* and raced speedboats with the Muchachos. "The idea that Pablo Escobar, George Morales, George H. W. Bush, cabinet members, CIA officials and top cocaine kingpins visited the club at one time or another could be considered just a coincidence; that they were in attendance at the same time would be, in legal terms, called 'proximity.'" Factor in what we know today about the Iran-Contra drugs-for-guns scenario, he said, "and you'd have to agree that this was more than just an exclusive Coconut Grove disco."

Sal Magluta graciously used his prison email account to correspond with me for nine months in 2012 and 2013—mostly daily Bible verses. He mentioned a memory about one debauched night at the Mutiny. And he asked me how Pammy (a gorgeous hostess from the Upper Deck) was doing. I wrote that I visited her in Indiana, and that she's well. And he was happy.

Both Willie and Sal were immortalized in Meek Mill's 2013 hip-hop track "Dope Dealer":

Sal Magluta, Willie Falcon . . .
From Monte Carlo to Los Muchachos . . .

Baruch Vega, sixty-nine, is a fashion photographer in Los Angeles. In his free time, the divorced father runs the "Colombian Traffickers Rehabilitation Program," where he has helped the US government flip 114 cocaine kingpins. "Dr. B," as he is called, has appeared on ABC News *Primetime* and on the front page of the *Wall Street Journal*. He is shopping his life's story.

Ricardo Morales's nieces say their uncle still visits them—in their dreams, where he is laughing and cursing and drinking. And he's still playing mind games with Miami.

In a 2005 *Miami Herald* article that mentioned Morales's allegations about who bombed that Cuban jetliner, a fingered exile in Hialeah strongly denied having any role in the affair—pointing blame back at Morales. "He can say what he wants," he told the reporter. "Request a direct line to hell, where he surely is, and ask him what his motives were."

TO THIS DAY, says Jorge Valdes, he cannot get his mind off the Federal Reserve, where he had that plum job as an undergrad. What if he had stuck with it? "The most important financial institution in the world," he says. "And I walked away from it when I was seventeen. I was making five dollars and working and studying full-time. Dead broke but, man, five dollars back then felt like a fortune, you know? I was one of the best finance kids at Miami. Where would I be now? Where would Willie and Sal be now?"

Ralph "Cabeza" Linero is similarly full of remorse. In the decade-plus he spent in prison, the former honor student at Miami Senior High lost his daughter to a car accident and had to attend her funeral in leg-irons and crowded by US Marshals. He had to listen in to his other daughter's wedding via prison phone. "At the end of the day," he asks, "was it all worth it? No!"

Nelson Aguilar, another retired cocaine dealer who has spent nearly half of his life in jail, concurred. "Every Mutiny story started in euphoria and ended in a crash. Done. Cocaine don't solve problems."

Miami's cocaine ghosts linger—defiantly. You see them in the bulging skyline, always a mortgage or two removed from drug money. Or on the fiftysomething restaurant owner with the dad bod and busted septum wearing an ankle monitor.

In January of 2016, Pablo Escobar's former 7,400-square-foot pink mansion in Miami Beach was demolished by its latest owner, a South Florida grilled chicken mogul. "I'm very excited to see the house of the devil disappearing right before our eyes," he declared to a throng of reporters on hand for the teardown. The chicken man's wife was adamant about having a Roman Catholic monsignor bless the grounds before they drafted plans for a new mansion.

But the devil refused such a speedy eviction. The demolition unearthed a dented-up but otherwise sealed seven-hundred-pound safe. Was it Escobar's cash? Coke? Diamonds? A bit of everything maybe?

"This is real. It's still locked," said the poultry pooh-bah. "It's very, very heavy. We can't believe it—now Pablito is my best friend."

Author's Note

I MET THE Mutiny—mostly collapsed and abandoned, save for vagrants and addicts—back in the spring of 1994, just before I thought I was leaving Miami for good to go to college. But that tableau on South Bayshore Drive kept bringing me back.

I've since spent the better part of two decades collecting public and law enforcement materials on the address. I've traveled the country and worked my "nights and weekend" minutes to meet its heyday's habitués, from retired kingpins and arms dealers to undercover cops, hostesses, ex-madams and the Mutiny's late founder, Burton Goldberg.

What follows is a list of everyone I've interviewed—in person, over the phone and via email (even prison email). Yet others agreed to participate only if I guaranteed their anonymity. Their recollections and candor are what bring the place back to life. (I was four in 1980.)

To those of you who (understandably) told me to go to hell, well, I still hope you enjoyed my book.

Willy Gomez

Nelson Aguilar

June Hawkins

Baruch Vega

Raul Diaz

Raul Martinez

Wayne Black

Al Singleton

Jerry Sanford

Vicky Gallas

Gary James

Johnny Hernandez

Kim Bacardi

Lourdes Castellon

Juan Cid

Todd R. Cimino

Magaly Migoya

Humberto Becerra

Carlos Quesada

Carlos Ruiz

Owen Band

Frank White

Robert Platshorn

Rodolfo Rodriguez Gallo

Rudy Rodriguez Jr.

Juan Cid

Sam Burstyn

Sam Smargon

Benny Lorenzo

Sal Magluta

Lauve Metcalfe

Alberto Bover, deceased

Joanna Christopher, deceased

Mike Wald, deceased

Mike McDonald, deceased

William Richey, deceased

Burton Goldberg, deceased

Enrique Bover

Christopher Clark

Pat Sullivan

Douglas Williams

Bonnie Tolentino

Pamela Besett

Bernardo de Torres

Bill Riley

Oscar Paz Jr.

Diosdado "D. C." Diaz

Nelson Andreu

Nancy Mira

Rene Rodriguez

Jorge Valdes

Mario Tabraue

Chuck Volpe

Ralph Linero

Juan Barroso

Tatico Martinez

Barbara Esposito

Deb Landsberger

Karen Landsberger-Tarpley

Audie Tarpley

Norman Canter

Cynthia Bettner

Cindy Proietti

Jay Weaver

Iris Salzman

Paul Risi

Nanette Pignato

Jennifer Boscan

Linda Scheller

Jennifer Kim James

Andrea James

Jane Podowski

Laura Costanzo

Bo Crane

Humberto Fleites

Walter Elmore

Clive Evenden, deceased

Julián Osca-Soriano

Stuart Abolsky

Alex Daoud

Richard Marx

Phil Mandina

Ken Avery

Joan Mellen

Carlos Suarez De Jesus

Mark Dachs

John Rothchild

Edwin Wilson Jr., deceased

Sarkis Soghanalian, deceased

Paul George

Seth Bramson

Mollie Hampton

Mario Ortiz

Acknowledgments

I'd never even have thought about writing this book had Gilda Nissenberg, my Spanish teacher at North Miami Beach High, not insisted that I go into the adult world *hablar español*—and with a Cuban twang at that. Thank you, Dr. Niss, for taking me under your wing; I love and cherish you. For Michael Fass, my hugely influential high school professor, I offer my gratitude in the shape of various Easter eggs in this book from the AP History and Psych exams.

I'm thankful for the deft editing advice of Mickey Meece, who mentored me during my summer at the *New York Times*. Brent Howard at Penguin Random House, who took on this project during the sleeplessness of new fatherhood, deserves a medal—or at least free Ambien. Thanks to Tracy Bernstein, Loren Jaggers, Danielle Perez, Yuki Hirose and Charlie Conrad, who acquired the title. Pilar Queen, my literary agent, believed in this project from our very first conversation.

Shout-outs to Mark Vamos and Hank Gilman; Justin Fox, who advised me in my transition from wealth management to financial

ACKNOWLEDGMENTS

journalism. Julian Sancton, Cullen Murphy, Keenan Mayo, Kevin Krim, Marion Maneker, Josh Brown, Barry Ritholtz, Tom Keene, Paul Barrett, Julie Cohen, Maia Samuel, Shannon High, John Brecher, Jesse Rodriguez; Hardy Green, Steve Baker, Lauren Young, Rob Hunter, Michael Orey, John Byrne and Ciro Scotti at *BusinessWeek* (43); Sarah Scully, Matt Miller and Pimm Fox at Bloomberg Television. Miriam Goderich and Jane Dystel. James Altucher, Bill Griffeth, Andrew Ross Sorkin, Sam Rega, Jay Yarow, Kerima Greene, Jonathan Wald, Ramona Schindelheim, Sue Herera, Ed Manigault, Alvaro Tafur, Vivian Gallagher, Erik Sorenson, James Harmon, Pete Finch, Nancy Smith, Bob Sabat, Terry Noland, Amy Choi, Becca Lehrer and Caitlin Thompson.

Thanks in Miami to Rondel Borless, Mitchell Kaplan, Lissette Mendez, Tim Elfrink, Lesley Abravanel, Gail L. Pacheco, Faquiry Diaz, Seth Bramson, Alam and Bill Berke, Joel Hirschhorn, Roy Black, Phil Mandina, Peter Zalewski, Francisco Alvarado, Chef Jeremiah, Dave Cypkin, Lindsey Snell, Paul George, Dawn Hugh, John Shipley, the Wolfson Archives and Isabel Brador, Terri Munn, Jim DeFede, Glenna Milberg, Michael Putney, Tim Chapman, Ian & Alanna Hochman. Gui Socarras, Charles Intriago, Carlos Suarez de Jesus, Alex Daoud, Joan Fleischman, Jaydee Freixas, Bobby Lickstein, Larry Lutness, Barron Sherer, Yami Alvarado, Paradise Afshar, Alberto Ibargüen, Wendy Zane, Tom Falco, and FiFi's in Miami Beach.

Jenny Van Leeuwen Harrington, Dan Roth, Adriana Cisneros, Steve Forrest, Adaora Udoji, Vinnie Malhotra, Geraldine Moriba, Chris Porter, J. B. Bunting, Jay Kernis, Wayne Kabak, Jane Friedman, Jeffrey Sharp, Julia Lee, Abhijay Prakhash, Steve Scully, Michelle Remillard, Geoffrey Bennett, Sara Just, Diane Lincoln, Anne Davenport, James Blue, Murrey Jacobson, Emily Carpaux, Judy Woodruff, Hari Sreenivasan, William Brangham, Frank Carlson,

ACKNOWLEDGMENTS

Jeffrey Brown, Kristen Doerer, Deirdre Bolton. Hugo Lindgren, Brad Weiners, Brad Stone, Barry Meier, Sara Sarasohn, Diane Brady, Jeremy Caplan, Sheelah Kolhatkar, Richard Turley, Josh Tyrangiel, Paula Dwyer, Brian Lehrer, David Rhodes. Sree Sreenivasan, Mamoon Hamid, Youngme Moon, Richard Tedlow, Moshe Oinounou, Chitra Wadhwani, Darcy Shean.

RVA props to Kim Zaninovich, Ed Ayers, Brian Balogh, Neil Patel and Ellie Hannibal; Erin Mahone, MSP Max, Matt Paxton, Craig Shealy, Brian Broadway, Josh Peck, Paul Spicer, Brandon Fox, Kendra Feather and John Murden. Rick & Molly Hood, Faissal Aridi, Swagger Jones, John Valentine, Helayne Spivak, Leslie Griles, P. J. Sykes, and the Brandcenter. Cece Cox Wolf, Dean and Johnny Giavos, Yackie and the essential Continental Westhampton. Carena Ives; Chris Tsui; Emily Shane, Avrum Elmakis, Fred Bryant, Russ Bencks, the Ukrops, Shane Emmett, Matt Rho, Chris Rogers, Darby O'Donnell, Tony Jones, Eric Martin, Prof. Sharon Burnham, Samuel Roukin, Ric & Rhona Arenstein, Big Cathy, Adam and Jay . . . and the intensely supportive and forgiving GG, Gwaanpa and Awneeta.

"Maybe this weight was a gift. . . ."

—NS

About the Author

Roben Farzad hosts the weekly programme *Full Disclosure* on NPR One and is a special correspondent on *PBS NewsHour*. He was previously a senior writer for *Bloomberg Businessweek*, where he covered Wall Street, international finance and Latin America. Farzad is a graduate of Princeton University and Harvard Business School.

Notes

8 **In the very week:** Phil Stanford, "The Bounty at the Mutiny," *Miami Magazine*, December 1981.

10 **According to one study:** Jerry Knight, "Underground Miami: The Land of Illegal Opportunity," *Washington Post*, July 22, 1981.

11 **So much marijuana:** James Kelly, "Trouble in Paradise," *Time*, November 23, 1981.

11 **Area McDonald's restaurants were:** "Spoons Redesigned," United Press International, December 11, 1979.

11 **Burger King, meanwhile, loaned:** Barbara Stewart, "The Way We Die Now," *Orlando Sentinel*, July 17, 1988.

11 **showing a five-billion-dollar:** Kelly, "Trouble in Paradise"

16 **developer set his sights:** "Developer Threatens a Suit Here," *Miami News*, June 14, 1966.

17 **Nineteen sixties South Florida:** Taylor Branch and George Crile III, "The Kennedy Vendetta: How the CIA Waged a Silent War Against Cuba," *Harper's*, August 1975.

19 **News of which:** Hank Tester, "Miami and the Bay of Pigs," NBC6 Miami, April 15, 2011.

20 **In 1963, Morales regaled:** Ricardo Morales to reporter Carlos Martinez, "Cuba Raider's Own Story on Attack," *Miami Herald*, June 24, 1963.

20 **mowing them down:** Taylor Branch, "Caracas Secret Police Chief: A Cuban Exile with CIA Past," *Miami News*, October 23, 1976.

20 **Morales took a bullet:** Glenn Garvin, "Anniversary Recalls Congo Rescue by Miami Cubans," *Miami Herald*, November 15, 2014.

21 **"Bombing Box Score":** Dave Nelson and Jon Nordheimer, "Two Bombs Rip Home of Underworld Figure," *Miami Herald*, August 22, 1967.

22 **Morales infiltrated the gang:** Margaret Carroll, "Bosch Is Guilty in Plot on Ship," *Miami Herald*, November 16, 1968.

22 **Down in Coconut Grove:** "Coconut Grove High-Rise Sets Opening for June 15," *Miami Herald*, May 5, 1968; "Security Insures Privacy," ad in *Miami Herald*, November 10, 1968; Fred Fogarty, "A Posh Palace: It's a 'Hand-Crafted High-Rise,'" *Miami Herald*, September 8, 1969.

24 **Adding urgency to their career:** "Florida Lobstermen Are Angry Over Bahamian Fishing Curbs," *New York Times*, July 20, 1975.

24 **Some of [these exiles]:** Peter Dale Scott and Jonathan Marshall, *Cocaine Politics: Drugs, Armies, and the CIA in Central America* (Updated Edition), University of California Press, 1998, p. 27.

29 **Perhaps he hadn't read:** Richard Rhodes, "A Very Expensive High," *Playboy*, January 1975.

32 **In February of 1977:** *United States of America, Plaintiff-appellee, v. Patricia Lynn Opager, Defendant-appellant*, 589 F.2d 799 (5th Cir. 1979), Feb. 14, 1979.

32 **Miami Dolphins players:** "2 Dolphins Out on Bail After Cocaine Arrest," *New York Times*, May 6, 1977.

47 **The cops flipped on:** John Rothchild, "The Informant," *Harper's*, January 1982.

48 **Police arrested Rudy Redbeard:** Joanne Hooker, "Prosecutor's Midnight Ride Preceded Big Drug Bust," *Miami News*, March 27, 1978; Hank Messick, *Of Grass and Snow: The Secret Criminal Elite*, Prentice-Hall, 1979, p. 56.

51 **Monkey Morales managed:** Danny Goodgame and Gloria Marina, "Cops Spy Familiar Face in Drug Bust," *Miami Herald*, April 7, 1978; John Rothchild, "The Informant"; "Judge Orders Lawmen to Leave Morales Alone," *Miami News*, April 26, 1978; "Monkey Says Jail Not the Right Place for Him," *Miami News*, May 24, 1978.

53 **A six-man jury:** Danny Goodgame, "Jury Acquits Former Spy in Pot Case," *Miami Herald*, July 30, 1978.

58 **His wife had to learn to live:** Jerome Sanford, *Odyssey into Politics*, Outskirts Press, 2012, pp. 13–14.

59 German Jimenez, a Colombian: Carl Hiaasen and Al Messer-
schmidt, "The Cocaine Wars," *Rolling Stone*, September 20, 1979; Billy
Corben, "Griselda Blanco: So Long and Thanks for All the Cocaine,"
Vice, September 4, 2012; Billy Corben and Alfred Spellman, *Cocaine
Cowboys*, Rakontur, 2006; Guy Gugliotta and Jeff Leen, *Kings of Co-
caine*, Simon & Schuster, 1990.

66 one of the largest cocaine: Jim DeFede, "Falcon and Magluta,"
Miami New Times, February 12, 1992.

68 Rewind to 1973: Jorge Valdes with Ken Abraham, *Coming Clean:
The True Story of a Cocaine Drug Lord and His Unexpected Encounter
with God*, WaterBrook Press, 1999.

68 Melvyn Kessler, a lawyer who: Jeff Leen, "Dirty Money," *Miami
Herald*'s *Tropic* magazine, September 2, 1990.

71 It so happened that Corona: Jay Weaver, "Feds Catch Convicted
Miami Lawyer on the Lam for 27 Years in Mexico," *Miami Herald*,
February 14, 2013.

82 Since their hotshot: "Death Trails Witnesses in Drug Case," Knight-
Ridder News Service, July 26, 1993.

87 After John F. Kennedy: Joan Mellen, *A Farewell to Justice: Jim Gar-
rison, JFK's Assassination, and the Case That Should Have Changed
History*, Potomac Books, 2007, pp. 86 to 90; "Answers Awaited on Gar-
rison Quiz," *New Orleans Times-Picayune*, February 20, 1967; Carlos
Martinez, "JFK Death Probe Sees Conspiracy," *Miami Herald*, Febru-
ary 19, 1967; Gaeton Fonzi, *The Last Investigation: What Insiders Knew
About the Assassination of JFK*, Thunder's Mouth Press, 1993; Larry
Hancock, *Someone Would Have Talked: The Assassination of President
John F. Kennedy and the Conspiracy to Mislead History*, JFK Lancer
Productions, 2010.

95 In 1978, Ralph Linero: Joanne Fishman, "Grand Prix Sailing Is in a
Critical Stage," *New York Times*, December 17, 1978.

96 Linero was a square: Verne Williams, "We Don't Want to Play
Hooky: Special Report from Our Kids," *Miami News*, February 26,
1968.

97 In June 1980: Jim DeFede, "The Drug Trafficker," *Loft*, March/April,
2002.

102 It would seem like: Charles Strouse, "Prosecutors Say Men Were
Kingpins," *Fort Lauderdale Sun-Sentinel*, February 14, 1996.

104 A sizable minority: John Rothchild, *Up for Grabs*, University Press
of Florida, 2000, p. 173.

104 **It took little time:** "Miami Homicide Rate Five Times Above Usual Among Cuban Exiles," Associated Press, May 31, 1981; Billy Corben and Alfred Spellman, *Cocaine Cowboys: Reloaded*, Rakontur Films.

104 **On May 8, 1980:** Nathan Adams, "Miami's Murderous Drug War," *Reader's Digest*, January 1981.

120 **The brothers used:** "$1 Million Credit Card Ring Cracked," United Press International, August 2, 1984.

122 **"If we didn't have them":** "Cuban Refugees Boost Miami's Murder Rate," Associated Press, June 1, 1981.

123 **That same week:** John Rothchild, "The Informant"

125 **What Raul Diaz had:** Carl Hiaasen, "Killer: The Life and Death of a Cocaine Cowboy," *Miami Herald*'s *Tropic* magazine, January 3, 1982.

131 **"Counting Casualties from One Miami Weekend":** Mike McQueen, "Counting the Casualties of One Miami Weekend," Associated Press, March 9, 1981.

133 **Frank White, a DEA sharpshooter:** Statement of Francis White given to DEA inspector William Ferris on May 15, 1981 re: GI-72-0025.

135 **Operation Tick-Talks:** Gary Moore, "The 'Operation Tick Talks' Tapes," *St. Petersburg Times*, June 1, 1982.

138 **"Time Runs Out on Suspected Coke Ring":** Ken Szymkowiak, "Tick-Talks: Time Runs Out for Cocaine Smuggling Ring," *Miami News*, August 5, 1981.

138 **Rafael Villaverde met:** Jay Ducassi, "Facing Charges, Villaverde Resigns Post," *Miami Herald*, August 7, 1981.

139 **Already in the first:** Randall Hackley, "Miami Pleads for Reprieve from Murders," Associated Press, January 3, 1982.

140 **Quesada appeared in court:** Al Messerschmidt and John Katzenbach, "Bond of $1 Million Upheld for Quesada," *Miami Herald*, August 7, 1981.

158 **Diaz immediately ordered 360-degree surveillance:** Paul Eddy, Hugo Sabogal and Sara Walden, *The Cocaine Wars*, Bantam, 1989, p. 57.

165 **In April, just as the:** John Rothchild, *Up for Grabs* and "The Informant."

168 *Newsday* ... **sported a vivid:** John Cummings, "Morales the Informer: License to Kill," *Newsday* magazine, June 1982.

177 **Not that this meant the real Miami:** Joan Fleischman, "Convict Charged with Executive's Slaying," *Miami Herald*, August 17, 1982.

180 **But Morales was not quite:** *"Historia de una Intriga"* interview, via YouTube.

189 **First-season *Miami Vice*:** Brett Sokol, "Perception Is Reality," *Miami New Times*, October 6, 2005.

189 **Cocaine smuggler Jon Roberts:** Jon Roberts and Evan Wright, *American Desperado*, Crown, 2011.

198 **For one, Jack Devoe:** Joel Brinkley, "Drug Smugglers Say Hard Part Is What to Do with Money," *New York Times*, November 29, 1984.

198 **On December 12:** Susan Sachs, "Drug Money Bought Bank, U.S. Charges; Government May Try to Seize Institution," *Miami Herald*, December 13, 1984.

198 **In Washington, no less than the attorney general:** "2 Miami Bankers Among 6 Linked to Drug Ring," *Reuters*, December 13, 1984.

199 **By the summer of 1985:** Susan Sachs, "Bad Boy of Miami Banking on the Ropes," *Miami Herald*, July 14, 1985.

202 **When its loan:** Dory Owens, "Peninsula Forecloses on Mutiny Hotel," *Miami Herald*, April 23, 1985; No. 86-2095-Civ and 663 F.Supp. 506 (1987): *Peninsula Federal S&L v. FSLIC, June 11, 1987*; Charles Kimball, "Lender Takes Back Mutiny," *Miami Herald*, January 5, 1986.

203 **In December and January:** Dory Owens, "Money Woes Force Mutiny to Cut Staff," *Miami Herald*, April 19, 1985.

204 **"It was the downfall":** Joel Achenbach, "Not Much Bounty Left for Grove's Mutiny Inn," *Miami Herald*, March 17, 1987.

205 **On May 28, 1985, Metro-Dade Police:** "Grand Jury Indicts Eight Men in Cocaine Smuggling Case," United Press International, July 3, 1985; "Drug Ring Called Area's Biggest Alleged Chief Modeled Self on Scarface," *Miami Herald*, October 22, 1985.

209 **1985 also saw:** George Ramos, "Judge Throws the Book at 'Miami Vice' Drug Dealer," *Los Angeles Times*, September 24, 1985.

209 **On a Saturday morning:** Joan Fleischman and Jim McGee, "Slain Restaurateur Feared He Might Be Killed, Pal Says," *Miami Herald*, January 15, 1985.

210 **mother was kidnapped:** Jim Defede, "Falcon and Magluta," *Miami New Times*, February 12, 1992.

211 **they did manage to:** Case 663 F. Supp. 506 (1987): *Peninsula Federal Savings & Loan Association v. FSLIC as receiver for Sunrise Savings & Loan*, No. 86-2095-Civ., June 11, 1987.

212 **Come 1987:** Bea Moss, "Business Booming at Private Clubs; Coconut Grove Nightspots Court Free Spenders," *Miami Herald*, August 21, 1986.

213 **detectives busted:** Joan Fleischman, "Cocaine, Conch Party at Mutiny Draws Hundreds, Then Cops," *Miami Herald*, March 16, 1987.

NOTES

213 **a month later, 250 former:** "Mutiny Survivors Reunite," *Miami News*, September 11, 1987.

214 **central banker, Ray Corona, was sentenced:** Stephen Hedges, "Coronas Get Prison for Bank Scheme," *Miami Herald*, October 22, 1987.

214 **As fate would have it:** Lynda Ann Ewen, *Social Stratification and Power in America: A View from Below*, Rowman & Littlefield, 1998, p. 169.

215 **By this point, the government:** *U.S. v. Robert C. Jacoby and Thomas Skubal, Defendants-appellants*, 955 F.2d 1527 (11th Cir. 1992), March 25, 1992; Jack Nease, "Time for Accounting in Sunrise S&L Trial," *Sun-Sentinel*, May 7, 1989.

217 **Associated Press reported:** Robert Parry, "How John Kerry Exposed the Contra-Cocaine Scandal," *Salon*, October 25, 2004; Robert Parry and Brian Barger, "Reports Link Nicaraguan Rebels to Cocaine Trafficking," Associated Press, December 20, 1985.

217 **Upper Deck speedboating phenom:** Deborah Petit, "Boat Racer Charged with Smuggling," *Sun-Sentinel*, June 18, 1986.

221 **In December of 1986:** James H. Tolpin, "Racer's Attorney to Cite National Security as Defense," *Sun-Sentinel*, December 13, 1986.

222 **Morales flew up to Washington:** Keith Schneider, "Iran-Contra Hearings: Smuggler Ties Contras to U.S. Drug Network," *New York Times*, July 16, 1987.

222 **Back down in South Florida:** Craig Davis, "Apache Gives Miami, Powerboats the Chance to Bring Out Their Best," *Sun-Sentinel*, September 21, 1986.

224 **In the spring of 1987:** "Fort Lauderdale Man Arrested in Bahamas Cocaine Seizure," United Press International, April 19, 1987.

225 **he could not resist:** Jim DeFede, "Falcon and Magluta," *Miami New Times*, February 12, 1992.

225 **failed to surrender:** *Magluta v. U.S./Supreme Court* (No. 05-0952), 2005.

225 **To make matters worse:** William Overend and William Nottingham, "Sports Figure Is Indicted—4 Days After Death," *Los Angeles Times*, November 26, 1987.

226 **November 1987 *Sports Illustrated* story:** Sam Moses, "Going Flat Out on the Briny: Key West's World Offshore Powerboat Championships Drew the Fastest, Fanciest Field of Racing Machines Ever," *Sports Illustrated*, November 23, 1987.

226 **Just a few months later:** Jim DeFede, "Falcon and Magluta," *Miami New Times*, February 12, 1992.

227 **upward of eighteen thousand dollars:** Peter Kerr, "Cocaine Glut Pulls New York Market into Drug Rings' Tug-of-War," *New York Times*, August 24, 1988.

227 **Justo Jay's 1988 indictment:** *U.S. v. Justo Enrique Jay* (No. 88-5635).

228 **Miami office supplies store:** Supreme Court: *Sal Magluta v. U.S. on petition for a writ of certiorari to the U.S. Court of Appeals*, 11th circuit. No. 05-952, 2005; Mike Clary, "'The Boys' Face Trial as New Tide of Drug Smuggling Rises," *Los Angeles Times*, January 13, 1996; Peter Slevin, Manny Garcia, Don Van Natta Jr., "Death Trails Witnesses in Drug Case," *Miami Herald*, July 26, 1993.

230 **Pro Bowl Dolphins wide receiver:** "Miami Dolphin Officials Denying Report," United Press International, December 7, 1988.

230 **Miami grand jury indicted:** *U.S. v. Falcon*, No. 88-327-CR, 1988.

231 **indicted the general:** Philip Shenon, "Noriega Indicted by U.S. for Links to Illegal Drugs," *New York Times*, February 5, 1988.

231 **praised him:** Michael Isikoff, "DEA Fights to Keep Office in Panama," *Washington Post*, October 4, 1988.

232 **seized KS&W Offshore Engineering:** Jim DeFede, "Falcon and Magluta," *Miami New Times*, February 12, 1992.

233 **How's this for irony:** "The Great S&L Fire Sale of 1990," *Fortune*, August 13, 1990.

233 **One last chance to reflect:** Fred Tasker, "A Last Chance to Reflect on Mutiny's Past," *Miami Herald*, April 6, 1990.

235 **Coca-Cola was cooperating:** Carol Marbin, "Second Trial Opens Against 'Coca-Cola' Ring; Murder of Witness Shouldn't Affect Outcome in Drug Case," *Palm Beach Post*, June 21, 1989.

235–36 **wife pleaded the Fifth:** Jim DeFede, "Falcon and Magluta," *Miami New Times*, February 12, 1992.

236 **Acosta got a call:** Linda Robinson, "The Panama Connection," *U.S. News & World Report*, December 9, 1991; Donna Gehrke, "Slain Attorney Mourned," *Miami Herald*, September 19, 1989.

237 **Colombian troops arrested Mono Abello:** "Medellín Suspect Extradited to U.S.," Associated Press, October 30, 1989.

237 **Avianca Flight 203:** Robert McFadden, "Drug Trafficker Convicted of Blowing Up Jetliner," *New York Times*, December 20, 1994.

238 **policemen surrounded Gacha:** Stan Yarbro, "Police Hunt Down Cartel Chieftain," Associated Press, December 16, 1989.

238 **Endara was sworn in:** Alma Guillermoprieto, *The Heart That Bleeds: Latin America Now*, Vintage Books, 1994, p. 220; Linda Robinson,

"The Panama Connection," *U.S. News & World Report*, December 9, 1991.

239 **in the MCC's "Dictator Suite":** "The Strongman in Stir," *Newsweek*, November 4, 1990.

241 **red underwear:** Joseph Treaster, "Noriega: Military Command Belittles General," *New York Times*, December 27, 1989.

241 **Valdes and his fiancée were:** Jorge Valdes with Ken Abraham, *Coming Clean: The True Story of a Cocaine Drug Lord and His Unexpected Encounter with God*, WaterBrook Press, 1999, p. 263.

242 **That November, Juan "Recotado" Barroso:** Steve Rothaus, "Like His Mates, Boat Racer in Trouble with Authorities," *Miami Herald*, November 30, 1990.

243 **Kessler had just been sentenced:** Jill Walker, "'For the Defense' Takes on a New Meaning," *Washington Post*, August 10, 1991.

244 **upped the stakes . . . "Venao":** Don Van Natta Jr. and David Lyons, "Slain Informant Recruited Drug-Case Witnesses," *Miami Herald*, June 25, 1993; Don Van Natta Jr., Manny Garcia and David Lyons, "Shooting Victim to Testify at Drug Trial Was Third Witness Shot in Case," *Miami Herald*, June 24, 1993.

255 **While her husband was in jail awaiting:** Ray Lynch, "Police at Galleria Mall Arrest Murder Suspect," *Sun-Sentinel*, August 13, 1992.

260 **The Hit List:** "Defense 'Rat Patrol' Raises Questions," United Press International, July 4, 1993; Mark Hansen, "An Ad Raises Controversy," *ABA Journal*, November 1993; Larry Rohter, "A Legal Advertisement, a Slaying and Then a Free-for-All Over Ethics," *New York Times*, October 8, 1993; Jim DeFede, "The Further Adventures of Willie and Sal," *Miami New Times*, November 10, 1993.

263 **hundreds of police and soldiers:** Steven Ambrus, "Colombian Drug Lord Escobar Dies in Shootout," *Los Angeles Times*, December 3, 1993.

264 **the security measures** Will Lester, "Attorney Says Pair 'Lived Like Kings,'" Associated Press, October 24, 1995; Mike Clary, "'The Boys' Face Trial as New Tide of Drug Smuggling Rises," *Los Angeles Times*, January 13, 1996.

265 **The *Miami New Times'* Jim DeFede billed:** Jim DeFede, "The Trial of Willie & Sal," *Miami New Times*, December 14, 1995.

271 **worked another front: jury tampering:** John Holland, "Juror Convicted of Taking Bribe," *Sun-Sentinel*, July 24, 1999; John Holland, "Bribed Foreman Gets 17 Years," *Sun-Sentinel*, March 4, 2000; Ann

O'Neil, "Two Miami Jurors Accused of Taking Bribes in Cocaine Cowboys Case," *Sun-Sentinel*, August 28, 2003; Billy Corben and Alfred Spellman, *Cocaine Cowboys III: Los Muchachos*, Rakontur, TBR 2017; Larry Lebowitz, "Moya's 'Date' Wild and Wired," *Sun-Sentinel*, September 19, 1998.

273 **at 6:30 p.m., the Boys were acquitted:** Jim DeFede, "The Impossible Victory," *Miami New Times*, February 29, 1996.

273 **In a past life:** Kirk Semple, "Crime & Nourishment," *Miami New Times*, April 11, 1996.

275 **the IRS accordingly slammed:** *Magluta v. United States*, 952 F. Supp. 798 (S.D. Fla. 1996); omnibus order on IRS jeopardy assessment.

277 **It took only until August:** 198 F. 3d 1265—*U.S. v. Magluta*, Magluta appeals from his conviction and sentence imposed in two separate cases: the "false identification case" and the "bond jumping case," December 23, 1999.

279 **Though *Miami Vice*:** Larry Lebowitz, "Moya's 'Date' Wild and Wired," *Sun Sentinel*, September 19, 1998.

280 **flipping Marilyn Bonachea:** U.S. Supreme Court: *Magluta v. U.S.* (05-952), via justice.gov.

280 **flew it to Israel:** No. 03-10694: 418 F. 3d 1166—*United States v. Magluta* via OpenJurist.

280 **Magluta pleaded guilty in:** Larry Lebowitz, "Fugitive Returns to Face the Music," *Sun-Sentinel*, November 25, 1998.

284 **inmate Gilbert Barrios:** "Drug Convict Says Ex-Boss Trying to Corrupt Jury in Trial," Associated Press, April 17, 2002.

286 **Villaverde—Tick-Talks' defendant:** David Green, "Slain Exile Was Eyed by Police in Killings," *Miami Herald*, June 16, 2002; Madeline BarM-s Diaz, "Castro Opponent's Death Still a Mystery," *Sun-Sentinel*, June 13, 2002.

287 **This second go-around:** Jay Weaver, "Magluta Murder Trial Begins," *Miami Herald*, May 15, 2002.

287 **the judge, siding with prosecutors':** Larry Lebowitz, "Magluta Guilty in Array of Crimes," *Miami Herald*, August 16, 2002.

288 **"205 Years for '*Scarface*'":** Jay Weaver, "A 'Message': 205 Years in Jail," *Miami Herald*, January 23, 2003; Jay Weaver, "Despite Tears, Humbled Magluta Receives 185 Years in Prison," *Miami Herald*, November 30, 2006.

289 **Willie Falcon pleaded guilty:** Jay Weaver, "Reputed Drug Lord Gets 20 Years in Trial-Fixing Scheme," *Miami Herald*, July 23, 2003.

NOTES

291   **Justo Jay testified for the government:** "Drug Lieutenant Breaks Long Silence," *Tampa Tribune*, July 18, 2006.

293   **Yuby Ramirez, a single mother:** Jay Weaver "Snitch-Killer's Girlfriend Released from Prison After 13 Years," *Miami Herald*, March 9, 2013.

300   **In 2001, O. J. Simpson:** George Rush, "O. J. Sex Tape," *New York Daily News*, June 4, 2006.

301   **The film *Scarface* . . . Oliver Stone:** Ken Tucker, *Scarface Nation: The Ultimate Gangster Movie and How It Changed America*, St. Martin's Griffin, 2008, p. 83.

301   **Universal Studios . . . Coen Brothers:** Bryan Alexander "*Scarface* Is Coming in 2018: Coen Brothers to Work on an 'Explosive' Remake," *USA Today*, February 10, 2017.

305   **pink mansion in Miami Beach:** "Bye-Bye Bandido: Demolition Begins on Florida Mansion Owned by Pablo Escobar," news.com.au, January 24, 2016; Sergio Candido, "Safe Found at Pablo Escobar House in Miami Beach Will Be Kept in Bank Vault—for Now," *Miami Herald*, January 25, 2016.

Index

INDEX

INDEX

INDEX

INDEX